VILLAGE LIFE IN CHINA

A STUDY IN SOCIOLOGY

BY

Rev. ARTHUR H. SMITH, D.D.

First published in 1899

This edition published by Read Books Ltd.
Copyright © 2018 Read Books Ltd.
This book is copyright and may not be
reproduced or copied in any way without
the express permission of the publisher in writing

British Library Cataloguing-in-Publication Data
A catalogue record for this book is available
from the British Library

CONTENTS

Arthur Henderson Smith...............................5

Foreword...9

Acknowledgment.....................................11

Glossary..13

PART I
The Village, Its Institutions,
Usages and Public Characters

I - THE CHINESE VILLAGE..........................17

II - CONSTRUCTION OF VILLAGES..................23

III - VILLAGE NOMENCLATURE 34

IV - COUNTRY ROADS.............................40

V - THE VILLAGE FERRY...........................44

VI - VILLAGE WELLS...............................51

VII - THE VILLAGE SHOP 56

VIII - THE VILLAGE THEATRE 62

IX - VILLAGE SCHOOLS AND TRAVELLING
   SCHOLARS......................................77

X - CHINESE HIGHER EDUCATION—THE VILLAGE
   HIGH SCHOOL—EXAMINATIONS—RECENT
   EDUCATIONAL EDICTS 116

XI - VILLAGE TEMPLES AND RELIGIOUS SOCIETIES141

XII - COÖPERATION IN RELIGIOUS OBSERVANCES.148

XIII - COÖPERATION IN MARKETS AND FAIRS 153

XIV - COÖPERATIVE LOAN SOCIETIES.............161

XV - SOCIETIES FOR WATCHING THE CROPS 170

XVI - VILLAGE AND CITY RAIN-MAKING..........179

XVII - THE VILLAGE HUNT 184

XVIII - VILLAGE WEDDINGS AND FUNERALS......189

XIX - NEW YEAR IN CHINESE VILLAGES 208

XX - THE VILLAGE BULLY 223

XXI - VILLAGE HEADMEN 238

PART II
Village Family Life

XXII - VILLAGE BOYS AND MEN 249

XXIII - CHINESE COUNTRY GIRLS AND WOMEN...270

XXIV - THE MONOTONY AND VACUITY OF

    VILLAGE LIFE 325

XXV - UNSTABLE EQUILIBRIUM OF

    THE CHINESE FAMILY 330

XXVI - INSTABILITY FROM FAMILY DISUNITY.....336

PART III
Regeneration of the Chinese Village

XXVII - WHAT CAN CHRISTIANITY

    DO FOR CHINA? 353

ARTHUR HENDERSON SMITH

Arthur Henderson Smith was born on 18th July 1845, in Vernon, Connecticut, U.S.A. He was a missionary of the American Board of Commissioners for Foreign Missions, particularly noted for spending a full fifty-four years as a missionary in China.

Smith served as a soldier in the American Civil War, before attending Beloit College (Wisconsin), and thereafter, Andover Theological Seminary, in Newton Massachusetts. Smith was awarded his degree from Union Theological Seminary, an independent, ecumenical, Christian seminary located in the Morningside Heights neighbourhood of New York City.

After marrying Emma Jane Dickinson, Smith was ordained into the Congregational ministry. The couple set sail for China in 1872, after which, they established themselves at Pangjiazhuang, a village in Shandong. Smith and Dickinson stayed there until the Boxer Rebellion of 1899 - 1901. This anti-imperialist uprising was motivated by proto-nationalist sentiments and opposition to foreign imperialism associated with Christian missionary activity – exactly the activities Smith was involved in. One of the missionaries there, possibly Smith, named the participants (who were mostly farmers), the 'Boxers' because of their athletic rituals.

The Boxer movement rapidly spread to several provinces in northern China and, eventually, received the support of the Chinese government. Smith and his wife were attending a missionary conference in Tongzhou in May 1900, when all the missionaries in Northern China found it necessary to seek safety from the Boxers by fleeing to Beiging or Tianin. The missionary William Scott Ament (1851 - 1909), rescued Smith, along with twenty-two other American missionaries and about one-hundred Chinese Christians in Tongzhou, and escorted them to Peking. They took refuge in the Legation Quarter during the 'siege of the legations' from 20th June until 14th August 1900.

Smith's role in the siege was a minor one as a gate guard, but he gathered material for his book, *China in Convulsion*, which is the most detailed account of the Boxer Rebellion. In 1906, Smith helped to persuade President Theodore Roosevelt to devote indemnity payments China was making to the United States, to the education of Chinese students. More than twelve million dollars was spent on this Boxer Indemnity Scholarship Program.

Smith wrote many books presenting China to foreign readers. These include *Chinese Characteristics* (1894), *Village Life in China* (1899), and *The Uplift of China* (1907). In the 1920s, Chinese Characteristics was still the most widely read book on China among foreign residents there. Due to his books, Smith was probably the best known American missionary of the day. His prominence was recognized in 1907, when he was elected the American co-chairman of the 'China Centenary Missionary Conference' in Shanghai; a conference attended by more than 1,000 Protestant missionaries.

Smith retired as a missionary in 1926, fifty-four years after his arrival in China. His wife died in the same year. Smith himself also died that year, in California in 1932, at the age of eighty-seven.

Chinese author Lu Xun (1881 - 1936; a leading figure of modern Chinese literature) has written that he was influenced by *Smith's Chinese Characteristics,* which was translated into Chinese, as well as Japanese and several European languages. He is remembered for speaking out against the Chinese practice of killing baby girls and drawing attention to this problem that was often ignored, even among other missionaries.

Chinese Villagers at Home

FOREWORD

These chapters are written from the standpoint of one who, by an extended experience in China, has come to feel a profound respect for the numerous admirable qualities of the Chinese, and to entertain for many of them a high personal esteem. An unexampled past lies behind this great race, and before it there may lie a wonderful future. Ere that can be realized, however, there are many disabilities which must be removed. The longer one is acquainted with China, the more deeply is this necessity felt. Commerce, diplomacy, extension of political relations, and the growing contact with Occidental civilization have, all combined, proved totally inadequate to accomplish any such reformation as China needs.

The Chinese village is the empire in small, and when that has been surveyed, we shall be in a better condition to suggest a remedy for whatever needs amendment. It cannot be too often reiterated that the variety in unity in China is such, that affirmations should always be qualified with the implied limitation that they are true somewhere, although few of them may hold good everywhere. On the other hand, the unity in variety is such that a really typical Chinese fact, although of restricted occurrence, may not on that account be the less valuable.

China was never so much in the world's thought as to-day, nor is there any apparent likelihood that the position of this empire will be less conspicuous at the opening of the twentieth century. Whatever helps to a better understanding of the Chinese people, is an aid to a comprehension of the Chinese problem. To that end this volume is intended as a humble contribution.

ACKNOWLEDGMENT.

The author desires to acknowledge his indebtedness to the Rev. Harlan P. Beach for his invaluable criticisms and the kindly services rendered in the proof-reading and piloting of this new voyager through the press.

For the use of original photographs from which engravings have been made, and are here published for the first time, the author and the publishers desire to acknowledge their obligations to Mr. Robert E. Speer, Mr. William Henry Grant, Albert Peck, M.D., Rev. W. C. Longden, and Miss J. G. Evans.

GLOSSARY

Boy, a term used by foreigners in China to denote the head-servant, irrespective of his age.

Cash, Chinese copper coin with a square hole for stringing. The value of a single cash may be taken as one-thousandth of a Mexican dollar. The cash vary greatly in size. A "string" theoretically consists of a thousand cash, but in many regions has but five hundred. The latter variety is at present equal to one-third of a gold dollar.

Catty, a Chinese pound, equal by treaty to one and one-third pounds avoirdupois.

Chin-shih, "Entered Scholar." The third literary degree; Doctor in Literature.

Chou, a Sub-prefecture, sometimes with Districts under it, and often without them.

Chü-Jên, "Selected man." The second full literary degree; a Master of Arts.

Compound, an enclosure or yard, usually containing a number of buildings belonging to a single family or establishment.

Fêng-shui, literally "wind and water." A complicated system of geomantic superstition, by which the good luck of sites and buildings is determined.

Fu, a Prefecture, governed by a Prefect, with several Districts under it.

Han-lin, "Forest of Pencils." The last literary degree, entitling to office.

Hsien, a District or Country, governed by the District Magistrate.

Hsiu-ts'ai, "Flourishing Talent." The lowest of the several literary degrees; a Bachelor of Arts.

K'ang, a raised platform of adobe or of bricks, used as a bed

13

and heated by means of flues.

K'o-t'ou or Kotow, the act of prostration and striking the head on the ground in homage or worship.

Li, a Chinese measure of length, somewhat more than three of which equal an English mile.

Squeeze, a forced contribution exacted by those through whose hands the money of others passes.

Tæl, a weight of money equivalent to a sixteenth of a Chinese pound; an ounce.

Tao-T'ai, an officer of the third rank who is intendant of a circuit.

Ya-mên, the office and residence of a Chinese official.

PART I

The Village, Its Institutions, Usages and Public Characters

I

THE CHINESE VILLAGE

There are in India alone over half a million villages. In all Asia, not improbably, there may be four times that number. By far the larger part of the most numerous people on the globe live in villages. The traveller in the Chinese Empire may start from some seaport, as Tientsin, and journey for several months together in the same general direction, before reaching its frontiers on the other side. In the course of such a tour, he will be impressed as only one who has ocular evidence can be impressed with the inconceivably great number of Chinese altogether outside of the great centres of urban population. Contrary to the current notions of Westerners, the number of great cities is not, relatively to the whole population, anything like so large in China as in Western lands. Many of the district cities, capitals of divisions analogous to what we call counties, are merely large villages with a wall and with government bureaus called yamêns. It is known that in India three-fourths of the population are rural. In China there is perhaps no reason for thinking the proportion to be less.

On such a journey as we have supposed, the traveller unacquainted with the Chinese, finds himself perpetually inquiring of himself: What are these incomputable millions of human beings thinking about? What is the quality of the life which they live? What is its content and its scope?

Questions like these cannot be answered intelligently without much explanation. The conditions and environment of Chinese life are so totally unlike those to which we are accustomed, that it is unsafe to take anything for granted. Amid certain fundamental unities the life of the Chinese is full of bewildering and inexplicable variety. No matter how long one may have lived in China, there is always just as much as ever that he never before heard of, but which every one is supposed to have known by intuition. The oldest resident is a student like the rest.

This state of things is the inevitable result of the antiquity of Chinese civilization, as well as of the enormous scale upon which it has operated to produce its effects. It is a sagacious remark of Mr. A. R. Colquhoun[1] that "the product resulting from duration multiplied by numbers must be immense, and if to this we add a third factor, isolation, we have no right to be surprised either at the complex character of Chinese civilization, or at its peculiarly conservative form." For this reason a connected and orderly account of the phenomena of Chinese life we believe to be a hopeless impossibility. It would require the combined information of all the residents of China to make it complete, to coördinate it would be the work of several life-times, and the resultant volumes would fill the Bodleian library. The only practicable way to extend our knowledge of so oceanic a subject, is to examine in more or less detail such phenomena as happen to have come within our restricted horizon. No two persons will have the same horizon, and no horizon will belt a sphere.

A good way to see what is happening in a building would be to take its roof off, could that be done without disturbing its inmates. If we wish to comprehend the Chinese, we must take the roof from their homes, in order to learn what is going on within. This no foreigner can do. But he can imitate the Chinese who apply a wet finger to a paper window, so that when the digit is withdrawn there remains a tiny hole, through which an observant eye may see at least something. The heterogeneous, somewhat disconnected, very unequally elaborated chapters which comprise this book, have this in common, that they are all studies of the phenomena seen at a peep-hole into the actual life of the Chinese people. Any one who knows enough about the subject to be entitled to have an opinion, cannot help perceiving how imperfect and inadequate they are. Yet they represent, nevertheless, realities which have a human interest of their own.

Southern Village Scene.

A Detail—The Village Well.

The traveller in China, constantly surrounded by countless towns and hamlets, naturally thirsts to know in a general way the population of the region which he is traversing. Should he venture, however, to ask any one the number of people in a city, or the district which it governs, he would get no other information than that there are "not a few," or "who knows?" Almost any intelligent person could tell approximately how many villages there are in his own county, but as some of them are large and some small, and as Chinese like other Orientals care absolutely nothing for statistics and have the crudest notion of what we mean by an average, one is none the wiser for their information.

It appears to be well settled that no real dependence can be placed upon the Chinese official returns, yet that they are the only basis upon which rational estimates can be based, and therefore have a certain value. So far as we are aware, efforts to come at the real population per square mile, have generally proceeded from such extensive units as provinces, or at least prefectures, the foundation and superstructure being alike a mere pagoda of guesses.

Some years ago an effort was made in a certain district to make a more exact computation of the population of a very limited area, as a sort of unit of measure. For this purpose a circle was taken, the radius of which was twenty li, the foreign residence being at the centre. A list was drawn up of every village having received famine relief in the year 1878, so that it was not difficult to make a proximate guess at the average number of families. The villages were 150 in number, and the average size was taken as eighty families, which, reckoning five persons to the family, gave a total of 60,000 persons. Allowing six miles to be the equivalent of twenty li, the population of the square mile would be 531, about the same as the average of the kingdom of Belgium (the most densely populated country in Europe), which had in 1890 an average of only 534 to the square mile.

At a distance of a few miles beyond this circle, there is a tract called the "Thirteen Villages," because that is the number within a distance of five li! This shows that the particular region in which this estimate was made, happens to be an unfavourable one for the purpose, as a considerable part of it is waste, owing to an old bed of the Yellow River which has devastated a broad band of land, on which are no villages. There is also a water-course leading from the Grand Canal to the sea, and a long depression much below the general average, thinly occupied by villages, because it is liable to serious inundation.

For these reasons it seemed desirable to make a new count in a better spot, and for this purpose a district was chosen, situated about ninety li east of the sub-prefecture of Lin Ch'ing, to which it belongs. The area taken was only half the size of the former, and instead of merely estimating the average population of the villages, the actual number of families in each was taken, so far as this number is known to the natives. The man who prepared the village map of the area is a native of the central village, and a person of excellent sense. He put the population in every case somewhat below the popular estimate so as to be certainly within bounds. The number of persons to a "family" was still taken at five, though, as he pointed out, this is a totally inadequate allowance. Many "families" live and have all things in common, and are therefore counted as one, although as in the case of this particular individual, the "family" may consist of some twenty persons. To the traveller in this region, the villages appear to be both large and thickly clustered, and the enumeration shows this to be the case. Within a radius of ten li (three miles) there are sixty-four villages, the smallest having thirty families and the largest more than 1,000, while the average is 188 families. The total number of families is 12,040, and the total number of persons at five to the family, is 60,200, or more than double the estimate for the region with twice the diameter. This gives a population of 2,129 to the square mile.

So far as appearances go, there are thousands of square miles in southern and central Chih-li, western and southwestern Shan-tung, and northern Ho-nan, where the villages are as thick as in this one tract, the contents of which we are thus able proximately to compute. But for the plain of North China as a whole, it is probable that it would be found more reasonable to estimate 300 persons to the square mile for the more sparsely settled districts, and from 1,000 to 1,500 for the more thickly settled regions. In any case a vivid impression is thus gained of the enormous number of human beings crowded into these fertile and historic plains, and also of the almost insuperable difficulties in the way of an exact knowledge of the facts of the true "census."

II

CONSTRUCTION OF VILLAGES

It is nearly 500 years since the great raid of the nephew of Hung Wu, founder of the Ming Dynasty, from the southern capital of China, to what is now known as Peking, then called the state of Yen. The celebrated raider is popularly believed to have destroyed the lives of all those whom he met, and to have reduced to an uninhabited desert the whole region from the Yang-tzŭ River to Peking. This is described as "Yen Wang's sweeping the North." After this ambitious youth had dispossessed his nephew, who was the rightful heir to the throne, he took the title of Yung Lo, which became a famous name in Chinese history. To repair the ravages which he had made, compulsory emigration was established from southern Shan-hsi and from eastern Shan-tung. Tradition reports that vast masses of people were collected in the city of Hung-tung Hsien in southern Shan-hsi, and thence distributed over the uncultivated wastes made by war. Certain it is that throughout great regions of the plain of northern China, the inhabitants have no other knowledge of their origin than that they came from that city.

It is a curious phenomenon that so practical a people as the Chinese, and one having so instinctive a sense of the points of the compass that they speak of a pain in "the east side" of the stomach, are indifferent to regularity of form in their towns. Every Chinese city seems to lie four square, but perhaps it is not too much to say that no Chinese city really does so lie. On the contrary a city wall is always found to have certain deliberate curves and irregularities which are designed for geomantic purposes. In other words they bring good luck, or they keep off bad luck, and are representations

23

of the mysterious science of fêng-shui or geomancy. It is for this reason that city gates must either not be opposite one another, or if they are so, some obstruction must intervene to prevent evil spirits from making a clean sweep of everything.

It is customary in Western lands to speak of "laying out" a city or a town. As applied to a Chinese village, such an expression would be most inappropriate, for it would imply that there has been some trace of design in the arrangement of the parts, whereas the reverse is the truth. A Chinese village, like Topsy, "just growed," how, or why, no one knows or cares. At some remote and generally unascertainable time in the dim past some families arrived from somewhere else, camped down, made themselves a "local habitation," (their name they probably brought with them), and that was the village. It has a street, and perhaps a network of them, but no two are parallel, except by accident, and no one of them is straight. The street is the path which has been found by long experience to be a necessary factor in promoting communication between the parts of the village and the outside world. It is not only liable to take sudden and inexplicable turns, but it varies in width at different points. Sometimes in a village a quarter of a mile long, there may not be a single crossroad enabling a vehicle to get from the front street to the back one, simply because the town grew up in that way, and no one either could or would remedy it, even if any one desired it otherwise. At right angles to the main street or streets, run narrow alleys, upon which open the yards or courts in which the houses are situated. Even the buildings which happen to stand contiguous to the main street offer nothing to the gaze but an expanse of dead wall. If any doorway opens on the highway, it is protected from the evil influences which might else result, by a screen wall, preventing any observation of what goes on within. A village is thus a city in miniature, having all the evils of over-crowding, though it may be situated in the midst of a wide and comparatively uninhabited plain. Whether land is dear or cheap, a village always has the same crowded appearance, and there is in either case the same indifference to the requirements of future growth.

The mountains furnish an abundance of stone, from which dwellings situated in such districts are built—dark, damp, and unwholesome at all seasons of the year, but especially so in the time of heavy rains. Even more unpleasant are the cave dwellings found in the loamy soil of loess regions, lighted only from the front, and quite free from any form of ventilation, a luxury for which no provision is made in the construction of a Chinese dwelling.

By far the most common material of which the Chinese build their houses is that which happens to be nearest at hand. Bricks are everywhere made in great quantities, almost always of the same colour as the clothes of the people, a bluish gray. This tint is secured by sealing up the brick-kiln perfectly tight, when the burning of the bricks is finished, and pouring upon the concave top several hundred buckets of water, which, filtering through the soil of which the top is composed, is instantly converted into steam when it reaches the bricks, and alters their hue. The scarcity of fuel, and an unwillingness to employ it where it seems like a waste leads to the almost universal practice of burning the bricks too little to make them valuable as a building material. Instead of becoming hard like stones as do foreign bricks, and coated with a thick glazing, a large percentage of Chinese bricks break merely by being handled, and when examined, they are found to be like well-made bread, full of air-holes. Each of these openings becomes a tube by which the bibulous bricks suck up moisture from below, to the great detriment of the building of which they generally form merely the foundations, or perhaps, the facings.

The vast majority of country dwellings are made simply of the soil, moulded into adobe bricks, dried till they cease to shrink. The largest of these bricks are two or three inches thick, and a foot wide, and perhaps twenty inches in length, weighing even when thoroughly dried more than forty pounds. The cost of making those which are only dried in a mould is not more than a cash a piece; those which are stamped while in the mould with a heavy stone rammer, are worth three or four times as much. If experts are employed to do this work, the outlay is greater as the owner of the earth not only provides a man to carry the necessary water, but he must furnish tea and tobacco for the workmen.

The foundations of adobe houses, like those of all others, must be of brick, and at the height of a foot or two above the ground will have a layer of reeds or some other substance, designed to prevent the dampness from rising into the walls, which crumble in such a case like candy houses in a rain. There is so much soda in the soil of all parts of the Great Plain of northern China, that unless extreme care is taken the best built structures will, in a very few years, show signs of decay.

The roof is meant to be supported by posts, no matter of what material the house is built, and this material is regarded as only the filling between them, but in the cheaper houses, the posts are often omitted to save expense. As a result, in a rainy year thousands of houses are literally soaked down whenever the moisture has sufficiently weakened the foundations. In this way many persons are killed and many more injured. In some districts one sees roofs made with the frame resembling that of a foreign house, but the ordinary form is with king and queen posts. In either case the timbers running lengthwise of the building support small purlines upon which rest thin bricks, or more frequently reeds, mats, or sorghum stalks, over which is spread the earth which forms the greater part of all roofs. Their enormous weight when well soaked make them highly dangerous after the timbers have become old and rotten. Where the roofs are flat, they serve as depositories for the crops, and for fuel.

If the village is situated in a low spot, the precaution is taken to throw up a mound of earth on which to build. But whatever the nature of the country, the removal of so much earth leaves a series of gigantic pits around every village, which catch the drainage of the surrounding region and the possession of which is disputed by ducks, geese, pigs and in summer by small children clad only in the skin garments furnished by nature.

The abundant moisture is an inducement to the growth of luxuriant groves of trees, which, seen at a distance, produce a charming effect. But on a nearer approach it is seen that the fine old trees are employed exclusively in shading the mud-holes, while the houses of the village are exposed to the fiercest rays of the summer sun. Trees are indeed to be met with in the village street, but they are not designed to shade a courtyard, which is almost invariably utterly destitute of trees of any sort. Even grapevines which would seem a natural and beautiful relief from the hideous bareness of the prevalent earth colour, are, in some regions at least, wholly tabooed. And why? Because, forsooth, the branches of the grape point down, while those of other trees point up, hence it would be "unlucky" to have grapevines, though not at all "unlucky" to roast all through the broiling summer for the lack of their grateful shade.

A man whose grandfather had been rich, and who was distinguished from his neighbours by owning a two-story dwelling, informed the writer that he could remember that his grandmother, who lived in the rear court, was constantly fretting at the lofty buildings in front, and at the magnificent elms which shaded the compound and left no place to dry clothes! In course of time the family was reduced to poverty, the two-story building was demolished, and the trees felled, so that the present generation, like other families, swelters in a narrow courtyard, with an unlimited opportunity (very little used) to dry their clothes. Luxuries which are denied to dwelling-houses, are cheerfully accorded to the gods, who have no clothes to dry, and a very small temple may have in front of it a grove of very old trees.

Sawyers Preparing Lumber.

Itinerant Blacksmiths Employed by Villagers.

The architecture of the Chinese has been compendiously and perhaps not inaccurately described as consisting essentially of two sticks placed upright, with a third laid across them at the top. The shape of some Chinese roofs, however they may vary among themselves, suggests the tent as the prime model; though, as Dr. Williams and others have remarked, there is no proof of any connection between the Chinese roof and the tent. Owing to the national reluctance to erect lofty buildings, almost all Chinese cities present an appearance of monotonous uniformity, greatly in contrast with the views of large cities to be had in other lands.

If Chinese cities are thus uninviting in their aspect, the traveller must not expect to find anything in the country village to gratify his æsthetic sense. There is no such word as "æsthetic" in Chinese, and, if there were, it is not one in which villagers would take any interest. The houses are generally built on the north end of the space reserved as a courtyard, so as to face the south, and if additional structures are needed they are placed at right angles to the main one, facing east and west. If the premises are large, the front wall of the yard is formed by another house, similar to the one in the rear, and like it having side buildings. However numerous or however wealthy the family, this is the normal type of its dwelling. In cities this type is greatly modified by the exigencies of the contracted space at disposal, but in the country it rules supreme.

The numerative of Chinese houses is a word which denotes division, signifying not a room, but rather such a part of a dwelling as can conveniently be covered by timbers of one length. As these timbers are seldom very large or very long, one division of a house will not often exceed ten or twelve feet in length, by a little less in width from front to back. An ordinary house will comprise three of these divisions, though there may be but one partition, forming one double and one single room. There is no ceiling, and the roof, which is usually not lofty, is in full view. Most doors are made with two leaves, projections above and below, like pins, serving as the hinges. There is a movable doorsill,

29

out of which a small hole is often cut to admit of entrance and exit for the dogs and cats. Such doors cannot be tightly closed, for the rude workmanship and the unequal shrinkage of the wood always render it easy to see through the many cracks.

Almost all parts of the eighteen provinces are very hot in summer, but it is only in some regions that a back door will be found opening opposite the front one. The wooden grating, which does duty as a window, is built into the wall, for security against thieves, and is often covered, even in the heat of summer, with oiled paper. Doors do not open directly from dwelling-houses to the street, and if there are any windows on the street side of the house, they are very small and very high.

Just inside the door is built the adobe support for the cooking-boiler, the latter shaped like a saucer and made very thin in order to economize fuel to the utmost. In all districts where provision is to be made for heating the room, it is done by conducting the smoke from this primitive range through a complicated set of flues, under the divan called a k'ang which serves as a bed, and which is merely an arrangement of adobe bricks. If the houses are thatched with straw the opening for smoke must be near the ground, as a precaution against fire.

On the end of the k'ang are piled the bed-quilts of the household and whatever trunks or boxes they may be able to boast, for this is the only part of the dwelling which is not likely to be damp. As the fire is so near to the outer door where drafts are strong, as the flues are very likely to get out of order, and as there are no chimneys worthy of the name, it is inevitable that the smoke should be distributed throughout the building with the greatest impartiality, often forming a coating of creosote an inch or more in thickness.

Above the cooking-range is fastened the image of the kitchen-god, popularly supposed to be a deification of Chang Kung, a worthy who lived in the eighth century of our era, and was able to live in perfect peace, although nine generations simultaneously inhabited the same yard. Even his hundred dogs were so polite as to wait for another, if any one of them was late at a meal.

The reigning emperor of the Tang Dynasty sent for Chang Kung, to inquire the secret of such wonderful harmony, and calling for a pen, he is said to have written the character denoting "Forbearance" a great number of times. According to tradition the picture of this patriarch was placed in every dwelling as a stimulus to the imitation of his example, a purpose for which it unfortunately proves quite inert.

That the dwellings of the Chinese are cold in winter, hot in summer, and smoky all the year round is inevitable. Even in the coldest weather there is no escape from the bitter cold, except as it may be got by curling upon the k'ang. For this reason Chinese women often speak of the k'ang as like an "own mother." A room in which there is none is considered almost uninhabitable. But from an Occidental point of view they are models of discomfort. The heat is but slowly diffused, and during a long night one may be alternately drenched with perspiration, and then chilled to the bone as the heat diminishes. The adobe bricks of which the k'ang is composed crumble if an uneven pressure is made upon them, so that one often finds the k'angs in an inn full of pitfalls. They are always the lodging places of a multitude of tiny monsters to which the Chinese are too much accustomed to complain. Even when the adobe bricks are broken up in the spring to be pulverized as manure—on account of the creosote—the animal life lodged in the walls is apparently sufficient to restock the universe.

It is not surprising that the title-deeds to land are in course of years destroyed or lost, for there is in a Chinese house no proper place in which they may be kept. The only closets are made by leaving out a few bricks from the wall. A small board, resting on two pegs often forms the only book-shelf to be found in the apartments even of men of letters. Doors are locked by passing the link of a chain over a staple in the door-frame above; but Chinese padlocks can generally be picked with a wire, a chopstick, or even with a dry weed, and afford no real protection. Thieves are always provided with an assortment of keys, and often get in by lifting the doors off the pins which serve as hinges. Nothing is easier than to dig through adobe walls. In some of the rich villages of Shan-hsi house-walls are built quite six feet thick to discourage such penetration.

The floor of all common dwellings is merely the earth, not smoothed but beaten into fixed inequalities; this we are assured (in reply to a question why smoothness is not cultivated) is much the best way, as by this means every fluid spilled will run out of itself! In the corners of the dwelling stand, lie, or hang, the numerous household articles for which there is no other place. Jars of grain, agricultural implements, clumsy looms for weaving cotton, spinning wheels, baskets of all sizes and shapes, one or two benches, and possibly a chair, all seem to occupy such space as is to be had, while from the sooty roof depend all manner of articles, hung up so as to be out of the way—some of which when wanted must be hooked down with a pole. The maxim "a place for everything, and everything in its place" is inappropriate to a Chinese dwelling, where there is very little place for anything.

The small yard is in as great confusion as the house, and for the same reason. Dogs, cats, chickens and babies enjoy a very limited sphere of action, and generally take to the street, which is but an extension of the court. If the family owns animals, some place must be found for them in the yard, though when not in use they spend their time anchored by a very short rope, attached to pegs sunk deep in the ground, in front of the owner's dwelling. Pigs are kept in a kind of well, with a brick wall to prevent its caving in, and by climbing a very steep flight of brick stairs they can ascend to a little kennel provided for them at the edge of their pits—in many regions the only two-story domiciles to be found!

The Chinese village is always a miniature city, not only by reason of its internal arrangements—or lack of it—but often also in the virtue of the fact that it is surrounded by a wall.

Not many years ago several regiments stationed near the Yellow River, in Shan-tung, mutinied, killed an officer and marched off to their homes. The intelligence of this event spread throughout the province, and each region feared to be visited by the soldiers who were sure to plunder and perhaps to kill. So great was the panic that cities hundreds of miles from the seat of the disturbance were packed with a multitude of farm-carts loaded with villagers who had left their homes and abandoned their crops at the beginning of the wheat harvest, trusting to find safety within city walls. The losses sustained in consequence were immense.

Events like this may occur at any time, and the great T'ai P'ing Rebellion of half a century ago, together with its resultant disorders, left an ineffaceable impression of the insecurity of an unwalled village. Although the walls are seldom more than fifteen or twenty feet in height, whenever a year of bad harvests occurs, and bands of plunderers roam about, the use of even such defences is made obvious. Slight as is their value against an organized, well-directed attack, experience shows that they are often sufficient to accomplish the object intended, by diverting the stream of invaders to other villages where they meet with no resistance. The least rumour of an uprising in any quarter is often sufficient to stimulate the villagers to levy a tax upon the land in order to repair their earthen ramparts, in which, not without good reason, they place much more dependence than in the cautious and dilatory movements of the local authorities who are generally in no condition to cope with an organized and resolute force, especially with those rebels who have a real grievance.

III

VILLAGE NOMENCLATURE

The Chinese is justly termed a poetical language. The titles of emperors, the names of men, the signs of shops, all have some felicitous meaning. It is therefore somewhat of a disappointment to discover that the names of Chinese villages, unlike those of cities, are not as a rule either poetical or significant. The drafts upon the language by the incessant multiplication of hamlets are too great to be successfully met. Nearly all Chinese surnames serve as the designation of villages, as in other lands the names of families are attached to the settlements which they make. Sometimes two or more surnames are linked together to denote the village, as Chang-Wang Chuang, the village of the Chang and the Wang families. It often happens that in the changes, wrought by time, of the families for whom the place was named not a single representative remains. In such cases the name may be retained or it may be altered, though all recollection of the circumstances of the change may be lost.

The most conspicuous object in a Chinese village is generally a temple, and this building often gives its name to the hamlet. Thus the wall surrounding a temple is covered with red plaster, and the village is dubbed Red Temple. In a few years the plaster falls off, but the name sticks. Temples are frequently associated with the families which were prominent in their construction, and the name of the village is very likely to be derived from this source, as Wang Chia Miao, the Temple of the Wang Family; the Hua Chia Ssŭ, the monastery of the Hua Family. If there happen to be two temples of a similar appearance, the village may get the title of Double Temple, and in general any peculiarity in edifices of this sort is likely to be stereotyped in the village name.

The habit of using the names of families and temples to indicate the villages is a fertile source of confusion through the indefinite multiplication of the same name. There is no postal system in China compelling each post office to have a designation which shall not be confounded with others in the same province. Hence the more common names are so exceedingly common that they lose all value as distinctive designations. "Chang, Wang, Li, and Chao," are the four surnames which the Chinese regard as the most prevalent, the first two of them far out-distancing all their competitors. The number of places in a given district bearing the same, or similar names, is past all ascertaining; as, say eight or ten Wang Family villages, the Larger Wang Village, the Smaller Wang Village, the Front Wang Village, the Rear Wang Village, the Wang Village Under-the-bank, and so forth. Even with this complexity, distinction would be a much easier matter if the same name were always used, but anything which has a Wang about it is like to be called simply Wang Village, and only on inquiry is it to be learned which of all these Wangs is the one intended.

A similar ambiguity is introduced along the line of imperial highways, where the hamlets at which food is sold, and where accommodations are offered to travellers, are called "shops," taking their distinctive title from the distance to the district city,—as Five Mile Shop, Ten Mile, Fifteen, Twenty, Thirty, and Forty Mile Shop. Each district city may have "shops" of this kind on each side of it, and while the one twenty miles (or li) north is Twenty Li Shop, so is the one twenty li south, to the great confusion of the traveller, who after all is not sure where he is. In addition to this ambiguity, the Thirty Li Shop of one city is liable to be confounded with the Thirty Li Shop of the next city. It is a common circumstance to find an insignificant hamlet with a name comprising four or five characters, the local pronunciation of which is generally difficult to catch, as the words are spoken as one prolonged, many-syllabled sound. This leads to abbreviations, the same long title having perhaps two or three different modes of utterance, to the bewilderment of strangers, and to the intense amusement of the rustic born on the spot, who cannot conceive what there can be so hard to understand about a name which is to him as familiar as his own.

Another source of confusion in the nomenclature of Chinese villages, is the almost universal habit of varying one or more characters of a name without any apparent reason. The alteration has no connection with euphony, ease of pronunciation, or with any known cause whatever, but seems to be due to an irresistible instinct for variety, and to an antipathy to a too simple uniformity. Thus a village the proper title of which is the Ancient Monastery of the Li Family, (Li Ku Ssŭ) is generally called Li Kuang Ssŭ; a village known as that of Benevolence and Virtue (Jên Tê Chuang), is ordinarily styled Jên Wang Chuang. Analogous to this habit, is that of affixing two entirely distinct names to the same little hamlet, neither name suggesting the other, and the duplication merely serving to confound confusion. Thus a village which has a name derived from a temple, like Hsüan Ti Miao (the temple to Hsüan Ti) is also known as Chang Chuang (the village of the Chang Family), but as there are many other villages of Chang families near by this, one will be known by way of distinction, as the "Chang Family village which has a temple to Hsüan Ti"! Many persons have occasion to write the names of villages, who have but the scantiest knowledge of Chinese characters, and they are as likely to indite a false character having the same sound as a right one—nay, far more so—and thus it happens that there is a perpetual uncertainty, never set at rest in any manner whatsoever, as to what the real name of a place ought to be, for to all Chinese one name is as good as another, and in such matters, as in many others, there appears to be no intuition of right and wrong.

Chinese villages are only individual Chinese amplified, and, like individuals, they are liable to be nicknamed; and, as often happens with human beings, the nickname frequently supplants the original, of which no trace may remain in memory. This helps to account for the singular appellations of many villages.

A market-town on the highway, the wells of which afford only brackish water, was called "Bitter Water Shop," but as this name was not pleasing to the ear, it was changed on the tax lists to "Sweet Water Shop." If any one inquires how it is that the same fountain can send forth at the same time waters both bitter and sweet, he is answered with conclusive simplicity, "Sweet Water Shop is the same as Bitter Water Shop!" A village situated on the edge of a river was named after the two leading families, but when the river rose to a great height this name sunk out of sight, and there emerged the title, "Look at the Water;" but even this alteration not being sufficient to satisfy the thirst for variety, the name is written and pronounced as if it meant, "Look at the Grave!" A hamlet named for the Liu Family had in it a bully who appeared in a lawsuit with a black eye, and hence was called the Village of Liu with the Black Eye. In another instance a town had the name of Dropped Tooth, merely because the local constable lost a central incisor (Lao Ya Chên); but in course of time this fact was forgotten, and the name altered into "Market-town of the Crows," (Lao Kua Chên) which it still retains.

A village in which most of the families joined the Roman Catholics and pulled down all their temples, gained from this circumstance the soubriquet of "No Gods Village" (Wu Shên Chuang). The following specimens of singular village names are all taken from an area but a few miles square, and could doubtless be paralleled in almost any other region. "The Imperial Horse Yard" (Yü Ma Yüan). This title is said to have been inherited from the times of the founder of the Sung Dynasty. It is generally corrupted into "Sesame Garden," (Chih Ma Yüan). "End of the Cave," a village situated on a great plain, with vague traditions of an underground passage. "Seeing the Horse"; "Horse Words Village," from a tradition of a speaking animal; "Sun Family Bull Village"; "Female Dog Village"; "Wang Family Great Melon Village"; "Separating from the King Village"; "Basket Village of the Liu Village"; "Tiger-catching Village," and "Tiger-striking Fair"; "Duck's Nest of the Chou Family"; "Horse Without a

Hoof"; "Village of Chang of the Iron Mouth"; "Ts'ui Family Wild Pheasant Village"; "Wang Family Dog's Tooth"; "Village of the Benevolent and Loving Magistrate"; "Village of the Makers of Fine-tooth Combs," (Pi-tzŭ-chiang Chuang), which is now corrupted into "The Village Where They Wear Pug-noses"!

The Village Cobbler.

Village Broom-Maker.

IV

COUNTRY ROADS

The contracted quarters in which the Chinese live compel them to do most of their work in the street. Even in those cities which are provided with but the narrowest passages, these slender avenues are perpetually choked by the presence of peripatetic vendors of every article that is sold, and by peripatetic craftsmen, who have no other shop than the street. The butcher, the baker, the candlestick-maker, and hundreds of other workmen as well, have their representatives in perpetual motion, to the great impediment of travel. The wider the street, the more the uses to which it can be put, so that travel in the broad streets of Peking is often as difficult as that in the narrow alleys of Canton. An "imperial highway" in China is not one which is kept in order by the emperor, but rather one which may have to be put in order for the emperor. All such highways might rather be called low-ways; for, as they are never repaired, they soon become incomparably worse than no road at all.

If this is true of the great tines of travel over the empire, we must not expect to find the village road an illustration of any doctrine of political economy. Each of them is simply a forced contribution on the part of the owner of the land to the general welfare. It is so much soil on which he is compelled to pay taxes, and from which he gets no more good than any one else. Each land-owner will, therefore, throw the road on the edge of his land, so that he may not be obliged to furnish more than half the way. But as the pieces of land which he happens to own may be, and generally are, of miscellaneous lengths, the road will wind around so as to accommodate the prejudices of the owner in this particular, which explains the fact that in travelling on village roads it is often necessary to go a great distance to reach a place not far off.

An ordinary road is only wide enough for one vehicle, but as it is often necessary for carts to pass one another, this can only be done by trespassing on the crops. To prevent this the farmer digs deep ditches along his land, resembling gas-mains. Each farmer struggles to protect his own land, but when he drives his own cart, he too becomes a "trespasser"; thus a state of chronic and immitigable warfare is established, for which there is absolutely no remedy. The Occidental plan of setting apart a strip of land of uniform width, free from taxes and owned by the state, the grade of which shall be definite, is utterly beyond the comprehension of any Chinese. Where land is valuable and is all private property, road repairs are out of the question. There is no earth to repair with, and without repair, the roads soon reach a condition beyond the possibility of any repairs. Constant travel compresses and hardens the soil, making it lower than the adjacent fields; perpetual attrition grinds the earth into banks, which by heavy gales are blown in the form of thick dust on the fields.

In the rainy season the fields are drained into the road, which at such times is constantly under water. A slight change of level allows the water to escape into some still lower road, and thus a current is set up, which becomes first a brook, and then a rushing torrent, constantly wearing out its bed. This process repeated for decades and for centuries turns the road into a canal, several feet below the level of the fields. It is a proverb that a road 1,000 years old becomes a river, just as a daughter-in-law of many years' standing gradually "summers into a mother-in-law."

By the time the road has sunk to the level of a few feet below the adjacent land, it is liable to be wholly useless as a thoroughfare. It is a canal, but it can neither be navigated nor crossed. Intercourse between contiguous villages lying along a common "highway," is often for weeks together entirely interrupted. The water drained from the land often carries with it large areas of valuable soil, leaving in its place a yawning chasm. When the water subsides, the owner of the land sallies out to see what has become of this section of his farm. It has been dissolved in the canal, but if the owner cannot find that particular earth he can find other earth just as good. Wherever the light soil called loam, or "loess," is found, it splits with a vertical cleavage, leaving high banks on each side of a rent in the earth. To repair these, the owner takes the soil which he needs from a pit excavated by the side of the road, or more probably from the road itself, which may thus in a single season be lowered a foot or more in depth. All of it is his land, and why should he not take it? If the public wish to use a road, and do not find this one satisfactory, then let the public go somewhere else.

If a road becomes so bad as to necessitate its abandonment, a new one must be opened, or some old one adapted to the altered circumstances. The latter is almost sure to be the alternative; for who is willing to surrender a part of his scanty farm, to accommodate so impersonal a being as the public? In case of floods, either from heavy rains or a break in some stream, the only feasible method is thought to be to sit still and await the gradual retirement of the water. A raised road through the inundated district, which could be used at all seasons, is a triple impossibility. The persons whose land must be disturbed would not suffer it, no one would lift a finger to do the work—except those who happened to own land along the line of the route—and no one, no matter where he lived, would furnish any of the materials which would be necessary to render the road permanent.

An illustration of this state of things is found in a small village in central Chih-li, where lives an elderly lady, in good circumstances, a part of whose land is annually subject to flood from the drainage of the surrounding region. The evil was so serious that it was frequently impossible to haul the crops home on carts, but they had either to be brought on the backs of men wading, or, if there were water enough, toilfully dragged along on stalk rafts. To this comparatively enlightened woman occurred the idea of having her men and teams dig trenches along the roadside, raise the road to a level above possible flooding, and thus remedy the trouble permanently. This she did wholly at her own expense, the emerging road being a benefit to the whole country-side. The following winter, during which the contagious influenza was world-prevalent, there were several cases in the village terminating fatally. After five or six persons had died, the villagers became excited to discover the latent cause of the calamity, which was traced to the new highway. Had another death occurred they would have assembled with spades and reduced it to its previous level, thus raising a radical barrier against the grippe!

The great lines of Chinese travel might be made permanently passable, instead of being, as now, interrupted several months of the year, if the Governor of a Province chose to compel the several District Magistrates along the line to see that these important arteries are kept free from standing water, with ditches in good order at all seasons. But for the village road there is absolutely no hope until such time as the Chinese villager may come dimly to the apprehension that what is for the advantage of one is for the advantage of all, and that wise expenditure is the truest economy—an idea of which at present he has as little conception as of the binomial theorem.

V

THE VILLAGE FERRY

In the northern part of China, although the streams are not so numerous as at the south, they form more of an obstruction to travel, on account of the much greater use made of animals and of wheeled vehicles. The Chinese cart is a peculiarly northern affair, and appears to be of much the same type as in ancient days. The ordinary passenger cart is dragged by one animal in the cities, and by two in the country. The country cart, employed for the hauling of produce and also for all domestic purposes by the great bulk of the population, is a machine of untold weight. We once put the wheel of one of these carts on a platform-scale and ascertained that it weighed 177 pounds, and the axle fifty-seven pounds in addition, giving a total of 411 pounds for this portion of the vehicle. The shafts are stout as they have need to be, and when the cart upsets—a not infrequent occurrence—they pin the shaft animal to the earth, effectually preventing his running away. Mules, horses, cows, and donkeys, are all hitched to these farm carts, each pulling by means of loose ropes anchored to the axle. To make these beasts pull simultaneously is a task to which no Occidental would ever aspire, nor would he succeed if he did aspire. General Wolseley mentions in his volume describing the campaign in 1860, when the army marched on Peking, that at Ho Hsi Wu all the Chinese carters deserted, and the British troops were totally unable to do anything whatever with the teams.

Under these conditions of travel, a Chinese ferry is one of the most characteristic specimens of the national genius with which we are acquainted. Ferries are numerous, and so are carts to be ferried. The interesting thing is to watch the process, and it is a spectacle full of delightful surprises.

At a low stage of water the ferry-boat is at the base of a sloping bank, down which in a diagonal line runs the track, never wide enough for two carts to pass each other. To get one of these large carts down this steep and shelving incline requires considerable engineering skill, and here accidents are not infrequent. When the edge of the ferry is reached the whole team must be unhitched, and each animal got on the boat as best may be. Some animals make no trouble and will give a mighty bound, landing somewhere or everywhere to the imminent peril of any passengers that may be already on board. None of the animals have any confidence in the narrow, crooked, and irregular gang planks which alone are to be found. The more crooked these planks the better, for a reason which the traveller is not long in discovering. The object is by no means to get the cart and animals on with the minimum of trouble, but with the maximum of difficulty, for this is the way by which hordes of impecunious rascals get such an exiguous living as they have. When an animal absolutely refuses to budge—an occurrence at almost every crossing—its head is bandaged with somebody's girdle, and then it is led around and around for a long time so as to induce it to forget all about the ferryboat. At last it is led to the edge and urged to jump, which it will by no means do. Then they twist its tail—unless it happens to be a mule—put a stick behind it as a lever and get six men at each end of the stick, while six more tug at a series of ropes attached to the horns. After a struggle lasting in many cases half an hour, often after prolonged and cruel beatings, the poor beasts are all on board, where the more active of them employ their time in prancing about among and over the human passengers, to their evident danger.

Sometimes the animals become excited and break away, plunging over the edge of the ferry, which has no guards of any kind, and in such cases it is not uncommon for them to be floated away, or even lost. The writer is cognizant of a case in which the driver was himself pulled into a swift and swollen stream while struggling to restrain his mules, and was drowned, a circumstance which probably caused his "fare"—a scholar on his way to or from a summer examination—endless delay, as he would be detained at the district yamên for a witness.

Waiting for the Boat.

Crossing the Ferry.

But while we have been busy with the animals, we have neglected the cart, which must be dragged upon the ferryboat by the strength of a small army of men. There may be only one man or a man and a boy on a ferry, but to pull a loaded cart over the rugged edges of the planks, up the steep incline, requires perhaps ten or fifteen men. This is accomplished by the process so familiar at Chinese funerals, the wild yelling of large bands of men as they are directed by the leader.

Every individual who so much as lays a hand upon the cart must be paid, and the only limit is the number who can cluster around it. As in all other Chinese affairs there is no regular tariff of charges, but the rule is that adopted by some Occidental railway managers to "put on all the traffic will bear." Suppose for example that the passenger cart only pays a hundred cash for its transport across the stream; this sum must be divided into three parts, of which the ferry gets but one and the bands of volunteer pullers and pushers on the two banks the other two-thirds. In this way it often happens that all that one of these loafing labourers has to show for his spasmodic toil may be four cash, or in extreme cases only two, or even one.

On the farther bank the scene just described is reversed, but occupies a much shorter time, as almost any animal is glad enough to escape from a ferry. The exit of the carts and animals is impeded by the struggles of those who want to get a passage the other way, and who cannot be content to wait till the boat is unloaded. There is never any superintendent of the boat, any more than of anything else in China, and all is left to chance or fate. That people are not killed in the tumultuous crossings is a constant wonder.

It is not unnatural for the Occidental whose head is always full of ideas as to how things ought to be done in the East, to devise a plan by which all this wild welter should be reduced to order. He would, to begin with, have a fixed tariff, and he would have a wide and gently sloping path to the water's edge. He would have a broad and smooth gang-plank, over which both animals and carts could pass with no delay and no inconvenience. He would have a separate place for human passengers and for beasts, and in general shorten the time, diminish the discomforts and occidentalize the whole proceedings.

Now stop for a moment and reflect how any one of these several "reforms" is to be made a fact accomplished. The gently sloping banks will wash away with the first rise of the river; who is to repair them? Not the boatman, for "it is not the business of the corn-cutter to pull off the stockings of his customers." If the ferry is an "official" one, that only means that the local magistrate has a "squeeze" on the receipts, not that there are any corresponding obligations toward facilitating travel. Who is to provide those wide gang-planks over which the passage is to be so easy? Not the boatman. Not the passenger, whose only wish is to get safely over for that single time. Not the swarm of loafers whose interest it is not to have any gang-planks at all, or as nearly as possible none.

And even if the roads were made, and the gang-planks all provided by some benevolent despot, it would not be a week before the planks would be missing, and all things going on as they have been since the foundation of the Chinese world. The appointment of inspectors, police, etc., etc., would do no manner of good, unless it should be to their interest to further the reform, which would obviously never be the case.

Imagine an Anglo-Indian official, whose knowledge of Oriental races and traits is profound, in charge of the ferries for a single stretch, say of the Grand Canal. What would he do?—what could he do, even if backed up by a force theoretically irresistible? Nothing whatever to any lasting or good purpose until the need of some alteration in their system, or rather lack of system, forces itself upon the Chinese mind. How long in the ordinary process of human evolution it would take to bring this about, it is easy to conjecture. Think for an instant of the objections which would be made on every hand to the innovations. Who are these fellows? What are their motives? No Chinese can for a moment comprehend such a conception as is embodied in the phrase Pro bono publico. He never heard of such a thing, and what is more he never wants to hear of it.

We have wasted an undue amount of time in crossing a Chinese river, for it is a typical instance of flagrant abuses which the Chinese themselves do not mind, which would drive Occidentals to the verge of insanity—if not over the brink—and which it seems easy, but is really impossible to remedy. Mutatis mutandis, these things are a parable of the empire. The reform must come. It must be done from within. But the impulse can come only from without.

VI

VILLAGE WELLS

On the Great Plain of North China the wells are generally shallow, ranging from ten to thirty feet in depth; one of fifty feet would be unusual, though they are occasionally much deeper. The well is a very important feature of the outfit of a Chinese village, though never the scene of ablutions as in India. To save the labour of carrying water, all the animals are led to the well to drink, and the resultant mud makes the neighbourhood, especially in winter, very disagreeable. Rarely have they a cover of any sort, and the opening being level with the surface of the ground, it would seem inevitable that animals, children and blind persons, should be constantly falling in,—as indeed, occasionally, but seldom happens. Even the smallest bairns learn to have a wholesome fear of the opening, and ages of use have accustomed all Chinese to view such dangers with calm philosophy.

The business of sinking wells is an art by itself, and in regions where they are commonly used for irrigation, the villagers acquire a great reputation for expertness in the process. A village which desires a new well sends an invitation to the experts, and a party of men, numbering perhaps fifteen or twenty, responds. Though the work is fatiguing, difficult, and often dangerous, no money payment is generally offered or desired, but only a feast to all the workers, of the best food to be had. If the well is to be anything more than a water-pit, it is dug as deep as can be done without danger of caving in, and then the brick lining is let down from above. The basis of this is a strong board frame of the exact size of the opening, and wide enough to place the walling upon. A section of the wall is built upon this base, and

51

the whole is firmly bound to the baseboard within and without by ropes or reed withes. The lining then resembles a barrel without the heads, and when completed is so strong that, though it be subjected to considerable and unequal strains, it will neither give nor fall apart.

Several feet of the lining are lowered into the cavity, and as the digging proceeds the lining sinks, and the upper wall is built upon it. If it is desired to strike a permanent spring, this is accomplished by means of a large bamboo tube to which an iron-pointed head is fixed. The tube is driven down as far as it will go, the earth and sand being removed from within, and when a good supply of water is reached the opening is bricked up as usual. Such wells are comparatively rare, and proportionately valuable.

Wherever the soil and water are favourable for market-gardens, the country-side abounds in irrigation wells, often only six feet in width, and provided with a double windlass or sweep. One may meet the gardeners carrying home the ropes, buckets, and the windlass itself, none of which can safely be left out over night. Village wells are often sunk on ground which is conjointly owned by several families. Like everything else Oriental, they furnish frequent occasions now, as in patriarchal times, for bitter feuds. Whenever one is especially unpopular in his village, the first threat is to cut off his water supply, though this is not often done.

In some districts quicksands prevent the sinking of any permanent wells. The villagers are obliged to be up all night in order to take their turn at the scanty water supply, and fights are not infrequent. In a dry year the suffering is serious. For evils of this sort tube-wells would seem to provide a remedy, but thus far there has been great difficulty in getting down to such a depth as to strike good water. The nature of the trouble was aptly described by a coolie employed by a foreigner on a work of this kind, who was asked why the pipe was not driven deeper. He replied that it was, but "the deeper they went the more there wasn't any water" It would appear that in the direction of a good water supply, Western knowledge might be applied for the benefit of great numbers of Chinese and on a large scale, or if not on a large scale, then on a small one.

As an illustration of the process by which this may be done, an experience of many years ago in a Shan-tung village is worthy of mention. One of the missionaries had the happiness of welcoming a second son to his household, an event which seemed to the Chinese of such happy omen that they were moved to unite in subscribing a fixed sum from each family in the village, to purchase a silver neck ornament for the infant. As the suggestion was not absolutely and peremptorily vetoed, the committee in charge went on and ordered the silver chain and padlock, after which the delicate question arose by what means this gift should be acknowledged. After canvassing many plans, one was at length hit upon which appeared to satisfy the requisite conditions, which were in brief that the thing bestowed should be a distinct benefit to all the people, and one which they could all appreciate. It was proposed to put a force-pump in a village well not far from the mission premises, where much water was daily drawn by a great many people with a great deal of labour. The force-pump would make this toil mere child's play. The plan was so plainly fore-ordained to success, that one of the missionaries—although not having the felicity of two sons—was moved to promise also a stone watering trough, which in Chinese phrase, would be a "Joy to Ten Thousand Generations." The village committee listened gravely to these proposals without manifesting that exhilaration which the obviously successful nature of the innovation seemed to warrant, but promised to consider and report later. When the next meeting of this committee with the missionaries took place, the former expressed a wish to ask a few questions. They pointed out that there were four or five wells in the village. "Was it the intention of the Western foreign 'shepherds' to put a 'water-sucker' into each of these wells?" No, of course not; it was meant for the one nearest the mission premises. To this it was replied that the trinket for the shepherd's child had been purchased by uniform contributions from each family in the village. Some of these families lived on the front street and some on the back one, some at the east end and some at the west end. "Would it be consistent with the ideal impartiality of Christianity to put a 'water-sucker' where it could only benefit a part of those for whom it was designed?"

After an impressive silence the committee remarked that there was a further question which had occurred to them. This village, though better off than most of those about, had some families which owned not a foot of land. These landless persons had to pick up a living as they could. One way was by carrying and selling water from house to house in buckets. According to the account of the shepherds the new "water-sucker" would render it so easy to get water that any one could do it, and the occupation of drawers of water would be largely gone. It could not be the intention of the benevolent shepherds to throw a class of workmen out of work. What form of industry did the shepherds propose to furnish to the landless class, to compensate them for the loss of their livelihood? At this point the silence was even more impressive than before. After another pause the village committee returned to their questions. They said that Western inventions are very ingenious, but that Chinese villagers "attain unto stupidity." As long as the Western shepherds were at hand to explain and to direct the use of the "water-suckers," all would doubtless go well; but they had noticed that Western inventions sometimes had a way of becoming injured by the tooth of time, or by bad management. Suppose that something of this sort took place with the "water-sucker," and suppose that no shepherd was at hand to repair or replace it, what should then be done after the villagers had come to depend upon it? This recalled the fact that a force-pump had been tried several years before in Peking, in the deep wells of that city, but the fine sand clogged the valves, and it had to be pulled up again! In view of these various considerations, is it surprising that the somewhat discouraged shepherds gave up the plan of interfering with Oriental industries, or that the obligation to the village was finally acknowledged by the payment of a sum of money which they used ostensibly for the repair of the rampart around the village, but which really went nobody knows where or to whom?

VII

THE VILLAGE SHOP

The Chinese have always divided themselves into the four classes of scholars, farmers, workmen, and merchants. Considering their singular penchant for trade, it is a surprise to find them putting traders at the foot of the list.

If any one has an idea that the life of a Chinese dealer is an easy one, he has a very inaccurate idea indeed, and the smallest investigation of any specific case will be sufficient to disabuse him of it. Indeed there are not many people in China whose life is an easy one, certainly not the officials and the rich, who are at once the most envied and the most misunderstood persons in the empire.

In Shan-tung, every village of any size has its little "tsa-huo-p'u," or shop of miscellaneous goods. It is not at all like a huckster's shop at home, for the goods kept are not intended to be disposed of at once. Many of them may remain in stock for many years, but they will probably all be worked off at last. Occidentals often suppose that the Chinese live on "curry and rice." Very few people in Shan-tung ever tasted rice in their lives, but there is generally a small quantity kept at the "tsa-huo-p'u" in case there should be a call for use at feasts, or for the sick. There is a good supply of red paper used for cards of invitation, and white paper for funeral announcements, the need for which must be met promptly, without waiting for a trip to a distant market-town. Besides this there is a large stock of fire-crackers which are wanted whenever there is a feast-day, a wedding or a funeral, and also paper money and other materials for the idolatrous ceremonies which these occasions involve. There are many other kinds of wares, for there is almost nothing for which a demand may not be made; but the greatest profit is derived from the articles last named.

Let not the reader, inexpert in Chinese affairs, suppose that the keeper of the "tsa-huo-p'u" sits all day in a chair awaiting customers, or spends the intervals between their infrequent arrivals in playing Chinese fox and geese or chess. He does nothing of the kind. If his shop is a very small one it is not tended at all, but simply open when occasion serves. If it is a larger affair, it requires the time of more than one person, not to tend it but to carry on the rural trade. For the larger part of the business of the "tsa-huo-p'u" is not at home, but at five-day markets all about. The proprietors of some shops take their wares to a fair every day in the month, on the first and sixth to one place, on the second and seventh to another, on the third and eighth to another, and on the fifth and tenth to still another, by which time the circle is completed.

Going to one of these markets is no holiday work. It is necessary to rise either at daylight or before, select the goods to be taken, pack them carefully, make an accurate list of them, and then wheel the barrow to the fair, sometimes over very bad roads in very bad weather. Arrived at the market-town there are no stalls or booths for the dealers to occupy, but each plants himself in a spot for which he has to pay a small ground-rent to the owner, who is always on hand to collect this rent. All day long the barrow must be tended assiduously, bickering with all sorts and conditions of men and women, and when the people have begun to scatter, the articles must be packed up again, and the barrow wheeled home.

Then comes the wearisome taking account of stock, in regard to which the proprietor is exceedingly particular. In China nobody trusts anybody else, for the excellent reason that he is aware that in similar circumstances it might not be safe to trust himself. Hence the owner of the little shop, or some one who represents him, looks carefully over the goods brought home and compares them with the invoice made out in the morning. This is a check upon the temptation to sell some things without giving an account of them. The sales which have been made during the day are for small sums only, and as all the cash has to be counted and strung on hemp cords so as to make the full string of 1,000 cash (or 500 in some parts of the country), this counting and stringing of the money takes a great deal of time, and is very tiresome work when done by the quantity—though this remark is applicable to most Chinese occupations viewed from an Occidental point of view.

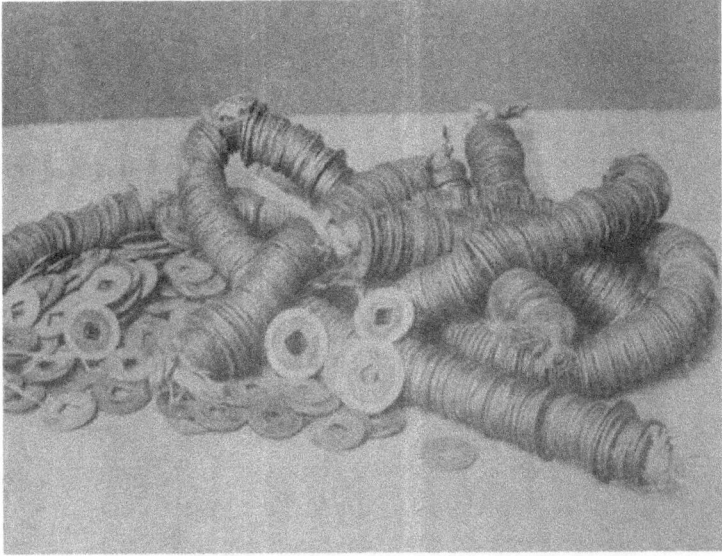

STRINGS OF CHINESE CASH.

PREPARING THE STRINGS.

The employee of the "tsa-huo-p'u" gets his meals when he can, which is after he has finished everything which his employer wants him to do. It is necessary for him to be a rare hand if he is to be so useful that he will not be sent away if business is slack when the year closes, or if the proprietor gets better service from some one else. The supply of labour of every description, is so excessive, that it is very hard to get a place, and harder still to keep it.

A country villager with whom the writer is well acquainted had too little land to support his family, so he accepted the offer of a neighbour to help him with the business which he had lately undertaken. This consisted of sending four wheel-barrows daily to different villages to sell meat at the markets. The men who did this had to rise long before daylight in order to get the meat ready, that is to cut it from the bones, which are disposed of at a separate rate. The weight of meat on each barrow had to be entered and also the weight of the bones. On the return of the barrows at night it was necessary to weigh what was left from the sales and compare it with the returns of cash. This must be gone through with for each barrow. The assistant to the meat-dealer had to keep in all fourteen different account books. "But," we said to him, "after the barrows are gone, and before they come back, there must be a little interval of comparative peace in which you can do what you like?" "Alas, no," was the reply, "it takes all of that time to balance up the fourteen entries of the day before;" and judging from what one knows of Chinese bookkeeping the time allowed would not be at all too much. Entries in Chinese account-books are not set down in columns, so as to be conveniently added, but strung along a page like stockings on a clothes-line. Each entry must be treated by itself on the suan-pan or reckoning-board, and there is no check against errors. Our informant was so tired of his contract that he seized the occasion of a funeral in a family with which he was connected, and which he was in theory bound to attend, to break away and make a brief call on the foreign friend who had generally been able to sympathize with certain of his previous woes.

A year later the writer met him again, ascertained that he had abandoned the intricate bookkeeping which selling meat appeared to involve, for another kind of account-keeping in a well-to-do family, where there is a good deal of land and much resulting activity. He was asked if he had any time to read his book—of which he seemed to be fond—and he replied with a decisive negative. Not if he got up early? No, indeed, he had to begin work the minute he was dressed. Not if he went to bed a little later? Certainly not; he had to go to bed late as it was—no time then. But he might at least snatch a little leisure while he was eating. "Far from it," was the response, "the woman who is at the head of affairs takes that opportunity to consult about the work."

In the case of firms having any considerable business, after the day's work is all over, the clerks are liable to be required to spend the evening in untying all the numerous strings of cash that have come in, with a view to the discovery of any rare coins that might be sold at a special price. All is fish that comes to a Chinese net, and sooner or later there is very little that does not find its way there to the profit of its owner. If the time should ever come, as come it may, when the far-distant West comes into close and practical competition with the patient Chinese for the right to exist, one or the other will be behind-hand in the race and it is safe to venture the prediction that it will not be the Chinese!

The village shop keeps different kinds of weighing poles for buying and for selling, works off all its uncurrent cash and bad bills on any one upon whom it can impose, and generally drives a hard bargain with those who deal with it, who retaliate in kind as opportunity offers. But as elsewhere in this mixed world, much depends upon the individuality of its head manager.

VIII

THE VILLAGE THEATRE

That the Chinese are extravagantly fond of theatrical representations, is well known to all who live in China. The Chinese trace the origin of the stage to the times of the Emperor Ming Huang, of the T'ang Dynasty (died 762) who, under an alias, is supposed to be worshipped as the god of play-actors. It is a popular saying that if the players neglect to do homage to this patron, they will altogether fail in their representations, whatever these may be.

With the history of the Chinese stage, we have in this connection no concern. According to the Chinese themselves, it has degenerated from its ancient function of a censor in morals, and has become merely a device for the amusement of the people. It is a remarkable circumstance that while the Chinese as a people are extravagantly fond of theatrical exhibitions of all sorts, the profession of play-actor is one of the few which debars from the privileges of the literary examinations. The reason for this anomaly is said to be the degradation of the theatre by pandering to vitiated or even licentious tastes. To what extent the plays ordinarily acted are of this sort, it is impossible for a foreigner to decide. The truth seems to be that the general (theoretical) contempt for the stage and its actors in China, is a product of the moral teachings of Confucianism, which uncompromisingly condemn the perversion of the right uses of dramatic representation. But while this (theoretical) view is the one which is constantly met, it is like many other Confucian doctrines, chiefly remarkable for the unanimity with which it is disregarded in practice.

In what we have to say of Chinese theatres, we must disclaim any knowledge of them at first hand, that is to say, by listening to acted plays. There are several obstacles to the acquisition of such knowledge by this method, even were other difficulties lacking. Most Chinese plays are laid out upon so extravagant a scale, as regards time, that they may be spread over many hours, or possibly several days. The most indefatigable European could not listen to the entire performance of any one of them, without becoming utterly exhausted. The dialect in which the actors speak is so different from the spoken language, that it is hard to form an idea of what they are saying. The tone adopted is that shrill falsetto, which is not only fatiguing to an Occidental hearer, but almost of necessity unintelligible.

When to these embarrassments are added the excruciating music, the discomfort attending the dense crowds, and the universal confusion which is an invariable concomitant of a Chinese theatre, it is not strange that these representations have for Westerners very few attractions, after the first glance has satisfied curiosity. This indifference on our part is almost unintelligible to the Chinese. That a foreign traveller, who is told of a theatre in full blast at the town at which he expects to spend the night, should feel no joy, but should deliberately push on so as to avoid spending the night at that place—this is to the Chinese profoundly incomprehensible.

Except in a few large cities, the Chinese have no theatres in our sense of the term, provided with seats and enclosed by walls and roof. The stage is a very simple affair, and is entirely open to inspection. Sometimes it is built like a temple with an open front. But by far the larger part of the rural representations of theatrical companies take place on a temporary scaffolding which is put up for the purpose the night before the plays begin, and is taken down the moment the last play closes. The players resemble their ancient Grecian prototypes in that they are a migratory band, going wherever they are able to find an engagement.

The stage equipments, like the stage itself, are of the simplest order, the spectator being required to supply by his imagination most of those adjuncts in the way of scenery, which in our days, are carried to such perfection in the theatres of the West. There is no division of a play into separate acts or scenes, and what cannot be inferred from the dress, or the pantomime of the actors, they must expressly tell to the audience, as for example who they are, what they have been doing, and the like. The orchestra is an indispensable accompaniment of a theatrical representation, and not only bursts into every interval of the acting, but also clangs with ferocity at such stirring scenes as a battle attack, or to add energy to any ordinary event.

Apropos of this resemblance between the Greek stage and the Chinese, which must have struck many observers, Mr. H. E. Krehbiel (in an article published in the Century for January, 1891) has declared that "the Chinese drama is to-day in principle a lyric drama, as much so as the Greek tragedy was. The moments of intense feeling are accentuated, not merely by accompanying music, as in our melodrama, but by the actor breaking out into song. The crudeness and impotency of the song in our ears has nothing to do with the argument. It is a matter of heredity in taste."

The village theatrical company owes its existence to some rich man, who selects this as a form of investment. As all the available land in the greater portion of China is wholly out of the market, it is not easy for one who has more money than he can conveniently use to decide what to do with it. If he should go into the theatrical business, it is not necessarily with the expectation that the money will yield him a large return, but in order to provide a popular amusement for a great number of people, and at the same time receive a larger or smaller interest on the amount invested.

The person whose capital is used in the costumes, which are the main part of the outfit of a Chinese theatre, is called the "Master of the chest." The whole outfit may be leased of him by an association of persons, who pay a fixed sum for the use of the costumes, which must be kept in good condition. In a first-class theatre, these costumes are very costly, and include what are called "dragon robes," and "python robes," each with double sets of inner garments, of fine quality, and handsomely embroidered. Of these there are at least two suits, five suits of armour, and numberless other articles of clothing, such as trousers, skirts, boots, buskins, etc. Another "chest" contains the accoutrements of the players, as swords, spears, and the like, made of gilded wood.

The value of all these various equipments, in a well-furnished theatre, is said to be fully $5,000, and in those of the cheaper sorts, two-thirds or half as much. Each of the three "chests" in which the stage accoutrements are stored, is in charge of three men, who are responsible for the security and the care of the contents of the cases.

The players are divided into classes which are called by different names, the members of each class receiving pay according to the dignity of their position. There are, for example, two individuals, one civil and one military, who represent high-class historical characters, like Chiang T'ai-kung, etc. These actors are called lao-shêng. Another class styled hu-shêng, represent personages like Wên Wang, or Chao K'uang-yin. A third class are assigned to characters like Lü Pu, etc., and these players are called hsiao-shêng. In addition to these are persons of less importance, who represent ladies, officials' wives, young girls, or others. After these come what may be called clowns, who are termed "flowery-faced," (hua-lien) subdivided into first, second and third. These represent the bad characters, such as Chou Wang, Ts'ao Ts'ao, and the like, down to the lowest class who take the most despised and hateful parts of all. In addition to these main characters, there is a considerable force detailed as soldiers, servants, messengers, or to personify boatmen, innkeepers, and the like. The rear is brought up with a large staff of cooks, water-carriers, etc., whose duty it is to provide for the material comfort of the players in their vagrant life.

Aside from the regular theatrical companies one frequently meets with companies of amateurs who have inherited the art of giving performances on a small scale called "a little theatre." They are young farmers who delight in the change and excitement of stage life, and who after the crops are harvested are open to engagements until the spring work begins. There may be only fifteen or twenty in the band, but the terms are low, and the food furnished them much better than they would have had at home, and when the season is over they may be able to divide a snug little sum to each performer.

The manager, or lessee of the theatrical equipment, is called a chang-pan, and engages the players for a term of about ten months, beginning early in the spring, and ending before the close of the year. The whole company may number between fifty and a hundred men, and the best actors may be engaged for sums ranging from the equivalent of a hundred dollars for the most skilled, down to a few tens of dollars for the inferior actors, their food in each case being furnished. It is thus easy to see that the expense of maintaining a theatre is a vast drain upon the resources of the lessee, and presupposes a constant succession of profitable engagements, which is a presupposition not infrequently at a great remove from the facts of experience.

The lessee of the theatre supplies himself with the material for the development of actors, by taking children on contract, or apprenticeship, for a fixed period (often three years) according to a written agreement. At the end of their apprenticeship, these pupils are at liberty to engage in any company which they may elect, for whatever they can get, but during their term of indenture, their time belongs to the man who has leased them of their parents. The motive for such a contract on the part of the parents, is to secure a support for the children. Sometimes children run away from home and make engagements on their own account, attracted by the supposed freedom of the player's life.

The amount which each child receives during the time of his apprenticeship, is the merest pittance, and it is said that in three months at most he can learn all that it is necessary for him to know. A large part of his duties will be to strut about on the stage, and mouth more or less unintelligible sentences in a grandiloquent tone. If the number of plays in which he appears is large, the tax upon the memory may be considerable, but Chinese children can learn by rote with amazing facility, and constant practice must in a short time fix in his memory everything which the young actor requires to remember.

From an Occidental point of view, it would be hard to imagine anything more remote from a life of pleasure, than the constant locomotion, routine drudgery, uncertain and inadequate remuneration of the average Chinese actor. We have never met one who did not admit that it was a bad life. A leading Japanese actor is quoted as saying that the popular notions in regard to the theatre of that country—which is probably in many respects analogous to that of China—are as different from the reality, as clouds from mud. "The hardships endured are as the suffering of Hades, and the world is not benefited a fraction by the actors' exertion, so they are not useful to society. It is a life to fear and to dread." There are probably very few Chinese actors who have progressed so far as to entertain, even for a moment, the thought whether their work is a good or an evil to "society."

It is not uncommon to hear of an exceptionally intelligent District Magistrate who issues proclamations strictly forbidding theatrical performances within his jurisdiction, exhorting the people to save their funds to buy grain and relieve the poor, or to set up public schools. But the only way to enforce these sensible orders of an unusually paternal official, is for him to make constant personal inspection, and see that his commands are heeded. Otherwise, a sum of money judiciously spent at the yamên, will buy complete immunity from punishment. Free schools and charity are too tame for the taste of the people, who demand something "hot-and-bustling," which a theatrical performance most decidedly is.

It is one of the contradictions which abound in the Chinese social life, that while play-actors are theoretically held in very light esteem, the representation of a play is considered as a great honour to the person on whose behalf it is furnished. Instances have occurred in China, in which such a representation has been offered by the Chinese to foreigners, as an expression of gratitude for help received in time of famine. The motives in such cases, however were probably very mixed, being composed largely of a desire on the part of the proposers to gratify their own tastes, while at the same time paying off in a public manner a technical debt of gratitude.

To suggest under such circumstances that the money which would have been absorbed in the expenses of the theatre, should rather be appropriated to the purposes of some public benefit, such as a free-school, would not commend itself to one Chinese in a thousand. Only a limited number of scholars could receive the benefit of a free-school, whereas a theatre is emphatically for everybody. Moreover, a theatre is demonstrative and obtrusively thrusts itself upon the attention of the general public in a manner which to the Oriental is exceedingly precious, while to set up a free-school would be "to wear a fine garment in the dark," when no one would know the difference.

The occasion for the performance of a play is sometimes a vow, which may have been made by an individual in time of sickness, the theatricals to be the expression of gratitude for recovery. In the case of an entire village, it is often the returning of thanks to some divinity for a good harvest, or for a timely rain. A quarrel between individuals is frequently composed by the adjudication of "peace-talkers" that one of the parties shall give a theatrical exhibition by way of a fine, in the benefits of which the whole community may thus partake. In view of the well-known propensities of the Chinese, it is not strange that this method of adjusting disputes is very popular. We have known it to be adopted by a District Magistrate in settling a lawsuit between two villages, and such cases are probably not uncommon.

Sometimes there is no better reason for holding a theatre than that a sum of public money has accumulated, which there is no other way to spend. A foreigner could easily propose fifty purposes to which the funds could be appropriated to much better advantage, but to the Chinese these suggestions always appear untimely, not to say preposterous.

When it has been determined to engage a theatre, the first step is to draw up a written agreement with the manager, specifying the price. This will vary from a sum equivalent to twenty-five dollars, up to several hundred dollars. The former amount is, indeed, a bottom price, and would be offered only to a very inferior company, which might be forced to accept it, or even a less sum, as better in a slack season than no engagement at all. During the time of the year, on the contrary, in which the demand for theatricals is at the maximum, a company may have offers from several villages at once. Rather than lose the double profit to be made, the troupe is often divided, and a number of amateurs engaged to take the vacant places, thus enabling the company to be in two places at the same date.

It is a common proverb that the country villager who witnesses a theatre, sees only a great hubbub, a generalisation strictly within the truth. It is upon this ignorance of the villager that the theatrical manager presumes when he furnishes an inferior representation, instead of the one for which his contract calls. But if the villager ascertains the fraud, consisting either in deficiency of players or inferior acting, he rises in democratic majesty, and "fines" the company an extra day or two, or even three days, of playing as a penalty, and from this decision it would be vain to appeal.

The individual who communicates with the village which hires the theatrical company, and who receives the money, is called the program bearer ("pao-tan ti"). The scorn in which theatrical folk are supposed to be held, appears to be reserved for this one individual alone. He makes arrangements for the conveyance of all the trunks containing the equipment from the previous place of playing, to the next one, and especially for the transportation of the staging.

In inland regions, where it is necessary to use animals, it

requires a great many carts to move about so much lumber, which must be done with great expedition in order not to waste a day, at a time when engagements are numerous; and, even to a Chinese, time is precious, because the food and pay of so many persons have to be taken into the account. The carts for this hauling are provided by the village which is to enjoy the exhibition, being often selected by lot. Sometimes, however, a small tax is levied on all the land in the village, and the carts are hired.

The day previous to a theatre in any village is a busy one. Great quantities of mats are provided, and in a short time some barren spot on the outskirts of the hamlet begins to assume the appearance of an impromptu settlement; for aside from the theatre itself, great numbers of small mat-sheds are put up to be used for cook-shops, tea-shops, gambling-booths, and the like. During the day, even if the village is but a small one, the appearance is that of the scene of a very large fair.

In the larger towns, where fairs are held at more or less regular intervals, it is usual, as already mentioned, to begin them with a theatrical exhibition, on the first day of which hardly any business will be done, the attendants being mainly occupied in gazing at or listening to the play. In such cases the attendants can frequently be safely estimated at more than 10,000 persons. In large fairs there is generally a performance every day as long as the fair holds, an arrangement which is found to be very remunerative from a financial point of view in attracting attendance, and therefore customers.

From a social point of view, the most interesting aspect of Chinese village theatricals is the impression which is produced upon the people as a whole. This impression may be feebly likened to that which is made upon children in Western lands, by the immediate imminence of Christmas, or in the United States by the advent of a Fourth of July. To theatrical holidays in China every other mundane interest must give way.

As soon as it is certain that a particular village is to have a theatre, the whole surrounding country is thrown into a quiver of excitement. Visits by young married women to their mothers' homes, always occasions to both mothers and daughters of special importance, are for a long time beforehand arranged with sole reference to the coming great event. All the schools in all the neighbouring villages expect at such times a holiday during the whole continuance of the theatricals. Should the teacher be so obstinate as to refuse it (which would never be the case, as he himself wishes to see the play) that circumstance would make no difference, for he would find himself wholly deserted by all his pupils.

It is not only brides who take advantage of this occasion to visit their relatives, but in general it may be said that when a village gives a theatrical representation, it must count upon being visited, during the continuance of the same, by every man, woman and child, who is related to any inhabitant of the village and who can possibly be present. Every Chinese family has a perfect swarm of relatives of all degrees, and the time of a theatrical performance is an excellent opportunity to look in upon one's friends. Whether these friends and relatives have been invited or not, will make no difference. In the case of ordinary villagers, the visitors would come even if they knew for certain that they were not wanted.

It has frequently been remarked that hospitality as such cannot be said to be a characteristic Chinese virtue, although there is at all times such a parade of it. But whatever one's feelings may be, it is necessary to keep up the pretence of overflowing hospitality, so that whoever comes to the yard must be pressed to stay to a meal and to spend the night, however anxious the host may be to get rid of him. On ordinary occasions, guests will not stay without such an amount of urging as may suffice to show that the invitation is bonâ fide, but during the continuance of a theatre it often makes very little difference how lacking the host may be in cordiality, the guests will probably decide to stay, as the play must be seen.

It is by no means an uncommon thing to find that in a village which has engaged a theatrical troupe, every family is overrun with such visitors, to such a degree that there is not space enough for them to lie down at night, so that they are forced to spend it in sitting up and talking, which may be easily conceived to be an excellent preparation for the fatiguing duties of the morrow. As a theatre seldom lasts less than three days, and sometimes more than four, it can be imagined what a tax is laid upon the village which is overrun. When it is considered that every married woman who returns to her home, as well as every woman who visits any relative, always brings all of her young children, and that the latter consider it their privilege to scramble for all that they can get of whatever is to be had in the way of food, it is obvious that the poor housekeeper is subjected to a tremendous strain, to which the severest exigencies of Western life afford very few analogies.

The cost of feeding such an army of visitors is a very serious one, and to the thrifty Chinese it seems hard that fuel which would ordinarily last his family for six months, must be burnt up in a week, to "roast" water, and cook food for people whom he never invited, and most of whom he never wished to see. It is a moderate estimate that the expense of entertainment is ten times the cost of the theatre itself, realizing the familiar saying that it is not the horse which costs but the saddle.

The vast horde of persons who are attracted to the village which has a theatre, has among its numbers many disreputable characters, against whom it is necessary for the villagers to be constantly upon their guard. For this reason, as well as on account of the necessity for being on hand to look after the swarms of guests, the people of the village have little or no opportunity to see the play themselves. Guests and thieves occupy all their time! Eternal vigilance is the price at which one's property is to be protected, and the more one has to lose, the less he will be able to enjoy himself, until the danger is over. It is a common observation that, after a theatrical performance, there is not likely to be a single chicken left in a village. To prevent them from being stolen by the expert chicken-thieves, the villagers must dispose of their fowls in advance.

Such being the conditions under which the Chinese village theatre is held, it is surprising that so great a number of theatrical troupes contrive to make a living—such as it is—out of so precarious an occupation, which is likely to fail altogether during years of famine or flood (never few in number), and also during the whole of each period of imperial mourning, when actors are often reduced to extreme misery. One reason for their passionate attachment to the theatre, must be found in the fact that for the Chinese people there are very few available amusements, and for the mass of the country people there is literally nothing to which they can look forward as a public recreation, except a few feast days (often only two or three in the year), the large fairs with accompanying theatricals, or theatricals without fairs.

It is evident that a form of exhibition which is so much valued by the Chinese, may become an important agency in inflaming the minds of the people. This is at times undoubtedly the case. Many instances have come to the knowledge of foreigners, in which theatricals representing the Tientsin massacre or some similar event, have been acted in the interior of China. In some cases this is doubtless done with the connivance of the magistrates, and it is easy to see that the effect upon the minds of the people must be very unfavourable, if it is held to be desirable to maintain among the Chinese respect for foreigners.

In China, as in other lands, it is easy for theatrical representations to deal with current events which have a general interest. In a certain case of warfare involving two different Counties, as to the right to make a bank to prevent inundation, several lives were lost and a formidable lawsuit resulted. The occurrences were of such a dramatic character that they were woven into a play, which was very popular at a little distance from the scene of the original occurrence.

The representation of historical events, by Chinese theatres, may be said to be one of the greatest obstacles to the acquisition of historical knowledge by the people. Few persons read histories, while every one hears plays, and while the history is forgotten because it is dull, the play is remembered because it is amusing. Theatricals, it is scarcely necessary to remark, do not deal with historical events from the standpoint of accuracy, but from that of adaptation to dramatic effect. The result is the greatest confusion in the minds of the common people, both as to what has really happened in the past, and as to when it took place, and for all practical purposes, fact and fiction are indistinguishable.

Among the most popular Chinese plays, are those which deal with everyday life, in its practical forms. Cheap and badly printed books, in the forms of tracts, containing the substance of these plays, are everywhere sold in great numbers, and aid in familiarizing the people with the plots.

Our notice of the Chinese drama may fitly conclude with a synopsis of one of these librettos, which contains a play of general celebrity, to which references are constantly made in popular speech. It is said to have been composed by a native of Shan-hsi, and is designed as a satire upon the condition of society in which, as so often in China at the present day, it is almost impossible for a teacher, theoretically the most honoured of beings, to keep himself from starvation.

It is a current proverb that in the province of Shan-tung, the number of those who wish to teach school is in excess of those who can read! The scene of this play is therefore appropriately laid in the land of the sages Confucius and Mencius, and in a district within the jurisdiction of the capital, Chi-nan Fu.

The characters are only two in number, a teacher called Ho Hsien-shêng who is out of employment, and reduced to extreme distress, and a patron named Li, who wishes to engage a master for his boys, aged nine and eleven. The teacher's remarks are mixed with extensive quotations from the Classics, as is the manner of Chinese schoolmasters, who wish to convey an impression of their great learning. He affirms that his success in instruction is such that he will guarantee that his pupils shall reach the first degree of hsiu-ts'ai, or Bachelor, in three years, the second of chü-jên, or Master, in six, and attain to the eminence of chin-shih, or Doctor, in twelve.

The teacher begins by a poetical lament that he had lost his place as a teacher, and that a scholar so situated is far worse off than a handicraftsman, who, he says, has always enough to eat. After this, the teacher comes on the stage, crying out like a peddler, "Teach School! Teach School!" Upon this Li comes forward, suggests that a man who offers to teach probably knows at least how to read, and explains that he feels the need of some one in the family who can decipher the tax bills, etc., but that he really cannot afford the expense of a teacher for his children.

He explains that his boys are dull, that the food of the teacher—the bill of fare of which he details—will be poor and coarse. There will be only two meals a day, to save expense, and at night there will be no fire. The coverlet is a torn dogskin, no mat on the bed, only a little straw, and no pillow. The salary is to be but 8,000 cash a year, but this is subject to a discount, 800 counting for 1000. The teacher is never to leave the schoolyard while school is in session.

The school will be held in a temple, hitherto occupied by nuns. These will be removed to a side room, and the teacher will be required to strike the bell, sweep out the building, and perform the other necessary services on the first and fifteenth of each month, and these duties must be executed with punctilious care. He is also cautioned not to allow his morals to be contaminated by the nuns whose reputation is so proverbially bad. None of his salary will be paid in advance, and a pro rata deduction will be made for every day of absence. During the summer rains the teacher must carry the children to school upon his back, that they may not spoil their clothes and make their mother trouble. Whenever school has been dismissed, the teacher is to carry water, work on the threshing floor, take care of the children, grind in the mill, and do all and everything which may be required of him. To all the foregoing conditions, the teacher cheerfully assents, and declares himself ready to sign an agreement upon these terms for the period of ten years!

Perhaps the most instructive aspect of Chinese theatricals, is that which takes account of them as indices to the theory of life which they best express, a theory in which most Chinese are firm, albeit unconscious, believers. It is a popular saying that "The whole world is only a stageplay; why then should men take life as real?" It is in strict accordance with this view, that the Chinese frequently appear as if psychologically incapable of discriminating between practical realities which are known to be such, and theoretical "realities" which, if matters are pushed to extremities, are admitted to be fictitious.

The spectacular theory of life is never for a moment lost sight of in China, and it demands a tribute which is freely, unconsciously, continually, and universally paid. It is upon this theory that a large proportion of Chinese revelling is based, the real meaning being, "You have wronged me, but I am not afraid of you, and I call upon all men to witness that I defy you." It is this theory upon which are grounded nine-tenths of the acts which the Chinese describe as being done "to save face," that is, to put the actor right with the spectators, and to prove to them that he is able to play his part and that he knows well what that part is. Never, surely, was it more true of any land than of China, that

"All the world's a stage,
And all the men and women merely players."

IX

VILLAGE SCHOOLS AND TRAVELLING SCHOLARS

The prominent place given to education in China renders the Chinese village school an object of more than common interest, for it is here that by far the greater number of the educated men of the empire receive their first intellectual training. While the schools of one district may be a little better or worse than those of another, there is probably no country in the world where there is so much uniformity in the standards of instruction, and in all its details, as in China.

There are in the Chinese Classics several passages which throw an interesting light upon the views which have been handed down from antiquity in regard to the education of children. One of these is found in the writings of Mencius. Upon one occasion he was asked why the superior man does not teach his own son. To this Mencius replied that the circumstances of the case forbid it. The teacher should inculcate what is correct. When he does so, and his lessons are not practiced, he follows it up by being angry. Thus he is alienated from his son who complains to himself that his father teaches one thing and practices another. As a result the estrangement becomes mutual and deepens. Between father and son, said Mencius, there should be no reproving admonitions to what is good, because these lead to such alienations. The ancients, he declared, exchanged sons, and one taught the son of another.

Another significant passage is found in the Confucian Analects, and is as follows, quoting, as before, Dr. Legge's translation, "Ch'ên K'ang asked Po Yü, the son of Confucius, saying, 'Have you heard any lessons from your father, different from what we have all heard?' Po Yü replied, 'No; he was once standing alone when I hurriedly passed below the hall, and he said to me, "Have you learned the Odes?" on my replying, "not yet," he added, "If you do not learn the Odes, you will not be fit to converse with." I retired and studied the Odes. Another day he was in the same way standing alone, when I hastily passed below the hall, and he said to me, "Have you learned the Rules of Propriety?" on my replying, "not yet," he added, "If you do not learn the Rules of Propriety, your character cannot be established." I then retired and studied the Rules of Propriety. I have heard only these two things from him.' Ch'ên K'ang retired, delighted, saying, 'I asked about one thing, and I have got three things. I have heard about the Odes, I have heard about the Rules of Propriety, and I have heard that the superior man maintains a distant reserve toward his son.'"

Confucius was a master who felt himself to be in possession of great truths of which his age was in deep need, and he offered his instructions to rich and poor alike, upon the sole condition of receptivity. "I do not open up the truth," he said, "to one who is not eager to get knowledge, nor help out any one who is not anxious to explain himself. When I have presented one corner of a subject to any one, and he cannot from it learn the other three, I do not repeat the lesson." For aught that appears, the son of Confucius was wholly dependent for whatever he knew or received, upon his father. According to Confucius, an acquaintance with the Odes, and with the Rules of Propriety, form a very considerable part of the equipment of a scholar. They embrace such subjects as could be comprehended and assimilated, one would suppose, only by the assistance of a competent teacher. That in the education of his own son, Confucius should have contented himself with a casual question, and a single hint, as to the pursuit of those branches which were in his eyes of preëminent importance, is a circumstance so singular that if it were not handed down upon the same authority as the other facts in the life of the sage, we might be disposed to doubt its credibility.

The theory upon which the master acted is happily epitomized by Ch'ên K'ang—"distant reserve." Even to his own son the superior man is a higher grade of being, whose slightest word contains fruitful seeds of instruction. He expects his pupil to act upon a hint as if it were the formal announcement of a law of nature. He is the sun around whom his planets revolve, in orbits proportioned to the force of the central attraction—an attraction which varies with the capacity to be attracted. Yet in every case there is a point beyond which no pupil can go, he must not come too near his sun.

According to Occidental thought, the ideal of teaching is exemplified in the methods of such educators as Dr. Arnold, of Rugby, whose stimulating influence was felt over an entire generation. Upon the plan of Confucius it is difficult to see, not how he could have won the love of his pupils—which was probably remote from his thought and from theirs—but how he could have permanently impressed himself upon any except the very apt. Few are the pupils, we may be sure, who after a chance question and a remark will retire and study unaided a branch of learning which, they are told, will enable them to converse, or to "establish" their characters.

Contrast with this method of Confucius that of James Mill, as detailed in the autobiography of his son, John Stuart Mill. Here was a father, not a professional philosopher, but a man of business, who amid the composition of historical and other works, found time to superintend the education of his son from the days of earliest infancy until mature manhood, not in the ancient language only, but in history, philosophy, political economy, composition, and even in elocution, and all with comprehensiveness of plan, a labourious and unwearying persistence in teaching principles and not rules, combined with scrupulous fidelity in minutest details. By this patient assiduity and his father's skillful direction, Mill was given a start over his contemporaries, as he himself remarks, of at least a quarter of a century, and became one of the most remarkably educated men of whom we have any record. One could wish that to his "imaginary conversations of literary men and statesmen," Walter Savage Landor had added a chapter giving a dialogue between Confucius and James Mill, "on distant reserve as a factor in the education of sons."

It is far from being the fact that every Chinese village has its school, but it is doubtless true that every village would like to have one, for there is everywhere the most profound reverence for "instruction." The reasons given for the absence of a school are always that the village is too poor, or too small, or both.

In China every educated man is a potential schoolmaster, and most of those who have the opportunity to do so take a school. It is one of the allegorical sayings of the flowery land that "in the ink-slab fields there are no bad crops," which signifies that literature is a vocation standing upon a firmer basis than any other. This is the theory. As a matter of fact the Chinese teacher is often barely able to keep soul and body together, and is frequently obliged to borrow garments in which to appear before his patrons. His learning may have fitted him to teach a school, or it may not. It has completely unfitted him to do anything else. It is therefore a period of great anxiety to the would-be pedagogue when the school cards are in preparation.

"When the ground is clean, and the threshing-floor bare,
The teacher's heart is filled with care,"

says the proverb, and another adage is current, to the effect that if one has a few bags of grain on hand, he is not obliged to be king over children.

To the enormous oversupply of school-teachers, it is due that one of the most honourable of callings is at the same time one of the most ill-paid. Teachers of real ability, or who have in some way secured a great reputation, are able to command salaries in proportion; but the country schoolmaster, who can compete for a situation within a very small area only, is often remunerated with but a mere pittance—an allowance of grain supposed to be adequate for his food, a supply of dried stalks for fuel, and a sum in money, frequently not exceeding ten Mexican dollars for the year. It is not very uncommon to meet teachers who have but one or two pupils, and who receive for their services little or nothing more than their food. To the natural inquiry whether it was worth his while to teach for such a slender compensation, a schoolmaster of this class replied, that it was better than staying at home with nothing to eat. It is a current saying that the rich never teach school, and the poor never attend one—though to this there are exceptions. It is a strange fact that one occasionally meets schoolmasters who have never studied anything beyond the Four Books, and who therefore know nothing of the Five Classics, an outfit comparable to that of a Western teacher who should only have perused his arithmetic as far as simple division!

The proposition to have a school is made by the parents of the children, and when it is ascertained that a sufficient number of names can be secured, these are entered on a red card, called a school list (kuan-tan). This is generally prepared by the time of the winter solstice (December 21st), though sometimes the matter is left in abeyance until the very end of the year, some six weeks later. On the other hand, in some regions, it is customary to have the school card ready by the 15th of the eighth moon, some time in August or September. The choice of a teacher, like many other things Chinese, is very much a matter of chance. It seems to be rather uncommon that a scholar should teach in his own village, though this does often happen. The reason generally given for this is that it is inconvenient for the pupils to be too near an ex-preceptor who may make demands upon them in later years. Sometimes the same teacher is engaged for a long series of years, while in other places there is an annual change.

Once the pupil's name has been regularly entered upon the school list, he must pay the tuition agreed upon, whether he ever attends the school or not, no matter what the reason for his absence.

Should serious illness prevent the teacher from beginning his duties at all, the engagement is cancelled; but if he enters upon them, and is then disabled, the full tuition is exacted from every scholar, just as if the engagement had been completed.

The wish of the school patron is to get as much work as he can out of the teacher for the money paid him. The endeavour of the teacher is to get as much money as he can, and to do as little work as he must. For this reason he is always glad to have the names added after the school list has been made out, because that will increase his receipts. The patrons frequently object to this, because they think their own children will be neglected, and unless all the patrons consent the addition cannot be made. They also dislike to have the teacher bring a son or a nephew with him, lest the slender salary should be insufficient for the food of both. In that event the master might abandon the school before the year is over, as sometimes occurs, but such teachers find it difficult to secure another school the following year.

The schoolhouse is an unoccupied room in a private house, an ancestral, or other temple, or any other available place borrowed for the purpose. Renting a place for a school seems to be almost or quite unknown. The teacher does his own cooking, or if he is unequal to this task, he is assisted by one of his pupils, perhaps his own son, whom he often brings with him, albeit, as already mentioned, there is classical authority against having a son taught by a father.

The furniture required for each pupil is provided by his parents, and consists simply of a table and a stool or bench. The four "precious articles" required in literature are the ink-slab with a little well to hold the water required to rub up the ink, the ink-cake, the brush for writing, and paper.

The Chinese school year is coincident with the calendar year, though the school does not begin until after the middle of the first moon, some time in February. There is a vacation at the wheat harvest in June, and another and longer one at the autumnal harvest in September and October. The school is furthermore dismissed ten or twenty days before the new year.

Should the master not have been reëngaged he is likely to do very little teaching during the last moon of the year, as he is much more interested in arranging for the future than in piecing out the almost dead present. The attendance of the scholars, too, is in any case irregular and capricious, amply justifying the saying:

"Once   entered   at   the   twelfth   month's   door,
The teacher rules his boys no more."

Chinese education is based upon the wisdom of the ancients, and of those ancients Confucius is held to be the chief. It is natural, therefore, that upon the beginning of a school there should be special respect paid to the Great Sage who is regarded as the patron of learning. Usages vary so much that no generalizations are ever safe in China, but it is a singular fact that instead of the altar, incense, candles, and formal prayers to Confucius, which in some parts of the empire are in use at the beginning of a year's school, in the province of Confucius himself the ceremonies are for the most part much simpler. At the feast to the teacher by the patrons, the scholars are introduced and make two obeisances, one meant for Confucius, and the other for the present preceptor. In this case there is not only no image of the Sage, but no written character to represent him. And even this modest ceremony is far from universal. A teacher of twenty-five or thirty years' experience declared that he had never seen this performed but once.

Threshing.

An Afternoon Siesta.

The scholars in a Chinese school are expected to be on hand at an early hour, and by sunrise they are, perhaps, howling vigourously away. When it is time for the morning meal they return to their homes, and as soon as it is finished, again return. About noon they are released for dinner, after which they go back as before to school. If the weather is hot, every one else—men, women, and children—is indulging in the afternoon siesta, but the scholars are in their places as usual, although they may be suffered to doze at their desks as well as they can, for half the rest of the day. In this way the discipline of the school is supposed to be maintained, and some allowance made at the same time for poor human nature. Were they allowed to take a regular nap at home, the teacher fears with excellent reason that he would see no more of them for the day.

If Chinese pupils are to be pitied in the dog-days, the same is even more true of the dead of winter, when the thermometer hovers between the freezing-point and zero. The village school will very likely have either no fire at all, or only such as is made by a pile of kindling or a bundle of stalks lit on the earth floor, modifying the temperature but for a few moments, and filling the room with acrid smoke for an hour. Even should there be a little brazier with a rudimentary charcoal fire, it is next to useless, and is mainly for the behoof of the master. The pupils will be found (if they can afford such luxuries) enveloped in long winter hoods, sitting all day in a state of semi-congelation.

They generally do not leave the schoolhouse until it is too dark to distinguish one character from another. When at length the scholars are released, it is not for a healthful walk, much less for a romp, but to return to their homes in an orderly and becoming manner, like so many grown Confucianists. In some schools the scholars are expected to come back in the evening to their tasks, as if the long and wearisome day were not sufficient for them, and this is, perhaps, universally the case in the advanced schools where composition is studied.

According to the Chinese theory, the employment of teacher

is the most honourable possible. Confucius and Mencius, the great sages of antiquity, were only teachers. To invite a teacher, is compared to the investiture of a general by the emperor with supreme command. In consequence of this theory, springing directly from the exalted respect for learning entertained by the Chinese, a master is allowed almost unlimited control. According to a current proverb, the relation of teacher and pupil resembles that of father and son, but the simile of a general would be a more correct expression of a teacher's powers. He is able to declare a sort of martial law, and to punish with the greatest rigour.

One of the earliest lines in the Trimetrical Classic declares that "to rear without instruction, is a father's fault"; "to teach without severity, shows a teacher's indolence." It is common for boys to run away, sometimes to great distances, because they have been punished at school. The writer was told by a man in middle life that when he was a lad he had been beaten by a preceptor of the same surname, because that teacher had himself been beaten as a child by the pupil's grandfather, the grudge being thus carried on to the third generation! The ferule always lies upon the teacher's desk, and serves also as a tally. Whenever a scholar goes out, he takes this with him, and is supposed to be influenced by the legend upon one side, "go out reverentially," and upon the other, "enter respectfully." Two pupils are not allowed to go out at the same time.

The most flagrant offence which a pupil can commit is the persistent failure to learn his task within the allotted time. For this misdemeanour he is constantly punished, and often to the extent of hundreds of blows. Considering how little correction is ever administered to Chinese children at home, and how slight are the attempts at anything resembling family government, it is surprising to what extreme lengths teachers are allowed to carry discipline. Bad scholars, and stupid ones—for a stupid scholar is always considered as a bad one—are not infrequently punished every day, and are sometimes covered with the marks of their beatings, to an extent which suggests rather a runaway slave than a scholar. As the pupil dodges about, with the hope of escaping some of the blows, he is not unlikely to receive them upon his head, even if they were not intended for it. In a case of this sort, a pupil was so much injured as to be thrown into fits, and such instances can scarcely be uncommon. As a general thing, no further notice appears to be taken of the matter by the parent than to see the master and ascertain the special occasion of his severity. The family of the pupil is naturally anxious that the pupil shall come to something, and is ready to assume as an axiomatic truth that the only road to any form of success in life is by the acquisition of an education. This can be accomplished only by the aid of the teacher, and therefore the rules laid down by him are to be implicitly followed, at whatever expense to the feelings of either father or son.

In one case within the writer's knowledge, a father was determined that his son should obtain sufficient education to fit him to take charge of a small business. The son, on the other hand, was resolved to return to his fork and manure basket, and the teacher was invited to further the plans of the boy's father. When the time came to begin his education at school, the lad absolutely declined to go, and like most Chinese parents in similar circumstances, the father was perfectly unable to force him to do what he did not wish to do. The only available plan was to have the boy tied hand and foot, placed in a basket slung to a pole, and carried by two men, like a pig. In this condition he was deposited at the schoolhouse, where he was chained to two chairs, and not allowed to leave the building. He was set the usual task in the Trimetrical Classic, to which, however, he paid no attention whatever, although beaten as often as the teacher could spare the time. The boy not only did not study, but he employed all his strength in wailing over his hard lot. This state of things continued for several days, at the end of which time it was apparent, even to the boy's father, that, as the proverb says: "You cannot help a dead dog over a wall;" and the lad was henceforth suffered to betake himself to those agricultural operations for which alone he was fitted.

Different teachers of course differ greatly in their use of punishment, but whatever the nature of the severities employed, a genuine Confucianist would much rather increase the rigour of discipline than relax it. To his mind the method which he employs appears to be the only one which is fitted to accomplish the end in view. The course of study, the method of study, and the capacity of the pupil, are all fixed quantities; the only variable one is the amount of diligence which the scholar can be persuaded or driven to put forth. Hence the ideal Chinese teacher is sometimes a perfect literary Pharaoh.

When the little pupil at the age of perhaps seven or eight takes his seat in the school for the first time, neither the sound nor the meaning of a single character is known to him. The teacher reads over the line, and the lad repeats the sounds, constantly corrected until he can pronounce them properly. He thus learns to associate a particular sound with a certain shape. A line or two is assigned to each scholar, and after the pronunciation of the characters has been ascertained, his "study" consists in bellowing the words in as high a key as possible. Every Chinese regards this shouting as an indispensable part of the child's education. If he is not shouting how can the teacher be sure that he is studying? and as studying and shouting are the same thing, when he is shouting there is nothing more to be desired. Moreover, by this means the master, who is supposed to keep track of the babel of sound, is instantly able to detect any mispronunciation and correct it in the bud. When the scholar can repeat the whole of his task without missing a single character, his lesson is "learned," and he then stands with his back to the teacher—to make sure that he does not see the book—and recites, or "backs," it at railway speed.

Every educator is aware of the extreme difficulty of preventing children from reading the English language with an unnatural tone. To prevent the formation of a vicious habit of this sort is as difficult as to prevent the growth of weeds, and to eradicate such habits once formed is often next to impossible. In the case of

Chinese pupils, these vices in their most extreme form are well-nigh inevitable. The attention of the scholar is fixed exclusively upon two things,—the repetition of the characters in the same order as they occur in the book, and the repetition of them at the highest attainable rate of speed. Sense and expression are not merely ignored, for the words represent ideas which have never once dawned upon the Chinese pupil's mind. His sole thought is to make a recitation. If he is really master of the passage which he recites, he falls at once into a loud hum, like that of a peg-top or a buzz, like that of a circular saw, and to extract either from the buzz or from the hum any sound as of human speech—no matter how familiar the auditor may be with the passage recited—is extremely difficult and frequently impossible.

But if the passage has been only imperfectly committed, and the pupil is brought to a standstill for the lack of characters to repeat, he does not pause to collect his thoughts, for he has no thoughts to collect—has in fact no thoughts to speak of. What he has, is a dim recollection of certain sounds, and in order to recall those which he has forgotten, he keeps on repeating the last word, or phrase, or sentence, or page, until association regains the missing link. Then he plunges forward again, as before.

Let us suppose, for example, that the words to be recited are the following, from the Confucian Analects, relating to the habits of the master: "He did not partake of wine and dried meat bought in the market. He was never without ginger when he ate. He did not eat much." The young scholar, whose acquaintance with this chapter is imperfect, nevertheless dashes on somewhat as follows: "He did not partake—he did not partake—partake—partake— partake—partake of wine and dried meat bought in—bought in—bought in the market—market—the market—the market. He was never without ginger—when—ginger—when-ginger— when he ate-he ate-he ate-he-ate-ate-he did not eat-eat-eat-eat- eat without ginger when he ate-he did not eat-did not eat much."

This is the method of all Chinese instruction. The consequence of so much roaring on the part of the scholars is that every Chinese school seems to an inexperienced foreigner like a bedlam. No foreign child could learn, and no foreign teacher could teach, amid such a babel of sound, in which it is impossible for the instructor to know whether the pupils are repeating the sounds which are given to them, or not. As the effect of the unnatural and irrational strain of such incessant screaming upon their voices, it is not uncommon to find Chinese scholars who are so hoarse that they cannot pronounce a loud word.

The first little book which the scholar has put into his hands, is probably the "Trimetrical Classic," (already mentioned) so called from its arrangement in double lines of three characters above and three below, to a total number of more than 1,000. It was composed eight centuries and a half ago by a preceptor for his private school, and perhaps there are few compositions which have ever been so thoroughly ground into the memory of so many millions of the human race as this. Yet of the inconceivable myriads who have studied it, few have had the smallest idea by whom it has written, or when. Dr. Williams has called attention to the remarkable fact that the very opening sentence of this initial text-book in Chinese education, contains one of the most disputed doctrines in the ancient heathen world: "Men at their birth, are by nature radically good; in their natures they approximate, but in practice differ widely." After two lines showing the modifying effects of instruction, and the importance of attention, the mother of Mencius is cited as an expert in object lessons for her famous son. The student is next reminded that "just was the life of Tou, of Yen; five sons he reared, all famous men."

The author then reverts to his main theme, and devotes several strenuous sentences to emphasizing the necessity for instruction in youth, "since gems unwrought can never be useful, and untaught persons will never know the proprieties." After a further citation of wonderful examples in Chinese history, accompanied with due moralizing, there follow more than sixty lines of a characteristically Chinese mosaic. The little pupil is enlightened on the progressive nature of numbers; the designations of the heavenly bodies; the "three relations" between prince and minister, father and son, man and wife; the four seasons; the four directions; the five elements; the five cardinal virtues; the six kinds of grain; the six domestic animals; the seven passions; the eight kinds of music; the nine degrees of relationship and the ten moral duties.

Having swallowed this formidable list of categories, the scholar is treated to a general summary of the classical books which he is to study as he advances. When he has mastered all the works adjudged "Classic," he is told that he must go on to those of philosophers and sages, as in the bill of particulars contained in the Trimetrical Classic. His special attention is invited to history, which suggests a catalogue of the numerous Chinese dynastic periods with the names, or rather the styles, of a few of the important founders of dynasties. The list is brought down to the first emperor of the present dynasty, where it abruptly stops at the year 1644. A pupil who wishes to know the titles of the later emperors of the Ch'ing Dynasty can be accommodated when the same shall have been overthrown, and therefore has become a suitable object of historical study. The pupil is urged to ponder these records of history till he understands things ancient and modern as if they were before his eyes, and to make them his morning study and his evening task.

The concluding section contains more of human interest than any of the preceding parts, since we are told that the great Confucius once learned something from a mere child; that the ancient students had no books, but copied their lessons on reeds and slips of bamboo; that to vanquish the body they hung themselves by the hair from a beam, or drove an awl into the thigh; that one read by the light of glow-worms, and that another tied his book to a cow's horn. Among the prodigies of diligence were two, who, "though girls, were intelligent and well informed." The closing lines strive to stimulate the ambition of the beginner, not only by the tales of antiquity, but by the faithfulness of the dog at night, and the diligence of the silk-worm and the bee.

"If men neglect to learn, they are inferior to insects." But "he who learns in youth, and acts when of mature age, extends his influence to the prince, benefits the people, makes his name renowned, renders illustrious his parents, reflects glory upon his ancestors and enriches his posterity." If every Chinese lad does not eventually become a prodigy of learning, it is certainly not the fault of the author of this remarkable compendium, the incalculable influence of which must be the justification of so extended a synopsis.

Another little book, to which the Chinese pupil is early introduced, is the list of Chinese surnames, more than 400 in number, and all to be learned by a dead lift of memory. The characters are arranged in quartettes, and when a Chinese tells another his own surname, it is common to repeat all four, whereupon his auditor recalls which of the several names having the same sound it may be. In some parts of the empire the "Thousand Character Classic" follows the Trimetrical Classic, while in other parts its use seems to be quite unknown. It comprises, as the name implies, a thousand characters, not one of which is repeated. It is common to use these characters instead of ordinal numbers to designate seats in the examination halls, so that it is desirable that scholars should be familiar with the book.

After the scholar has mastered the smaller ones, he passes on to the "Four Books," the Confucian Analects, the Great Learning, the Doctrine of the Mean, and the works of Mencius. The order in which these books are taken up varies in different places, but, as already observed, the method of study is as nearly as possible invariable. Book after book is stored away in the abdomen (in which the intellectual faculties are supposed to be situated), and if the pupil is furnished with the clew of half a sentence, he can unravel from memory, as required, yards, rods, furlongs or miles of learning.

After the Four Books, follow in varying order the Poetical Classic, the Book of History, the Book of Changes, and the historical work of Confucius, known as the Spring and Autumn

Annals. To commit to memory all these volumes, must in any case be the labour of many years. Usage varies in different localities, but it is very common to find scholars who have memorized the whole of the Four Books, and perhaps two of the later Classics—the Odes and the History—before they have heard any explanations even of the Trimetrical Classic, with which their education began. During all these years, the pupil has been in a condition of mental daze, which is denoted by a Chinese character, the component parts of which signify a pig in the weeds (mêng). His entrance upon study is called "lifting the darkness" (ch'i mêng), and to teach the beginner is to "instruct darkness." These expressive phrases correspond to a fixed reality. Of those who have committed to memory all the books named, some of the brightest have no doubt picked up here and there, and as it were by accident, an idea.

Thoughtful Chinese teachers, familiar with the capacity of their pupils, estimate that the most intelligent among them can not be expected to understand a hundredth part of what they have memorized. The great majority of them have about as accurate a conception of the territory traversed, as a boy might entertain of a mountainous district through which he had been compelled to run barefooted and blindfolded in a dense fog, chased for vast distances by a man cracking over his head a long ox-whip. How very little many scholars do grasp of the real meaning, even after explanations which the teacher regards as abundantly full, is demonstrated by a test to which here and there a master subjects his scholars, that of requiring them to write down a passage. The result is frequently the notation of so many false characters as to render it evident, not only that the explanations have not been apprehended, but that notwithstanding such a multitude of perusals, the text itself has been taken only into the ear as so many sounds, and has not entered the mind at all.

The system of explanations adopted by Chinese teachers, as a rule, is almost the exact opposite of that which, to an Occidental, would seem rational. "In speech," said Confucius, "one should be intelligible, and that is the end of it." The Confucian teacher, however, is often very far indeed from feeling that it is necessary to be intelligible—that is to say, to make it absolutely certain that his pupils have fully comprehended his meaning. He is very apt to deliver his explanations—when a sufficient number of years has elapsed to make it seem worth while to begin them at all— ex cathedra, and in a stately, formal manner, his attention being much more fixed upon the exhibition of his own skill in displaying his own knowledge, than upon imparting that knowledge to his scholars. It is common to hear it said of a teacher who has attained distinction, that when he opens his mouth to explain the Classics, "every sentence is fit for an examination essay." This is considered to be the acme of praise. Sentences which are suited to be constituent parts of examination essays, are not, it is superfluous to remark, particularly adapted to the comprehension of young schoolboys, who know nothing about examination essays, the style of which is utterly beyond their powers.

The commentary upon the Classics written by Chu Hsi, in the twelfth century, A. D., has come to have an authority second only to that of the text itself. That no Chinese school- teacher leads his pupils to question for an instant whether the explanation is accurate and adequate, is a matter of course. The whole object of a teacher's work is to fit his pupils to compete at the examinations, and to prepare essays which shall win the approval of the examiners, thus leading to the rank of literary graduate. This result would be possible only to those who accept the orthodox interpretation of the Classics, and hence it is easy to see that Chinese schools are not likely to become nurseries of heresy. The very idea of discussing with his pupils either text or commentary, does not so much as enter the mind of a Chinese schoolmaster. He could not do so if he would, and he would not if he could.

The task of learning to write Chinese characters is a very serious one, in comparison with which it is scarcely unfair to characterize the mastery of the art of writing any European language, as a mere pastime. The correct notation of characters is, moreover, not less important than the correct recognition of them, for success in some of the examinations is made to depend as much upon caligraphy as upon style.

The characters which the teacher selects for the writing exercises of his pupils, have no relation, strange as it may seem, to anything which he is studying. These characters may at first be taken from little books of rhymes arranged for the purpose, containing characters at once simple and common.

The next step is to change to books containing selections from the T'ang Dynasty poets, an appreciation of which involves acquaintance with tones and rhyme, of which the pupil, as yet, knows nothing. The characters which he now learns to write he has very likely never seen before, and they do not at all assist his other studies. The only item of which notice is taken, is whether the characters are well or ill-formed. Review there is none.

The reason for choosing T'ang Dynasty poetry for writing lessons, instead of characters or sentences which are a part of the current lesson, is that it is customary to use the poetry, and is not customary to use anything else, and that to do so would expose himself to ridicule. Besides this, poetry makes complete sense by itself (if the pupil could only comprehend it) while isolated characters do not. The consequence of this method of instruction is that hundreds of thousands of pupils leave school knowing very little about characters, and much of what they do know is wrong. The method of teaching characters explains in part what seems at first almost unaccountable, that so few ordinary persons know characters accurately. It is an inevitable incident of the system, that to write some of the commonest characters, referring to objects used in daily life, is quite beyond the power of a man who has been for years at school, for he has never seen them either written or printed. Thus in taking an inventory of household property, there is not one chance in ten that the characters will be written correctly, for they do not occur in the Classics, nor in T'ang Dynasty poetry. Not only so, but it is altogether probable that an average graduate of the village school cannot indite a common letter, or set down a page of any miscellaneous characters, without writing something wrong.

If the teacher is a man of any reputation, he has a multitude of acquaintances, fellow students, any of whom may happen to call upon him at the schoolhouse, where he lives. Chinese etiquette requires that certain attentions should be paid to visitors of this sort, and while it is perfectly understood that school routine ought not to be broken in upon by unnecessary interruptions, as a matter of fact in most schools these interruptions are a serious nuisance, to which the teacher often cannot and oftener will not put a stop.

The system here described, by which the whole time of the master is supposed to be devoted to instructing his pupils, makes no allowances for any absences whatever. Yet there are few human beings blessed with such perfect health, and having such an entire freedom from all relations to the external world, as to be able to conduct a school of this kind month after month, with no interruptions.

It frequently happens that the teacher is himself one of the literary army who attends the examinations in hope of a degree. If this is the case, his absences for this purpose will often prove a serious interruption to the routine of the school. Some patrons appear to consider that this disadvantage is balanced by the glory which would accrue to their school in case its master were to take his degree while in their service. Moreover, aside from the regular vacations at the feast times and harvests, every teacher is sure to be called home from time to time by some emergency in his own family, or in his village, or among his numerous friends. Under these circumstances he provides a substitute if he happens to find it convenient to do so. Such are nicknamed "remote-cousin-preceptors" (su-pai lao-shih), and are not likely to be treated with much respect. When the teacher is absent for a day, instead of dismissing the school, he perhaps leaves it theoretically in the charge of one of the older scholars. The inevitable consequence is, that at such times the work of the school is reduced not merely to zero, but to forty degrees below zero. The scholars simply bar the front door, and amuse themselves in using the teacher's ferule for a bat, and the Trimetrical Classic, or the Confucian Analects, for a ball. The demoralization attending such lawlessness is evidently most injurious to the efficiency of the school.

The irregularities of the master's attendance are more than matched by those of his scholars. The pressure of domestic duties is such that many poorer families on one pretence or another are constantly taking their children out of school. To-day the pupil must rake up fuel, next week he must lead the animal that draws the seed drill, a month later he is taken for two or three days to visit some relatives. Not long after there is in the village, or perhaps in some neighbouring village, a theatrical entertainment, but in either case the whole school expects a vacation to go and see the sport. As already remarked when describing theatricals, if this vacation were denied they would take it themselves. Besides interruptions of this sort, there are the spring and autumn harvests, when the school is dismissed for two months and perhaps for three, and the New Year vacation, which lasts from the middle of the twelfth moon to the latter part of the first moon. But, extensive as are these intermissions of study, the dog-days are not among them, and the poor pupils go droning on through all the heat of summer.

As the Chinese child has no Saturdays, no Sundays, no recesses, no variety of study, and no promotion from grade to grade, nor from one school to another, it is probable that he has enough schooling such as it is. As every scholar is a class by himself, the absence of one does not interfere with the study of another. Even if two lads happen to be reciting in the same place, they have no more connection with each other than any other two pupils. Of such a thing as classification the teacher has never heard, and the irregular attendance of the scholars would, he tells you, prevent it, even were it otherwise possible. Owing to the time required to hear so many recitations, an ordinary school does not contain more than eight or ten pupils, and twenty are regarded as beyond one teacher's capacity.

There is very little which is really intellectual in any part of the early schooling of an ordinary Chinese boy. As a rule, the teacher does not concern himself with his pupils further than to drag them over a specified course, or at least to attempt to do so. The parents of the lad are equally indifferent, or even more so. If the father himself can read, he remembers that he learned to do so by a long and thorny road, and he thinks it proper that his son should traverse it likewise. If the father can not read, he at least recognizes the fact that he knows nothing at all about the matter, and that it is not his business to interfere. The teacher is hired to teach—let him do it. As for visiting the school to see what progress his son is making, he never heard of such a thing, and he would not do it if he had heard of it. The teacher would say in his manner if not in his words, "What business have you here?"

A sufficient reason for spending all his time in the schoolroom is the fact that it is practically impossible for a Chinese child to do any studying amid the distractions of a Chinese household. Even for adult scholars it is almost always difficult to do so. At his home the pupil has no mental stimulus of any sort, no books, magazines or papers, and even if he had them, his barren studies at school would not have fitted him to comprehend such literature.

The object of Chinese education is to pump up the wisdom of the ancients into the minds of the moderns. In order to do this, however, it is necessary to keep the stream in a constant flow, at whatever cost, else much of the preceding labour is lost. According to Chinese theory, or practice, a school which should only be in session for six months of the year, would be a gross absurdity. The moment a child fails to attend school, he is supposed (and with reason) to become "wild."

The territory to be traversed is so vast that the most unremitting diligence is absolutely indispensable. This continues true, however advanced the pupil may be; as witness the popular saying, "Ten years a graduate (without studying), and one is a nobody." The same saying is current in regard to the second degree, and with not less reason.

The necessity of confining one's attention to study alone, leads to the selection of one or more of the sons of a family as the recipient of an education. The one who is chosen is clothed in the best style which his family circumstances will allow, his little cue neatly tied with a red string, and he is provided, as we have seen, with a copy of the Hundred Surnames and of the Trimetrical Classic. This young Confucianist is the bud and prototype of the adult scholar. His twin brother, who has not been chosen to this high calling, roams about the village all summer in the costume of the garden of Eden, gathering fuel, swimming in the village mud-hole, busy when he must be busy, idle when he can be idle. He may be incomparably more useful to his family than the other, but so far as education goes he is only a "wild" lad.

If the student is quick and bright, and gives good promise of distinguishing himself, he stands an excellent chance of being spoiled by thoughtless praises. "That boy," remarks a bystander to a stranger, and in the lad's hearing, "is only thirteen years old, but he has read all the Four Books, and all of the Book of Poetry, etc. By the time he is twenty, he is sure to become a graduate." When questioned as to his attainments, the lad replies without any of that pertness and forwardness which too often characterize Western youth, but, as he has been taught to do, in a bashful and modest manner, and in a way to win at once the good opinion of the stranger. His manner leaves nothing to be desired, but in reality he is the victim of the most dangerous of all flatteries, the inferiority of what is around him. In order to hold his relative position, it is necessary, as already pointed out, to bestow the most unwearied attention on his books. His brothers are all day in the fields, or learning a trade, or are assistants to some one engaged in business, as the case may be, but he is doing nothing, absolutely and literally nothing, but study.

So much confinement, and such close application from the

very earliest years, can scarcely fail to show their effects in his physical constitution. His brother hoes the ground, bare-headed throughout the blistering heats of July, but such exposure to the sun would soon give him the headache. His brother works with more or less energy all day long (with intermittent sequence), but were he compelled to do the same the result would not improbably be that he would soon begin to spit blood. That he is physically by no means so strong as he once was, is undeniable. He has very little opportunity to learn anything of practical affairs, and still less disposition. The fact that a student has no time to devote to ordinary affairs is not so much the reason of his ignorance, as is the fact that for him to do common things is not respectable. Among the four classes of mankind, scholars rank first, farmers, labourers, and merchants being at a great remove.

The two things that a pupil is sure to learn in a Chinese school are obedience, and the habit of concentrating his attention upon whatever he is reading, to the entire disregard of surrounding distractions. So far as they go these are valuable acquirements, although they can scarcely be termed an education.

Every pupil is naturally anxious to get into the class of scholars, and this he does as soon as he gives all his time to study; for whether he is a real scholar or not, he plainly belongs to neither of the other classes. We are told in the Confucian Analects that the master said, "The accomplished scholar is not a utensil." The commentators tell us that this means that whereas a utensil can only be put to one use, the accomplished scholar can be used in all varieties of ways, ad omnia paratus, as Dr. Legge paraphrases it. This expression is sometimes quoted in banter, as if in excuse for the general incapacity of the Chinese literary man—he is not a utensil. The scholar, even the village scholar, not only does not plow and reap, but he does not in any way assist those who perform these necessary acts. He does not harness an animal, nor feed him, nor drive a cart, nor light a fire, nor bring water—in short, so far as physical exertion goes, he does as nearly as possible nothing at all. "The scholar is not a utensil," he seems to be thinking all day long, and every day of his life, until one wishes that at times he would be a utensil, that he might sometimes be of use. He will not even move a bench, nor make any motion that looks like labour. Almost the only exception to this general incapacity, is an exception for which we should hardly be prepared; it is a knowledge, in many cases of the art of cooking, in so far as it is necessary for the practice of the scholar, who often teaches in a village other than his home, where he generally lives by himself in the schoolhouse.

We have already alluded to the great oversupply of teachers of schools. Many of them, owing to their lack of adaptation to their environment, are chronically on the verge of starvation. It is a venerable maxim that poverty and pride go side by side, and nowhere does this saying find more forcible exemplification than in the case of a poor Chinese scholar. He has nothing, he can do nothing, and in most cases he is unwilling to do anything. In short, viewed from the standpoint of political economy, he is good for nothing.

One specimen of this class the writer once saw, who had been set at work by a benevolent foreigner molding coal balls, an employment which doubtless appeared to him and to the spectators as the substantial equivalent of the chain-gang, and yet, to the surprise of his employer, he accepted it rather than starve. A certain scholar of this description was so poor that he was obliged to send his family back to her mother's house, to save them from starvation. The wife, being a skillful needle-woman, was employed at good wages in a foreign family, but when her husband heard of it he was very angry, not because he was unwilling to have her associate with foreigners, who he was kind enough to say were very respectable, but because it was very unsuitable that she, the wife of a scholar, should work for hire! The wife had the sense and spirit to reply that, if these were his views, it might be well for him to provide his family with something to eat, to which he replied with the characteristic and ultimate argument for refractory wives, namely, a sound beating!

When one of these helpless and impecunious scholars calls upon a foreigner whom he has met only once, or perhaps never even seen, he will not improbably begin by quoting a wilderness of classical learning to display his great—albeit unrecognized—abilities. He tells you that among the five relations of prince and minister, husband and wife, father and son, brother to brother, and friend to friend, his relationship to you is of the latter type. That it would do violence to his conception of the duties of this relation, if he did not let you know of his exigencies. He shows you his thin trousers and other garments concealed under his scholar's long gown, and frankly volunteers that any contribution, large or small, prompted by such friendship as ours to him will be most acceptable.

While the conditions of the life of the village scholar are thus unfavourable for his success in earning a living, they are not more favourable to his own intellectual development. The chief, if not the exclusive sources of his mental alimentation have been the Chinese Classics. These are in many respects remarkable products of the human mind. Their negative excellencies, in the absence of anything calculated to corrupt the morals, are great. To the lofty standard of morality which they fix, may be ascribed in great measure their unbounded and perennial influence, an influence which has no doubt powerfully tended to the preservation of the empire. Apart from the incalculable influence which they have exerted on the countless millions of China for many ages, there are many passages which in and of themselves are remarkable.

But taken as a whole, the most friendly critic finds it impossible to avoid the conviction, which forces itself upon him at every page, that regarded as the sole text-books for a great nation they are fatally defective. They are too desultory, and too limited in their range. Epigrammatic moral maxims, scraps of biography, nodules of a sort of political economy, bits of history, rules of etiquette, and a great variety of other subjects, are commingled without plan, symmetry, or progress of thought. The chief defects, as already suggested, are the triviality of many of the subjects, the limitation in range, and the inadequacy of treatment. When the Confucian Analects are compared, for example, with the Memorabilia of Xenephon, when the Doctrine of the Mean is placed by the side of the writings of Aristotle and Plato, and the bald notation of the Spring and Autumn Annals by the side of the history of Thucydides, when the Book of Odes is contrasted with the Iliad, the Odyssey, or even the Æneid, it is impossible not to marvel at the measure of success which has attended the use of such materials in China.

Considering what, in spite of their defects, the Classics have done for China, it is not surprising that they have come to be regarded with a bibliolatry to which the history of mankind affords few parallels. It is extremely difficult for us to comprehend the effect of a narrow range of studies on the mind, because our experience furnishes no instance to which the case of the Chinese can be compared. Let us for a moment imagine a Western scholar, who had enjoyed a profound mathematical education, and no other education whatever. Every one would consider such a mind ill-balanced. Yet much of the ill effect of such a narrow education would be counteracted. Mathematical certainty is infallible certainty; mathematics leads up to astronomy, and a thorough acquaintance with astronomy is of itself a liberal education. Besides this, no man in Western lands can fail to come into vital contact with other minds. And there is what Goethe called the Zeit-geist, or Spirit of the Age, which exerts a powerful influence upon him. But in China, a man who is educated in a narrow line, is likely, though by no means certain, to remain narrow, and there is no Chinese Zeit-geist, or if there is, like other ghosts, it seldom interposes in human affairs.

The average Chinese scholar is at a great disadvantage in the lack of the apparatus for study. In a Western land, any man with the slightest claim to be called a scholar, would be able to answer in a short time, a vast range of questions, with intelligent accuracy. This he would do, not so much by means of his own miscellaneous information, as by his books of reference. The various theories as to the location of the Garden of Eden, the dimensions of the Great Pyramid, the probable authorship of the Junius Letters, the highest latitude reached in polar exploration, the names of the generals who conducted the fourth Peloponnesian war—all these, and thousands of similar matters, could be at once elucidated by means of a dictionary of antiquities, a manual of ancient or modern history, a biographical dictionary, and an encyclopedia. To the ordinary Chinese scholar, such helps as these are entirely wanting. He owns very few books; for in the country where printing was invented, books are the luxury of the rich.

The standard dictionary of Chinese, is that compiled two centuries ago in the K'ang Hsi period, and is alleged to contain 44,449 characters, but of these an immense number are obsolete and synonomous, and only serve the purpose of bewildering the student. Within the past two generations the Chinese language has undergone a remarkable development, owing to the contact of China with her neighbours. All the modern sciences have obtruded themselves, but there is no interest in the coördination of these new increments to their language on the part of Chinese scholars, to whom K'ang Hsi's lexicon is amply sufficient.

In order to attain success in Chinese composition, it is necessary to be acquainted with the force of every character, as a means to which, access to this standard dictionary, would seem to be indispensable. Yet, though invaluable, it is not in the possession of one scholar in fifty. Its place is generally taken by a small compendium, analogous to what we should call a pocket-manual, in which the characters are arranged according to the sound, and not according to the radicals, as in K'ang Hsi.

Pupils are seldom taught the 214 radicals, and many persons who have spent years at school have no idea how to use K'ang Hsi's dictionary, when it is put into their hands. Within a circle of eight or ten villages, there may be only a single copy, and if it is necessary to obtain more accurate information than is to be had in the pocket-dictionary, the inquirer must go to the village where there is a copy of K'ang Hsi, and "borrow light" there.

But such an extreme measure is seldom considered necessary. The incessant study of the Classics has made all the characters in them familiar. Those who write essays can compose them with the aid of these characters only, and as for miscellaneous characters—that is, those not found in the Classics—why should one care for them? A good edition of K'ang Hsi, with clear type and no false characters, might cost, if new, as much as the village schoolmaster would receive for his whole year's work.

At examinations below that for the second degree, a knowledge of history is said to be as superfluous as an acquaintance with the dictionary. Nine out of ten candidates at the lower examinations know little of the history of China, except what they have learned from the Trimetrical Classic, or picked up from the classics. The perusal of compendiums of history, even if such are available, is the employment of leisure, and the composition of essays as a business once entered upon, there is no leisure.

One occasionally meets a teacher who has made a specialty of history, but these men are rare. Historical allusions often lie afloat in the minds of Chinese scholars, like snatches of poetry, the origin and connection of which are unknown. Many scholars who have the knack of picking up and appropriating such spiculæ of knowledge, acquire the art of dextrously weaving them into examination essays and owe their success to this circumstance alone, whereas if they were examined upon the historical connection of the incidents which they have thus cited, they would be unable to reply. But as long as the use of such allusions in essays is felicitous, no questions are asked, and the desired end is attained. "The Cat that catches the Rat is a good Cat," says the adage, and it is no matter if the Cat is blind, and the Rat is a dead one!

The Peking Gazette occasionally contains memorials from officers asking that certain sums be set apart for the maintenance of a library in some central city, to aid poor students in the prosecution of their studies. If there were libraries on a large scale in every district city, they would be valuable and much-needed helps. But so far as appears, for all practical purposes, they scarcely exist at all.

The Chinese method of writing history, is what Sydney Smith called the antediluvian, that, namely, in which the writer proceeds upon the hypothesis that the life of the reader is to be as long as that of Methuselah. Projected upon this tremendous plan, the standard histories are not only libraries in size, but are enormously expensive in price. In a certain District (or County) it is a well-known fact that there is only one such history, which belongs to a wealthy family, and which one could no more "borrow," than he could borrow the family graveyard, and which even if it could be borrowed would prove to be a wilderness of learning. It is indeed a proverb, that "He that would know things ancient and modern, must peruse five cartloads of books."

But even after this labour, his range of learning, gauged by Occidental standards, would be found singularly inadequate. According to Chinese ideas, the history of the reigning dynasty is not a proper object of knowledge, and histories generally end at the close of the Ming Dynasty, about 250 years ago. If any one has a curiosity to learn of what has happened since that time, he can be gratified by waiting a few decades or centuries, when the dynasty shall have changed, and the records of the Great Pure Dynasty can be impartially written. Imagine a History of England which should call a halt at the House of Hanover!

The result of the various causes here indicated, combined with the grave defects in the system of education, is that multitudes of Chinese scholars know next to nothing about matters directly in the line of their studies, and in regard to which we should consider ignorance positively disgraceful. A venerable teacher remarked to the writer with a charming naïveté that he had never understood the allusions in the Trimetrical Classic (which stands at the very threshold of Chinese study), until at the age of sixty he had an opportunity to read a Universal History, prepared by a missionary, in which for the first time Chinese history was made accessible to him.

The encyclopedias and works of reference, which the Chinese have compiled in overwhelming abundance, are as useless to the common scholar as the hieroglyphics of Egypt. He never saw these works, and he has never heard of them. The information condensed into a small volume like Mayers' Chinese Reader's Manual, could not be drawn from a whole platoon of ordinary scholars. Knowledge of this sort the scholar must pick up as he goes along, remembering everything that he reads or hears; and much of it will be derived from cheap little books, badly printed, and full of false characters, prepared on no assignable plan, and covering no definite ground.

The cost of Chinese books being practically prohibitory to teachers who are poor, they are sometimes driven to copy them, as was the habit of the monks in the middle ages. The writer is well acquainted with a schoolmaster who spent the spare time of several years in copying a work in eight octavo volumes, involving the notation of somewhere between 50,000 and 100,000 characters, to the great injury of his health and of his eyesight.

The whole plan of Chinese study has been aptly called intellectual infanticide. The outcome of it is that it is quite possible that the village scholar who has the entire Classics at his tongue's end, who has been examined before the Literary Chancellor more times than he can remember, may not know fact from fiction, nor history from mythology. He is, perhaps, not certain whether a particular historical character lived in the Han Dynasty or in the Ming Dynasty, though the discrepancy involves a matter of 1,000 or 1,200 years. He does not profess to be positive whether a given name represents a real person, or whether it may not perhaps have been merely one of the dramatis personæ of a theatrical play.

He cannot name the governors or governors-general of three out of the eighteen provinces, nor does he know the capitals of a third of those provinces. It is enough for him that any particular place in China, the location of which he is ignorant of, is "south-side." He never studied any geography ancient or modern, he never saw an ancient atlas nor a modern map of China—never in fact heard of one.

An acquaintance of the writer's, who was a pupil in a mission school, sent to a reading man of his village a copy of a Universal Geography in the Mandarin Colloquial, the explanations of which would seem to render mistake as to its purport almost impossible. Yet the recipient of the work, after protracted study of it, could make nothing whatever of the volume, and called to his aid two friends, one of whom was a literary graduate, and all three of them puzzled over the maps and text for three days, at the end of which time they all gave the matter up as an insoluble riddle, and determined in despair to await the return of the donor of the book, to explain what it was about!

This trait of intellectual obtuseness, is far enough from being exceptional in Chinese scholars. With a certain class of them, a class easily recognized, it is the rule, and it is a natural outcome of the mode and process of their education. Although the education of a Chinese scholar is almost exclusively devoted to acquiring facility of composition, it is composition of one variety only, the examination essay. Outside of examination halls, however, the examination essay, even in China, plays a comparatively small part, and a person whose sole forte is the production of such essays often shows to very little advantage in any other line of business. He cannot write a letter without allowing the "seven empty particles" to tyrannize over his pen. He employs a variety of set forms, such as that he has received your epistle and respectfully bathed himself before he ventured to open it (a very exaggerated instance of hyperbole), but he very likely neglects to inform you from what place he is writing and if he is reporting, for example, a lawsuit, he probably omits altogether several items of vital importance to a correct comprehension of the case. In a majority of instances he is miserably poor, often has no employment whatever, and no prospect of obtaining any. If he becomes acquainted with a foreigner, you are aware, before he has made three calls, that he is in quest of a situation. You inquire what he can do, and with a pathetic simplicity he assures you that he can do some things, and is really not a useless person. He can indeed, write from a copy, or from dictation if an eye be constantly kept upon him to prevent the notation of wrong characters. But it will not be surprising if his employer finds that at whatever task he is set, he either does it ill, or cannot do it at all.

There are several criticisms which the average Occidental is sure to make on the average Chinese schoolmaster. He always lacks initiative and will seldom do anything without explicit directions. He is also painfully deficient in finality, especially in the statement of his own affairs, often consuming an hour wheeling in concentric circles about a point to which he should have come in three minutes—that is, had he been constructed intellectually as most Westerners are. Yet he has undoubted intellectual abilities, not frequently surprising one by the keenness and justice of his criticisms and comments. But his mind has been trained for one line of work, and often for that alone. Every one knows that the minds of the Chinese are not by nature analytic; neither are they synthetic. They may suppose themselves to have the clearest perception of the way in which a statement ought to be made, but a whole platoon of teachers will not seldom spend several days in working over and over an epitome of some matter of business which happens to be somewhat complicated, and after all with results unsatisfactory to themselves, and still more so to the Occidental who fails to understand why it could not have been finished in two hours. The same phenomenon is often witnessed in their efforts to assimilate unfamiliar works which are not geographical. If a reading man is invited to peruse one and make an abstract of it, he generally declines, remarking that he does not know how, a proposition which he can speedily prove with a certainty equal to any demonstration in Euclid.

The inborn conservatism of the Chinese race is exhibited in the average literary man, whatever the degree of his attainments. To change his accustomed way of doing anything is to give his intellectual faculties a wrench akin to physical dislocation of a hip-bone. Chinese writing is in perpendicular columns, and if horizontal reads from right to left—the reverse of English. A fossilized Chinese whom the writer set to noting down sentences in a ruled foreign blank-book could not be induced to follow the lines as directed, but wished to make columns to which he was used. When the foreign way was insisted upon, he simply turned the book partly around and wrote on the lines perpendicularly as before! He would not be a party to violent rearrangement of the ancient symbols of thought. Such a man's mind resembles an obsolete high bicycle—very good if one but knows how to work it, but not quite safe for any others. There is another similarity likewise in the circumstance that many Chinese who have some degree of scholarship are not expecting to employ their intellectual faculties except when they happen to be called for. One is often told by Chinese who have gone from home for some considerable time, that he cannot read something which has been offered to him, as he has left his glasses at home, not supposing that he should have any use for them. A greater intellectual contrast between the East and the West it might not be easy to name.

To almost all Chinese the form of a written character appears to be of indefinitely greater importance than its meaning. Those who are learning to read, or who can read only imperfectly, are generally so completely absorbed in the mere enunciation of a character, that they will not and probably cannot pay the smallest attention to any explanation as to its purport, the consideration of which appears to be regarded as of no consequence whatever, if not an interruption. But the scholar and the new beginner have this admirable talent in common, that they are almost always able completely to abstract themselves from their surroundings, disregarding all distractions. This valuable faculty, as already remarked and a phenomenally developed verbal memory are perhaps the most enviable results of the educational process which we are describing. As an excellent example, however, of the degree to which verbal memory extinguishes the judgment, may be mentioned a country schoolmaster (a literary graduate) whom the writer interviewed in a dispensary waiting-room as to the respective deserts of Chou, the tyrant whose crimes put an end to the Ancient Shang Dynasty, and Pi Kan, a relative whom Chou ordered disemboweled in mere wantonness in order to see if a Sage really has seven openings in his heart. The teacher recollected the incident perfectly, and cited a passage from the Classics referring to it, but declined to express any judgment on the merits of these men as he had forgotten what "the small characters" (the commentary) said about them!

We have already adverted to some of the principal defects in the routine of Chinese schools, but there is another which should not be omitted. There is scarcely a man, woman or child in China, who will not spend a considerable fraction of life in handling brass cash, in larger or smaller quantities. It is a matter of great importance to each individual, to be able to reckon, if not rapidly, at least correctly, so as to save trouble, and what is to them of far more importance, money. It seems almost incredible that for instruction in this most necessary of arts, there is no provision whatever. To add, to subtract, to divide, to multiply, to know what to do with decimal fractions, these are daily necessities of every one in China, and yet these are things that no one teaches. Such processes, like the art of bookkeeping in Western lands fifty years ago, must be learned by practical experience in shops and places of business. The village schoolmaster not only does not teach the use of the abacus, or reckoning board, but it is by no means certain that he understands it himself. Imagine a place in England or in the United States where the schoolboy is taught nothing of the rules of arithmetic at school, and where he is obliged, if he desires such knowledge, to learn the simple rules of addition, etc., from one person, those for compound numbers from another person, not improbably in a distant village, the measurement of land from yet a third individual, no one of them being able to give him all the help he requires.

The Chinese reckoning board is no doubt a very ingenious contrivance for facilitating computation, but it is nevertheless a very clumsy one. It has the fatal defect of leaving no trace of the processes through which the results have been reached, so that if any mistake occurs, it is necessary to repeat them all, on the reiterative principle of the House that Jack Built, until the answer is, or is supposed to be correct. That all the complicated accounts of a great commercial people like the Chinese, should be settled only through such a medium, seems indeed singular. An expert arrives at his conclusions with surprising celerity, but even those who are familiar with ordinary reckoning, become puzzled the moment that a problem is presented to them beyond the scope of the ordinary rules. If one adult receives a pound of grain every ten days, and a child half as much, what amount should be allotted to 227 adults and 143 children, for a month and a half? Over a problem as simple as this, we have seen a group of Chinese, some of whom had pretensions to classical scholarship, wrestle for half an hour, and after all no two of them reached the same conclusion. Indeed the greater their learning, the less fitted do the Chinese seem to be, in a mathematical way, to struggle with their environment.

The object of the teacher is to compel his pupils, first to Remember, secondly, to Remember, thirdly and evermore to Remember. For every scholar, as we have seen, is theoretically a candidate for the district examinations, where he must write upon themes selected from any one of a great variety of books. He must, therefore, be prepared to recall at a moment's notice, not only the passage itself, but also its connections, and the explanations of the commentary, as a prerequisite for even attempting an essay.

Under the conditions of the civil service examinations, as they have been conducted for many hundred years, a system of school instruction like the one here described, or which shall at least produce the same results, is an imperative necessity in China. A reform cannot begin anywhere until a reform begins everywhere. The excellence of the present system is often assumed and in proof, the great number of distinguished scholars which it produces, is adduced. But, on the other hand, it is absolutely necessary to take into account the innumerable multitudes who derive little or no benefit from their schooling. Nothing is more common than to meet men who, although they have spent from one to ten years at school, when asked if they can read, reply with literal truth that their knowledge of characters has been "laid aside"—in other words they have forgotten almost everything that they once knew, and are now become "staring blind men," an expression which is a synonym for one who cannot read.

It is a most significant fact that the Chinese themselves recognize the truth that their school system tends to benumb the mental faculties, turning the teachers into machines, and the pupils into parrots. On the supposition that all the scholars were to continue their studies, and were eventually to be examined for a degree, it might be difficult to suggest any system which would take the place of the one now in use, in which a most capacious memory is a principal condition of success.

In the Village School, however, it is within bounds to estimate that not one in twenty of the scholars—and more probably, not three in a hundred—have any reasonable prospect of carrying their studies to anything like this point. The practical result, therefore, is to compel at least ninety-seven scholars to pursue a certain routine, simply because it is the only known method by which three other scholars can compete for a degree. In other words, nineteen pupils are compelled to wear a heavy cast-iron yoke, in order to keep company with a twentieth, who is trying to get used to it as a step towards obtaining a future name! If this inconvenient inequality is pointed out to teachers or to patrons, and if they are asked whether it would not be better to adopt, for the nineteen who will never go to the examinations, a system which involves less memorizing, and a wider range of learning in the brief time which is all that most of the pupils can spend at school, they reply, with perfect truth, that so far as they are aware there is no other system; that even if the patrons desired to make the experiment (which would never be the case), they could find no teacher to conduct it; and that even if a teacher should wish to institute such a reform (which would never happen), he would find no one to employ him.

The extreme difficulty which men of some education often find in keeping from starvation, gives rise to a class of persons known as Strolling Scholars, (yu hsiao), who travel about the country vending paper, pictures, lithographs of tablets, pens and ink. These individuals are not to be confounded with travelling pedlars, who, though they deal in the same articles, make no pretension to learning, and generally convey their goods on a wheelbarrow, whereas the Strolling Scholar cannot manage anything larger than a pack.

When a Strolling Scholar reaches a schoolhouse, he enters, lowers his bundle, and makes a profound bow to the teacher, who (though much displeased at his appearance) must return the courtesy. If there are large pupils, the stranger bows to them and addresses them as his Younger Brothers. The teacher then makes some inquiries as to his name, etc. If he turns out to be a mere pretender, without real scholarship, the teacher drops the conversation, and very likely leaves the schoolroom. This is a tacit signal to the larger scholars to get rid of the visitor. They place a few cash on the table, perhaps not more than five, or even three, which the Strolling Scholar picks up, and with a bow departs. If he sells anything, his profits are of the most moderate description—perhaps three cash on each pen, and two cash on each cake of ink. With a view to this class of demands, a small fund is sometimes kept on hand by the larger scholars, who compel the younger ones to contribute to it.

If, however, the Strolling Scholar is a scholar in fact, as well as in name, so that his attainments become apparent, the teacher is obliged to treat him with much greater civility. Some of these roving pundits make a specialty of historical anecdotes, and miscellaneous knowledge, and in a general conversation with the teacher, the latter, who has not improbably confined himself to the beaten routine of classical study, is at a disadvantage. In this case, other scholars of the village are perhaps invited in to talk with the stranger, who may be requested to write a pair of scrolls, and asked to take a meal with the teacher, a small present in money being made to him on his departure.

It is related that a Strolling Scholar of this sort, being present when a teacher was explaining the Classics, deliberately took off his shoes and stockings in presence of the whole school. Being reproved by the teacher for this breach of propriety, he replied that his dirty stockings had as good an "odour" as the teacher's classical explanations. To this the teacher naturally replied by a challenge to the stranger to explain the Classics himself, that they might learn from him. The Strolling Scholar, who was a person of considerable ability, had been waiting for just such an opportunity, and taking up the explanation, went on with it in such an elegant style, "every sentence being like an examination essay," that the teacher was amazed and ashamed, and entertained him handsomely. If a teacher were to treat with disrespect one whose scholarship was obviously superior to his own, he would expose himself to disrespect in turn, and might be disgraced before his own pupils, an occurrence which he is very anxious to avoid.

In China the relation between teacher and pupil is far more intimate than in Western lands. One is supposed to be under a great weight of obligation to the master who has enlightened his darkness, and if this master should be at any time in need of assistance, it is thought to be no more than the duty of the pupil to afford it. This view of the case is obviously one which it is for the interest of teachers to perpetuate, and the result of the theory and of the attendant practice is that there are many decayed teachers roving about, living on the precarious generosity of their former pupils.

X

CHINESE HIGHER EDUCATION—
THE VILLAGE HIGH SCHOOL—
EXAMINATIONS—RECENT EDUCATIONAL EDICTS

When it is definitely decided that a pupil is to study for the examinations, he enters a high school, which differs in many respects from the ones which he has hitherto attended. The teacher must be a man of more than average attainments, or he can neither gain nor hold such a place. His salary is much greater than that given by the ordinary school. The pupils are much harder worked, being compelled to spend almost all their waking hours in the study of model examination essays. These are to be committed to memory by the score and even by the hundred, as a result of which process the mind of the student gradually becomes so saturated with the materials of which they are composed, that he will always be able to take advantage of the accumulations of his patient memorizing in weaving his own compositions in the examination hall.

During the preceding years of study he has already committed to memory the most important parts of the literature of his native land. He is now intimately familiar with the orthodox explanations of the same. He has been gradually but thoroughly inducted into the mystery of tones and rhymes, the art of constructing poetry, and the weaving of antithetical couplets, beginning with the announcement that the heaven is high, balanced by the proposition that the earth is thick, and proceeding to the intricate and well-nigh inscrutable laws by which relation and correlation, thesis and antithesis are governed. He has now to learn by carefully graded stages the art of employing all his preceding learning in the production of the essay, which will hereafter constitute the warp and the woof of his intellectual fabric. In future he will eat, drink, write, talk, and sleep essays, essays, essays.

Measured by Chinese standards, the construction of a perfect essay is one of the noblest achievements of which the human mind is capable. The man who knows all that has been preserved of the wisdom of the ancients, and who can at a moment's notice dash off essays of a symmetrical construction, lofty in sentiment, elevated in style, and displaying a wide acquaintance not only with the theme, but also with cognate subjects, such a man is fit not only to stand before kings, but before the very Son of Heaven himself.

A high official called a provincial Literary Chancellor, (Hsiao Yüan), is despatched from Peking to the provinces, to hold periodical examinations once in three or twice in five years. Upon the occasion of an emperor's ascending the throne, his marriage, the birth of an heir, etc., there are extra examinations bestowed as a favour (ên k'o). When the village scholar is able to produce an essay, and to write a poem that will pass the scrutiny of this formidable Literary Chancellor, he may hope to become a hsiu-ts'ai or graduate. In order to fit him for this ordeal, which is regarded by outsiders with awe, and is anticipated by the young candidate himself with mingled hope and terror, it is necessary that he should run the gauntlet of a long series of preliminary test examinations.

Some months before the visit of the Chancellor is to take place, of which notice is communicated to the Governor of the Province, and from him to the District Magistrates, preparations are made by the latter officer for the first examination, which is held before him, and in the District city. It is part of the duty of some of the numerous staff of this official to disseminate the notice of such an impending examination. In any Western country, this would be accomplished by the insertion of a brief advertisement in the official newspaper of the District, or County. In China, where there are no newspapers, the message must be orally delivered. The high schools in which pupils are trained with special reference to such examinations, are visited, and the day of the examination notified. Literary graduates within the district, who must be examined with reference to passing a higher grade, are also informed of the date. A small sum, the equivalent of fifteen or twenty cents, is expected by the yamên messengers as a solace for the "bitterness" which they have suffered in distributing the notices. Notwithstanding this clumsy method of circulating the notifications, it is rare that any one concerned fails to receive the message.

Those who intend to be examined, make their way to the city, a day or two in advance of the time fixed, that they may rent quarters for the half month which they will be obliged to spend there. If the student chance to have friends in the city, he may avoid the expense of renting a place, and if his home should be near the city, he may be able to return thither at intervals, and thus lessen the expenditure; for all these trifles are important to the poor scholar, who has abundant need of money. As many scholars combine to rent one room or one house, the cost to each is not great, perhaps the equivalent of one or two dollars. Each candidate must furnish himself with provisions for half a month. In some district cities there are special examination buildings, capable by crowding, of seating 600 or 800 persons. In other cities, where these buildings have either never been built, or have been allowed to go to ruin, the examination is conducted in the Confucian temple, or at the yamên of the District Magistrate.

On the first day of the examination, two themes are given out at daylight, by which time every candidate must be in the place assigned him, and from there he must not stir. The themes are each taken from the Four Books, and the essay is not expected to exceed 600 characters. By nine or ten o'clock the stamp of the examiner is affixed to the last character written in the essay, preventing further additions if it should not be finished, and the essays are gathered up. About eleven o'clock, the third theme is given out. This is an exercise in poetry, the subject of which may be taken from the Book of Odes, or from some standard poet. The poem is to be composed of not more than sixty characters, five in each line. A rapid writer and composer, may be able to hand in his paper by three or four in the afternoon, and many others will require much longer. The limit of time may be fixed at midnight, or possibly at daylight the next morning. The physical condition of a scholar who has been pinned to his seat for four and twenty hours, struggling to produce an essay and poem which shall be regarded by the severest critic as ideal, can be but faintly imagined by the Occidental reader.

The next two days being devoted to the inspection of the wilderness of essays and poems, the product of this first trial, the unhappy competitors have leisure for much needed rest and sleep. On the morning of the fourth day, the "boards are hung," that is, the list of those whose essays have passed, is exposed. If the whole number of candidates should be 500—an extremely moderate estimate for a reasonably populous district—the proportion of those whose hopes are at once wrecked may be half. Only those whose names are posted after the first trial can enter the succeeding one. If the subordinates of the magistrate perceive that a great many names are thrown out, they may come kneeling before the magistrate, knocking their heads, and begging that he will kindly allow a few more names to pass. If he happens to be in good humour at the moment, he may grant their request, which is not in the smallest degree prompted by any interest in the affairs of the disappointed candidates, but on the important principle, that the fewer the sheep, the smaller will be the crop of wool.

The only fee required for the examination is that paid for registration, which amounts to about twenty cents. Not the name of the candidate only, but those of his father and grandfather are to be recorded, to make it sure that no one legally disqualified is admitted. The paper upon which the examination essays and poems are written is of a special kind, sold only at the yamên, and at a cost for each examination equivalent to about ten cents, or fifty cents for the whole five examinations, but the candidate must pay three-fifths of this amount for the first supply, whether he is admitted to a further examination or not. If he is, he becomes entitled to a rebate of this amount on his subsequent purchases.

On the fifth or sixth day, those who have been selected from the whole number examined, again file into the examination hall, and are seated according to their newly-acquired rank for the second test. Three themes are again propounded, the first from the Four Books, the second from one of the Five Classics, the third a poetical one, in a manner similar to the first examination. A day or two is allowed for the inspection of these essays, when the boards are again hung, and the result is to drop out perhaps one-half of the competitors.

At the third examination the themes, which are given out somewhat later than in the previous trials, are two in number, one from the Four Books, the other poetical. About noon of this day, the magistrate has a meal of vermicelli, rice, etc., sent to the candidates. By four in the afternoon the hall is empty. After the interval of another day the boards are again hung, indicating that all but perhaps fifty are excluded from further competition.

The fourth examination begins at a later hour than the third, and while the number of the themes may be larger than before—all of them from the Four Books—time is not allowed for the completion of any of them. In addition to the classical themes, a philosophical one may be given. Besides this, there are poetical themes, to be treated in a way different from those in the preceding examinations, and much more difficult, as the lines of poetry are subject also to the rules governing the composition of antithetical couplets.

The metre, whether five characters to a line, or seven, (the only varieties to choose from), is left to the option of the candidate, who, if he be a fine scholar and a rapid penman, may treat the same theme in both ways. A meal is served as at the preceding trial, and by five or six o'clock, the hall is empty. After the interval of another day, the fourth board is hung, and the number who have survived this examination is found to be a small one—perhaps twenty or thirty.

A day later the final examination occurs. The theme is from the Four Books, and may be treated fully or partially according to the examiner's orders at the moment. A poem is required in the five-character metre, and also a transcript of some section of the "Sacred Edicts" of the Emperor Yung Chêng. The design of the latter is to furnish a specimen of the candidate's handwriting, in case it should be afterward needed for comparison. A meal is furnished as before, and by the middle of the afternoon the hall is cleared. The next day the board is again hung, announcing the names who have finally passed. The number is a fixed one, and it is relatively lowest where the population is most dense. In two contiguous districts, for example, which furnish on an average 500 or 600 candidates, the number of those who can pass is limited, in the one case to twenty and in the other to seventeen. In another district where there are often 2,000 candidates, only thirty can pass. It thus appears that the chances of success for the average candidate, are extremely tenuous.

Every candidate for a degree, is required to have a "surety." These are selected from graduates of former years, who have advanced one step beyond that of hsiu-ts'ai, to that of ling-shêng hsiu-ts'ai. The total number of sureties is not necessarily large, perhaps four from each district, and many of them may be totally unacquainted with the persons for whom they become thus responsible. The nature of this responsibility is twofold, first to guarantee that the persons who enter under a particular name, really bear that name, and second that during the examination they will not violate any of the established rules. If a false name is shown to have been entered, or if a violation of the rules occurs, the ling-shêng would be held responsible, and would be likely to lose his own rank as a graduate. Each candidate is required to furnish not only a surety, but also an alternate surety, and in consideration of a present of from ten cents to five or six dollars, the ling-shêngs are quite willing to guarantee as many candidates as apply. They must be paid in advance, or they will prevent the candidate from entering the examination hall.

The preliminary examinations in the District city, having been thus completed, are followed about a month later by similar ones in the Prefectural city, before the Prefect, (chih-fu). Here are gathered candidates from all the districts within the jurisdiction of the Fu city, districts ranging in number according to density of population, from two or three, to twelve or more. Those who have failed to pass the District examinations are not on that account disqualified from appearing at the Prefectural examinations, which, like the former, are intended to act as a process of sifting, in preparation for the final and decisive trial before the Literary Chancellor. The details of the Prefectural examinations are similar to those already described, and the time required is about the same. The number of candidates in a thickly-settled Prefecture, will often amount to more than 10,000. As no ordinary examination building will accommodate so many at once, they are examined in relays. The examinations are conducted by the Prefect, but it by no means follows that those who have been first in the District examinations will be so now. The order changes, indeed, from day to day, but those who are constantly toward the head of the list, are regarded as certain to pass the Chancellor's examination.

The writer is acquainted with a man who at his examination for the first degree, stood last in a list of seventeen, at the trial next before the final one. But in that test he was dropped one number, missing his degree by this narrow margin. His grief and rage were so excessive as to unbalance his mind, and for the greater part of his life he has been a heavy burden on his wife, doing absolutely nothing either for her support or for his own.

Those who have already attained the degree of hsiu-ts'ai, are examined by themselves for promotion. The expense of obtaining sureties is confined to the last two sets of examinations. The final trial before the Literary Chancellor is conducted with far greater care and caution than the preliminary ones before the local officials. The candidates having been duly guaranteed and entered, are assigned to seats, distinguished by the characters in the Millenary Classic, which as already mentioned, affords a convenient system of notation, being familiar, and having no repeated characters. The students are closely packed together, fifteen or twenty at each table. The first table is termed "Heaven" after the first character in the Millenary Classic, and its occupants are denoted as "heaven one," "heaven two," etc. Each candidate notes his designation; for in the final lists of those who have passed, no names are used, but only the description of the seat as above described. Every student is carefully searched as he enters the hall, to ascertain whether he has about him any books or papers which might aid him in his task. The examination begins at an extremely early hour, the theme being given out by sunrise. This theme is written on a large wooden tablet, and is carried about to all parts of the room, that each candidate may see it distinctly. It is also read out, in a loud voice. By nine or ten o'clock another subject is announced from the Four Books and a poetical theme in five-metre rhythm. A rapid writer and composer might finish his work by one or two o'clock in the afternoon. As in other examinations, those who have completed their tasks are allowed to leave the hall at fixed times, and in detachments. By five or six P. M. the time is up, and the fatal stamp is affixed to the last character, whatever the stage of the composition. During the whole of this examination, no one is allowed on any pretext whatever to move from his position. If one should be taken deathly sick, he reports to the superintendent of his section, and requests permission to be taken out, but in this case he cannot return. A student who should merely rise in his seat and look around, would be beaten a hundred blows on his hand, like a schoolboy (as indeed he is supposed to be), would be compelled to kneel during the whole of the examination, and at the close would be ejected in disgrace, losing the opportunity for examination until another year.

Some years ago the examination hall of the city of Chi-nan Fu, the capital of Shan-tung, was in a very bad condition. The Chancellor held the summer examinations at that city, because the situation is near to hills, and to water, and thus was supposed to be a little cooler than others. At one of these examinations, a violent rain came on, and the roof of the building leaked like a sieve. Many of the poor candidates were wet to the skin, their essays and poems being likewise in soak, yet there they were obliged to remain, riveted to their seats. The unhealthy season caused much sickness, and many of the candidates suffered severely, seven or eight dying of cholera while the examinations were in progress. That this is not an exceptional state of things, is evident from the fact that it has since been repeated. In the autumn examinations for 1888, at this same place, it was reported that over one hundred persons died in the quarters, either of cholera or of some epidemic closely resembling it. Of these, some were servants, some copyists, some students, and a few officials. On the same occasion one of the main examination buildings fell in, as a result of which several persons were said to have been killed. The utterly demoralizing effect of such occurrences is obvious.

On the second or third day after the examinations the boards are hung, and the number of those successful appears. Yet to make the choice doubly sure, and to guard against fraud and accidents, still another examination is added, which is final and decisive. In addition to the twenty or thirty who have passed, half as many more names are taken of those next highest, making perhaps thirty or forty candidates, between whom the final choice will lie. At this examination a theme from the Four Books is again announced, on which only a fragment, the beginning, middle or end of an essay, is to be produced, under the immediate eye of the Chancellor himself. The number of those examined being so limited, it is easy to supervise them strictly, and changes in the previous order are sure to occur.

When the results of this examination are posted, the persons who have finally passed, and whose talents are definitely adjudged to be "flourishing," are for the first time known. Those who have failed at any stage of the trial may return to their homes, but those who have "entered school" must remain at the Prefectural city, to escort the Chancellor upon his way to the next city where he is to hold examinations.

The expenses of the Chancellor's examination, to those who fail to pass, are the same as those of the preceding ones. But for those who have "entered" there are other and most miscellaneous expenses, illustrating the Chinese aphorism that it is the sick man who must furnish the perspiration. The fee to the ling-shêng who is surety, has been already mentioned. There are also other fees or gratuities, the amount of which will depend upon the circumstances of the student, but all of which must be paid. The underlings who transact the business of the examination receive presents to the amount of several dollars, the "board-hangers" must be rewarded with a few hundred cash, etc., etc.

As soon as the candidate is known to have "entered," a strip of red paper is prepared, announcing this fact, and a messenger is posted off to the graduate's home. For this service, a fee of several thousand cash is expected. Large proclamations, called "Joyful Announcements," are prepared by establishments where characters are cut on blocks, and sold to successful competitors, at the rate of three or four cents apiece. A poor scholar may not be able to afford these luxuries, but those who can afford it buy great numbers of them, sending them in every direction to friends and relatives, who take care to have them properly posted. On receipt of these notifications, it is customary for the friends of the fortunate family to pay a visit of congratulation, at which they must be handsomely entertained at a feast. Each one brings with him a present in money, varying according to his circumstances, and his relations to the family of the graduate. If the newmade Bachelor has a wide circle of relatives and friends, especially if some of them happen to be occupying official positions, he will not improbably receive enough in gifts of this sort, to reimburse himself for the costs attending his examinations, and in exceptional instances, his congratulatory presents may greatly exceed the total of his expenses.

The style of these notices is the same, a blank being left for the name and rank of the graduate which is inserted in writing. It is a very common practice in some regions to announce that the person concerned, "entered as first on the list," though as a matter of fact he may have been one of the last. This is considered a very easy and desirable way to get a name, though no one is deceived by the fraud, for when a dead wall is covered by scores of these announcements, each recording the entry of some one as the "first name," it is obvious that the phrase is merely employed for display.

It would naturally be supposed that the result of competition so severe and so protracted as that for the degree of hsiu-ts'ai, would be certified in the most careful manner, such as by a diploma bearing the seal of the Chancellor. There is, however, nothing of the kind. The essays of the successful candidates are supposed to be forwarded to the Board of Rites in Peking, where it is to be hoped they eventually grow mouldy and disappear, else the capital might be buried beneath the enormous mass. But the individual whose talent is at last flourishing, has of that fact no tangible evidence whatever. When it becomes desirable to investigate the claim of a hsiu-ts'ai, he is asked in what year he graduated, the name of the examiner, the several themes propounded, etc. It will be difficult to manufacture plausible replies, which will not give some clew to their falsity. In one case of this sort within the writer's knowledge, a man who had been examined, but who did not pass, on being questioned gave the name, the subjects, etc., which belonged to his own brother, who really was a graduate. The man himself, as afterward appeared, was in prison at the very time when he professed to have graduated.

This absence of credentials for a degree so much coveted, makes it easy for scholars of shrewdness, and real ability, to pass themselves off in districts remote from their own, as having attained to a rank which they have not in reality reached.

A graduate is allowed to wear a plain brass button on his cap, which he prefers to the pewter one given him on graduating. In case of violations of law, the Magistrate of the District in which the offender lives, may have his button taken away, and the graduate reduced to the level of any other person. As long, however, as he continues to be a graduate, he cannot be beaten like other Chinese, except on the palm of the hand. If a Magistrate were to violate the rights of any graduate, the act would raise a tornado about his head, before which he would be glad to retreat, for the whole body of graduates would rise like a swarm of hornets to resent the insult.

The financial exigencies of the past generation or two have led to the open sale of literary degrees, a practice resorted to on a great scale by the Chinese Government, whenever there is any unusual pressure for funds, such as the repair of the disasters caused by the change in the Yellow River. It is often quite possible to buy the degree of hsiu-ts'ai, for about $100, and the purchaser is provided with a certificate, being in this respect on a better footing than the graduate. But subscription degrees are regarded with merited contempt, and their sale great as it has been, does not appear to have seriously affected the regular examinations, by diminishing the number of contestants.

There are other methods than purchase of a degree, by which the candidate for literary honours, whose means admit of it, may try to weight the wheel of fortune in his favour. There are three common ways of providing oneself with examination essays without undergoing the labour of composing them. Of these the first is known as the "box plan," (hsiang-tzŭ), and it is not so much cramming, as padding. The Four Books and Five Classics seem at first sight to afford an almost unbounded field for subjects of essays, and as the Chancellor does not announce his themes until he enters the hall, it is hopeless to attempt to ascertain them in advance. But the shrewd Celestial has an empirical, if not a scientific acquaintance with the doctrine of chances and of averages. He knows that in the course of years, the same themes recur, and that essays which were composed long before he was born are just as good in the present year as they ever were. The "padding" method consists in lining one's clothing with an immense number of essays, the characters of which are of that minute kind known as "fly-eye," scarcely legible without a magnifying glass. Upon this scale, it is easy to reduce an essay with 300 characters to a compass of extreme insignificance, and a moderately "padded" scholar might be provided with 8,000 or 10,000 such essays. Sometimes they are concealed in the baskets in which the students bring their provisions to the hall. By dint of a complete index, the student who is padded, can readily ascertain whether he is provided with an essay upon the passage desired, and though the withdrawal of an essay from a pack might seem a more difficult feat, it is easily done by the judicious expenditure of a fee to the guards both at the door and within the hall. A variation of the padding method is to have essays written all over the lining of the inner jackets, which are made of white silk for this purpose.

A second and very common way of obtaining essays without writing them, is by purchase. In furtherance of this plan, there is a special system of machinery, which (with appropriate financial lubrication) may be easily set in motion.

The purchase of an essay is one of those acts which in China can by no possibility be concealed. "There is no hedge that excludes the wind," and the close proximity of so many witnesses would, in any case, render the transaction in a manner a public one. Why then do not those scholars who are honestly toiling for a degree, agree to expose the frauds by which every one of them is so seriously wronged? It is not, indeed, an unknown circumstance for a scholar to cry out, so as to attract the attention of the examiners, when he witnesses the transfer of essays, but it is not apparently a common act. The custom of selling essays, like other abuses in China, is too universal and too ancient to be broken up, without the steady coöperation of many forces, for which it is hopeless to look. The Chinese dread to give offence by any such burst of indignation as would be, for an Occidental, irrepressible. And so things go on in the old way. As to the morality of the affair, if the consideration of it ever occurs to any one, it is hard to make that appear culpable in a poor scholar, which is legitimate for the emperor.

The proportion of students who obtain their degrees unfairly must be large, but there is no means of ascertaining the facts, even approximately. No two examinations are alike, and in all of them much depends upon the temper and vigilance of the presiding officer. In one district in which the writer lived, there was an examination in which so many persons obtained their degrees by fraud, that even the patience of the most patient of peoples was exhausted. Some defeated candidate wrote a complaint of the wrong, and tossed it into the examination hall where it was brought to the attention of the Chancellor, who had all the successful candidates examined on their essays, an examination which eleven out of fifteen were unable to pass, having bought their essays, and the result was their summary disgrace. Since this occurrence, much greater care has been exercised at this particular examination than was formerly the rule. In another district a candidate known to the writer succeeded in passing the first of the two examinations before the Chancellor, but the second was too much for him. His essay and poem were adjudged bad, and he was beaten a hundred blows on the hand. It was then the custom to publish the names of those who passed the best examination on the first trial before the Chancellor, as already having attained a degree. This notice had already been sent to the home of the candidate, who now had the exquisite mortification of having his name erased, when the prize was already within his grasp. The subordinates in the yamên of the Chancellor kneeled to his Excellency, and implored him to overlook the amazing stupidity of this candidate, which the great man was kind enough to do, and thus a degree was wrested even from fate itself.

At all varieties of examinations, there are present many persons who act as essay brokers and as middle-men between those who have essays to sell, and those who wish to buy. It is supposed that both the seller of the essay and the purchaser will be among those examined, but the practical difficulty arises from the uncertainty whether their respective seats in the hall, which cannot be known in advance, will be within reach of each other. As any two persons are very liable to be so far apart that communication will be impossible, it is usual for the essay broker to introduce a number of essay vendors to each intending purchaser, so that the chances of effecting a transfer between any two of them may be increased. To bind the bargain, before the essay is composed, a brief but explicit contract is signed by the purchaser in the hall. The terms are arranged on a sliding scale, called "first two and after two," "first five and after five," etc. This signifies that it is agreed that the person who furnishes the essay shall receive in any event a first payment of 20,000 cash, or 50,000 cash, as the case may be, and should the purchaser win a degree, there is to be an after payment of 200,000 cash, or 500,000 cash, according to the terms. These payments are enforced by the brokers, who must be well acquainted with the financial circumstances of the several parties. These obligations, like gambling debts, cannot of course be legally prosecuted, but the Chinese have in all such cases simple ways of enforcing payment, such as raising a disturbance in an annoying and public way.

The reputation of having bought an examination essay is not one which any candidate wishes to have made public authentically, however notorious the fact may be, but the reputation of having bought an essay and of having declined payment, would be intolerable. Some essay vendors frequent examinations for a long series of years, with no view to obtaining a degree for themselves, but in order to reap more substantial benefits from their scholarship than a degree is likely to confer. If they have once taken a degree themselves, they can only carry on this trade by assuming the name of some candidate, to whom a fee must be paid for the privilege of personating him. Graduates of the rank of Selected Men also carry on this business, sometimes in a double way, taking a degree for the person whom they personate, and also having leisure to write essays for sale, after their own are finished, thus killing two birds with one stone. In either case, it is necessary to bribe the ling-shêng who is the guarantee of the identity of the undergraduate.

The third method of obtaining the essays of other persons, is called "transmission" (ch'uan ti). This can only be accomplished by the coöperation of the inspectors (hsün ch'ang) who, like all other mortals, are supposed to be perfectly open to considerations of temporal advantage, if only arguments of sufficient strength are employed. As soon as the Chancellor's theme is announced, it is copied, and at a preconcerted signal thrown over the wall of the examination premises to persons waiting for it. Several scholars outside may have been previously engaged to write essays for different persons within the hall. When the essays are finished they are carefully done up, and at a signal, such as a call for a dog or for a cat, are thrown over the wall to the watchman, who has been previously paid to receive them. The inspector, also liberally fed, ascertains from a private mark on each essay, for whom it is intended, and while pacing back and forth through the hall, contrives to deliver them, without being seen by the Chancellor. In one case, six persons were known to have received their degrees, on the merits of essays which were brought into the hall after being thrown over the wall in a single bundle. Sometimes essays are concealed in the body of a harmless-looking bread-cake, which is tossed carelessly from one candidate to another when the lunches are eaten, with the connivance, no doubt, of the inspectors. The District Magistrates sometimes post the Secretaries at the corners of the examination hall, where it is easy to see all that goes on. But much more often, it is probable, that the Magistrate takes little interest in such details.

In some examinations, the Chancellors are very strict, and forbid any of the watchmen to enter the hall at all, which, of course, checkmates the plan last described. Such instances are much more than offset by others, in which the Chancellor does not remain through the examination himself, but entrusts the conduct of affairs to his Secretaries. These functionaries are then at liberty to furnish essays to candidates who can afford to pay the heavy price necessary. In such cases, while ostensibly examining the essays, the Secretaries find it easy to throw one of their own under a stool, or in some place from which it may be readily captured by the purchaser.

In a case reported in the Peking Gazette some years since, a bold vendor of essays succeeded in getting his paper conveyed to the individual for whom it was intended, by hooking it on the garments of the venerable Chancellor himself, who thus unconsciously became the bearer of the very documents which he was endeavouring to suppress! The candidates at the Chancellor's examination are generally seated in such proximity, that including those on each side, most of the students are within easy reach of ten or fifteen other persons. This renders the transfer of papers an easy matter. In the second of these trials, when the number is reduced to a mere handful, the students are often seated just as compactly as before.

A scholar with whom the writer is acquainted, once found himself near a poor fellow, who was utterly at a loss how to treat the theme from Mencius, "Like climbing a tree to catch a fish." A verbal arrangement was hastily made for the purchase of an essay, but the usual written agreement was omitted. The essay was indited in the lawless style of chirography known as the "grass character," and handed to the purchaser to be copied. Here an untoward accident occurred, for the man who bought the essay mistook two characters, when he copied out the paper, for two others which they much resembled, thus ruining the chances of success. The poor scholar begged off from the amount which he had agreed to pay, (which was about ten dollars) on the plea of poverty. The angry essay-seller then raised a kind of mob of students, went to the lodgings of his debtor and made an uproar, the result of which was to extract from the latter about a dollar and a half, which was all that could be got! The preceptor of the man who sold the essay, who was himself one of the candidates at this examination, claimed, with many others, that the essay which was sold, as represented by the author, must certainly have resulted in a degree for the poor scholar if he had not blundered in inditing false characters.

Should an examiner overlook a wrong character, and the fact be afterward made public, he might be degraded for his carelessness. A case of this sort was reported a few years ago in the Peking Gazette. At the triennial examination for the Han-lin, in the year 1871, after the essays had been submitted to the Han-lin examiners, the nine most meritorious ones were selected, and were sent in to the Empress Dowager—the Emperor being under age—to have the award formally confirmed. The work of greatest merit was placed uppermost, but the old lady, who had an imperial will of her own, was anxious to thwart the decision of the learned pundits; and, as chance would have it, the sunlight fell upon the chosen manuscript, and she discovered a flaw, a thinness in the paper, indicating a place in the composition where one character had been erased and another substituted. The Empress rated the examiners for allowing such "slovenly work" to pass, and proclaimed another man, whose name was Hsiang, as victor. This individual hailed from the province of Kuang-tung—a province which had produced a Senior Wrangler but once in 250 years. On his return to his native province the successful scholar was received by the local authorities with the highest possible honours. All the families owning his surname who could afford to do so paid enormous sums to be permitted to come and worship at his ancestral hall, for by this means they established a pseudo claim to relationship, and were allowed to place tablets over the entrances of their own halls inscribed with the title Chuang Yüan, or Senior Wrangler. The superstitious Cantonese believed that the sunbeam which revealed the fatal flaw was a messenger sent from heaven!

The fact that a man has taken the degree of hsiu-ts'ai, does not release him from the necessity of studying. On the contrary, this is called "entering school," and the graduate is required to present himself at each triennial examination, to compete for the next step in the scale of honours, that of ling-shêng hsiu-ts'ai. The number of graduates who can attain the rank of ling-shêng in any one year is limited. In a district which graduates seventeen hsiu-ts'ai, there may be but one or two ling-shêng graduates passed at a time. There are, however, extra examinations, as already explained, in case of the accession of an Emperor, etc., and when a vacancy in the fixed number takes place through death, an additional candidate is allowed to pass to fill the place. A hsiu-ts'ai is not allowed to decline the examination merely on account of the improbability of his passing it; on the contrary, every graduate is required to compete as often as examinations occur. This is the theory, but as a matter of fact, the payment of about a dollar and a half to the underlings of the Superintendent of Instruction for the District will enable the candidate to have an entry opposite his name, signifying that he is "incapacitated by illness," or is "not at home." But after the graduate has been examined ten times, and has persistently failed to show any capacity for further advance, he is excused from examination thereafter, and his name is dropped. At these examinations the candidates are divided into four classes according to the respective merits of their essays. If any candidate fails to get into the first three classes, he is regarded as having forfeited his title to the grade of hsiu-ts'ai, and he loses his rank as such, unless the Chancellor can be prevailed upon to excuse his "rotten scholarship," and give the unfortunate student another trial. Hence the proverb, "The hsiu-ts'ai dreads the fourth class." The ling-shêng is entitled to a small allowance of about $10 a year, from the Government, to assist him in the prosecution of his studies, though the amount can hardly be regarded as proportioned to the difficulty of attaining the rank which alone is entitled to receive this meagre help.

The ling-shêng graduates are required to compete at the triennial examinations, for the next step, which is that of kung-shêng. Only one candidate can enter this rank at one examination unless there should be a special vacancy.

There are five varieties of kung-shêng, according to the time at which and the conditions under which they have graduated. These scholars do not, like the ling-shêng, act as bondsmen for undergraduates, nor do they like them, have an allowance. They are permitted to wear a semi-official robe, and are addressed by a title of respect, but in a pecuniary point of view their honours are empty ones, unless they secure the place of Superintendent of Instruction, which must, however, be in some district other than their own. The kung-shêng and the hsiu-ts'ai are at opposite ends of one division of the long educational road. The former is regarded as a schoolboy, and the latter is for the first time a man, and need be examined no more, unless he chooses to compete for the rank of Selected Man, (chü-jên) an examination which has intricacies and perils of its own. "The hsiu-ts'ai," says the proverb, "must have talent, but the chü-jên must have fate," that is, no amount of talent, by itself, will suffice to win this higher rank, unless the fates are on one's side, a proposition which we are prepared to believe, from what has already been seen of the lower grades of scholarship.

At any part of the long process which we have described, it is possible to become a candidate for honours above, by purchasing those below. A man of real talent, studiously inclined, might for example buy the rank of ling-shêng, and then with a preceptor of his own, and great diligence, become a kung-shêng, a chü-jên, and perhaps at last an official, skipping all the tedious lower steps. The taint of having climbed over the wall, instead of entering by the straight and narrow way, would doubtless cling to him forever, but this circumstance would probably not interfere with his equanimity, so long as it did not diminish his profits. As a matter of experience, however, it is probable that it would be more worth while to buy an office outright, rather than to enter the field, by the circuitous route of a combination of purchase and examinations.

Whether to be examined or not is not always optional in China. A father was determined that his son should study for a degree, which the son was very unwilling to do, yielding however to compulsion. He was so successful that at the age of nineteen he became a Bachelor, only to find that his father's ambition was far from satisfied, and that he now required him to go on and work for the next degree of Selected Man. Perceiving that there was no hope of escaping this discouraging task, the youth hung himself, and was examined no more!

The office of Superintendent of Instruction, is considered a very desirable one, since the duties are light, and the income considerable. This income arises partly from a large tract of land set apart for the support of the two Superintendents, partly from "presents" of grain exacted twice a year after the manner of Buddhist priests, and partly from fees which every graduate is required to pay, varying as all such Chinese payments do, according to the circumstances of the individual. The Superintendent is careful to inquire privately into the means at the disposal of each graduate, and fixes his tax accordingly. From his decision there is no appeal. If the payment is resisted as excessive, the Superintendent, who is theoretically his preceptor, will have the hsiu-ts'ai beaten on the hands, and probably double the amount of the assessment. If any of the graduates in a district are accused of a crime, they are reported to the District Magistrate, who turns them over to the Superintendent of Instruction, for an inquiry. The Superintendent and the Magistrate together, could secure the disgrace of a graduate, as already explained.

The Government desires to encourage learning as much as possible, and to this end there are in many cities, what may be termed Government high-schools or colleges, where preceptors of special ability are appointed to explain the Classics, and to hold frequent examinations, similar to those in the regular course, as described. The funds for the support of such institutions, are sometimes derived from the voluntary subscriptions of wealthy persons, who have been rewarded by the gift of an honourary title, or perhaps from a tax on a cattle fair, etc. Where the arrangement is carried out in good faith, it has worked well, but in two districts known to the writer, the whole plan has been brought into discredit of late years, on account of the promotion to office of District Magistrates who have bought their way upward, and who have no learning of their own. In such cases, the management of the examination is probably left to a Secretary, who disposes of it as quickly and with as little trouble to himself as possible. The themes for the essays are given out, and prizes promised for the best, but instead of remaining to superintend the competition, the Secretary goes about his business, leaving the scholars who wish to compete to go to their homes, and write their essays there, or to have others do it for them, as they prefer. In some instances, the same man registers under a variety of names, and writes competitive essays for them all, or he perhaps writes his essays and sells them to others, and when they are handed in, no questions are asked. It would be easy to stop abuses of this sort, if it were the concern or the interest of any one to do so, but it is not, and so they continue. A school-teacher with whom the writer is acquainted, happening to have a school near the district city, made it a constant practice for many years, to attend examinations of this sort. He was examined about a hundred times, and on four occasions received a prize, once a sum in money equivalent to about seventy-five cents, and three other times a sum equal to about half-a-dollar!

It is a constant wonder to Occidentals, by what motives the Chinese are impelled, in their irrepressible thirst for literary degrees, even under all the drawbacks and disadvantages, some of which have been described. These motives, like all others in human experience are mixed, but at the base of them all, is a desire for fame and for power. In China the power is in the hands of the learned and of the rich. Wealth is harder to acquire than learning, and incomparably more difficult to keep. The immemorial traditions of the empire are all in favour of the man who is willing to submit to the toils that he may win the rewards of the scholar.

Every village as already explained, has its headmen. Among them the literary graduate, provided he is also a practical man, will inevitably take the lead. He will often come into relations with the District Magistrate, which makes him a marked man among his fellows. He will be constantly called upon to assist in the settlement of disputes, and every such occasion will afford opportunities for the privilege, so dear to the Chinese, of enjoying a feast at the expense of his neighbours, besides putting them under an obligation to him for his trouble. At the weddings and funerals within the large circle of his acquaintance he will be a frequent guest, and always in the place of honour due to his literary degree. This is especially the case in funeral ceremonies of those who are buried with the most elaborate ritual. On these occasions the ancestral tablet of the deceased is to be written, and as an important part of the exercises a red dot over one character signifying King is to be placed, thus changing it into the symbol denoting Lord. It is not uncommon to have the performances connected with such funerals extended over several days, each furnishing three excellent feasts, as well as abundant supplies of opium for those who wish to smoke. In a country like China the participation in revels such as these approach more nearly to paradisaic bliss than anything of which the Chinese mind can conceive. Every scholar is desirous of getting into such relations with his environment that honours of this sort come to him as a matter of course. If he happens to be very poor, they furnish a not unimportant part of his support, as well as of his happiness.

The village graduate who knows how to help in lawsuits by preparing complaints, and by assisting in the intricate proceedings ensuing at each stage is often able by means of the prestige thus gained, to get his living at the expense of others more ignorant. No country offers a better field for such an enterprise than China. Unbounded respect for learning coexists with unbounded ignorance, and the experienced literary man knows how to turn each of these elements to the very best account. In all lands and in all ages, the man who is possessed with what is vulgarly termed the "gift of the gab," is able to make his own way, and in China he carries everything before him.

The range of territory which any aspirant for literary honours in China must expect to traverse, is, as we have seen, continental. In order to have any hope of success, he must be acquainted with every square inch of it, and must be prepared to sink an artesian well from any given point to any given depth. To the uneducated peasant, whose whole being is impregnated with a blind respect for learning, amounting at times to a kind of idolatry, such knowledge as this seems an almost supernatural acquirement, and inspires all the reverence of which he is capable. The thought of the estimate in which they will be held for the whole term of their lives, is thus a powerful stimulus to scholars of ambition, even under the greatest discouragements.

There could scarcely be a better exemplification of what the Chinese saying calls "superiority to those below, and inferiority to those above," than the position of the hsiu-ts'ai. While he is looked upon by the vulgar herd in the light we have described, by the educated classes above him he is regarded, as we have so often termed him, as a schoolboy who is not yet even in school. The popular dictum avers that though the whole body of hsiu-ts'ai should attempt to start a rebellion, and should be left undisturbed in the effort for three years, the result would be failure, albeit this proverb finds no support in the history of the great rebellion, which originated with a discontented undergraduate who was exasperated at his repeated failures to get his talent recognized. Literary examinations, as we have abundantly seen, are like the game of backgammon, an equal mixture of skill and luck, but the young graduate easily comes to regard the luck as due to the skill, and thus becomes filled to the full of that intellectual pride which is one of the greatest barriers to the national progress of China.

Differing by millenniums from the system just described is that recently decreed after successful agitation by a few reformers. During the summer of 1898 His Majesty Kuang Hsü, Emperor of China, issued several Edicts which abolished the "eight-legged examination essay" as an avenue to the attainment of literary degrees, and introduced in their place what was termed Practical Chinese Literature, and Western Learning, which were to be combined in Provincial and County Academies. Existing institutions were to be remodelled after a more or less definite pattern set in Peking. All except official temples (that is, those where offerings or services were required from the Magistrates) were to be surrendered as seats of the New Learning. Reports were demanded from Provincial Governors as to the present status of these temples, and the future prospects for income from them.

These Edicts potentially revolutionized the intellectual life of China. They were received very differently in different parts of the empire, but there is no reason to doubt that they would have been widely welcomed by an influential minority of the literati of China, who had in various ways come to realize the futility of the present instruction for the needs of to-day. The immediate effect was to bring Western Learning into universal demand. Scholars who had never deigned to recognize the existence of foreigners, were now glad to become their pupils and purchasers of their text-books on a large scale. For a few weeks examination themes were strongly tinctured with Western topics, and those who were able to show any familiarity with those branches of learning were almost sure of a degree. Correct answers to simple mathematical, geographical, or astronomical questions are said to have rendered success certain, and it is even alleged that a candidate in one place took his honours by writing out and commenting upon the Ten Commandments, which he represented as The Western Code of Laws.

Toward the close of September, 1898, the Empress Dowager seized the reins, suppressed her nephew, and nearly all reforms, educational and political, were extinguished. A new Imperial University in Peking survived the storm, but almost all of the extended and beneficent program of His Majesty was relegated to the Greek Kalends. It is only a question of time when the pendulum shall swing back, but every well-wisher of China hopes that it may not be delayed until the national existence of the Chinese shall have been lost.

XI

VILLAGE TEMPLES AND RELIGIOUS SOCIETIES

The process by which the inconceivably great numbers of Chinese temples came to be is not without an interest of its own. When a few individuals wish to build a temple, they call the headmen of the village, in whose charge by long custom are all the public matters of the town, and the enterprise is put in their care. It is usual to make an assessment on the land for funds; this is not necessarily a fixed sum for each acre, but is more likely to be graded according to the amount of land each owns, the poor being perhaps altogether exempt, or very lightly taxed, and the rich paying much more heavily. When the money is all collected by the managers, the building begins under their direction. If the temple is to be a large one, costing several hundred tæls, in addition to this preliminary tax, a subscription book is opened, and sent to all the neighbouring villages, and sometimes to all within a wide radius, the begging being often done by some priest of persuasive powers, dragging a chain, or having his cheeks pierced with spikes, or in some way bearing the appearance of fulfilling a vow. The only motive to these outside contributions is the strong impetus to the "practice of virtue," which exists among the Chinese, and which can be played upon to almost any extent. Lists of contributions are kept in the larger temples, and the donors are expected to receive the worth of their money, through seeing their names posted in a conspicuous place, as subscribers of a certain sum. In some regions it is customary to set down the amount given as much larger than it really is, by a fiction equally agreeable to all concerned. Thus the donor of 250 cash sees his name paraded as the subscriber of 1,000 cash, and so throughout.

These subscriptions to temples are in reality a loan to be repaid whenever the village subscribing finds itself in need of similar help, and the obligation will not be forgotten by the donors.

It is seldom safe to generalize in regard to anything in China, but if there is one thing in regard to which a generalization would seem to be more safe than another, it would be the universality of temples in every village throughout the empire. Yet it is an undoubted fact that there are, even in China, great numbers of villages which have no temple at all. This is true of all those which are inhabited exclusively by Mohammedans, who never take any part in the construction of such edifices, a peculiarity which is now well known and respected though at the first appearance of these strangers, it caused them many bitter struggles to establish their right to a monotheistic faith.

The most ordinary explanation of a comparatively rare phenomenon of a village without a temple, is that the hamlet is a small one and cannot afford the expense. Sometimes it may have been due to the fact that there was no person of sufficient intelligence in the village to take the initial steps, and as one generation is much influenced by what was done and what was not done in the generations that have passed, five hundred years may elapse without the building of a temple, simply because a temple was not built five hundred years ago. In the very unusual cases where a village is without one, it is not because they have no use for the gods; for in such instances the villagers frequently go to the temples of the next village and "borrow their light," just as a poor peasant who cannot afford to keep an animal to do his plowing may get the loan of a donkey in planting time, from a neighbour who is better off.

The two temples which are most likely to be found, though all others be wanting, are those of the local god, and of the god of war. The latter has been made much of by the present dynasty, and greatly promoted in the pantheon. The former is regarded as a kind of constable in the next world, and he is to be informed promptly on the death of an adult, that he may report to the city god ("Ch'êng Huang,") who in turn reports to Yen Wang, the Chinese Pluto.

In case a village has no temple to the T'u-ti, or local god, news of the death is conveyed to him by wailing at the crossing of two streets, where he is supposed to be in ambush.

Tens of thousands of villages are content with these two temples, which are regarded as almost indispensable. If the village is a large one, divided into several sections transacting their public business independently of one another, there may be several temples to the same divinity. It is a common saying, illustrative of Chinese notions on this topic, that the local god at one end of the village has nothing to do with the affairs of the other end of the village.

When the temple has been built, if the managers have been prudent, they are not unlikely to have collected much more than they will use in the building. This surplus is used partly in giving a theatrical exhibition, to which all donors are invited—which is the only public way in which their virtue can be acknowledged— but mainly in the purchase of land, the income of which shall support the temple priest. In this way, a temple once built is in a manner endowed, and becomes self-supporting. The managers select some one of the donors, and appoint him a sort of president of the board of trustees, (called a shan chu, or "master of virtue"), and he is the person with whom the managers take account for the rent and use of the land. Sometimes a public school is supported from the income of the land, and sometimes this income is all gambled away by vicious priests, who have devices of their own to get control of the property to the exclusion of the villagers. When temples get out of repair, which, owing to their defective construction, is constantly the case, they must be rebuilt by a process similar to that by which they were originally constructed; for in China there are as truly successive crops of temples as of turnips.

There is no limit to the number of temples which a single village may be persuaded into building. Some villages of three

143

hundred families have one to every ten families, but this must be an exceptional ratio. It is a common saying among the Chinese that the more temples a village has, the poorer it is, and also the worse its morals. But, on the other hand, the writer has heard of one village which has none at all, but which has acquired the nickname of "Ma Family Thief Village." It seems reasonable to infer from the observed facts that, when they have fallen into comparative desuetude, temples are almost inert, so far as influence goes. But when filled with indolent and vicious priests, as is too often the case, they are baneful to the morals of any community. In the rural districts, it is comparatively rare to find resident priests, for the reason that they cannot live from the scanty revenue, and a year of famine will starve them out of large districts.

Temples that are a little distance from a village are a favourite resort of thieves, as a convenient place to divide their booty, and also are resting-places for beggars. To prevent this misuse, it is common to see the door entirely bricked up, or perhaps a small opening may be left for the divinity to breathe through!

The erection of a temple is but the beginning of an interminable series of expenses; for, if there is a priest, he must be paid for each separate service rendered, and will besides demand a tax in grain of every villager after the wheat and autumn harvests—exactions which often become burdensome in the extreme. In addition to this, minor repairs keep up an unceasing flow of money. If there is an annual chanting of sacred books (called ta chiao), this is also a heavy expense.

Temples which are not much used are convenient receptacles for coffins, which have been prepared in the Chinese style before they are needed, and also for the images of animals, made of reeds and paper, which are designed to be burnt at funerals that they may be thus transported to the spirit world. If the temple has a farm attached, the divinities are quite likely to be obscured, in the autumn, by the crops which are hung up to dry all about and even over them; for storage space under a roof is one of the commodities most rare in the village.

The temples most popular in one region may be precisely those which are rarely seen in another, but next to those already named perhaps the most frequently honoured divinities are the Goddess of Mercy (Kuan Yin P'u Sa), some variety of the manifold goddess known as "Mother" (Niang Niang), and Buddha. What is called the "Hall of the Three Religions" (San Chiao T'ang), is one of the instructive relics of a time when the common proposition that the "three religions are really one" was not so implicitly received as now. In the Hall of the Three Religions, Confucius, Lao-tzǔ (the founder of Taoism, or Rationalism), and Buddha, all stand together on one platform; but Buddha, the foreigner, is generally placed in the middle as the post of honour, showing that even to the Chinese the native forms of faith have seemed to be lacking in something which Buddhism attempts to supply. This place has not been obtained, however, without a long struggle.

Another form of genial compromise of rival claims, is what is called "The Temple of All the gods" (Ch'üan shên miao), in which a great variety of deities are represented on a wall, but with no clear precedence of honour. Temples to the god of Literature, (Wên Ch'ang), are built by subscriptions of the local scholars, or by taxes imposed by the District Magistrate. It is impossible to arrive at any exact conclusions on the subject, but it is probable that the actual cost of the temples, in almost any region in China, would be found to form a heavy percentage of the income of the people in the district.

The World's Oldest Sacred Mountain, T'ai Shan.

Scenery Along The River Lin.

XII

COÖPERATION IN RELIGIOUS OBSERVANCES

The genius of the Chinese for combination is nowhere more conspicuous than in their societies which have a religious object. Widely as they differ in the special purposes to which they are devoted, they all appear to share certain characteristics, which are generally four in number—the contribution of small sums at definite intervals by many persons; the superintendence of the finances by a very small number of the contributors; the loan of the contributions at a high rate of interest, which is again perpetually loaned and re-loaned so as to accumulate compound interest in a short time and in large amounts; and lastly, the employment of the accumulations in the religious observance for which the society was instituted, accompanied by a certain amount of feasting participated in by the contributors.

A typical example of the numerous societies organized for religious purposes may be found in one of those which have for their object a pilgrimage to some of the five sacred mountains of China. The most famous and most frequented of them all is the Great Mountain (T'ai Shan) in Shan-tung, which in the second month of the Chinese year is crowded with pilgrims from distant parts of the empire. For those who live at any considerable distance from this seat of worship, which according to Dr. Williamson is the most ancient historical mountain in the world, the expense of travel to visit the place is an obstacle of a serious character. To surmount this difficulty, societies are organized which levy a tax upon each member, of (say) one hundred cash a month. If there are fifty members this would result in the collection of 5,000 cash as a first payment. The managers who have organized the society, proceed to loan this amount to some one who is willing to pay for its use not less than two or three per cent. a month. Such loans are generally for short periods, and to those who are in the pressing need of financial help. When the time has expired, and principal and interest is collected, it is again loaned out, thus securing a very rapid accumulation of capital. Successive loans at a high rate of interest for short periods, are repeatedly effected during the three years, which are generally the limit of the period of accumulation. It constantly happens that those who have in extreme distress borrowed such funds, find themselves unable to repay the loan when it is called in, and as benevolence to the unfortunate forms no part of the "virtue practice" of those who organize these societies, the defaulters are then obliged to pull down their houses or to sell part of their farms to satisfy the claims of the "Mountain Society." Even thus it is not always easy to raise the sum required, and in cases of this sort, the unfortunate debtor may even be driven to commit suicide.

"Mountain Societies" are of two sorts, the "Travelling," (hsing-shan hui), and the "Stationary," (tso-shan hui). The former lays plans for a visit to the sacred mountain, and for the offering of a certain amount of worship at the various temples there to be found. The latter is a device for accomplishing the principal results of the society, without the trouble and expense of an actual visit to a distant and more or less inaccessible mountain peak. The recent repeated outbreaks of the Yellow River which must be crossed by many of the pilgrims to the Great Mountain, have tended greatly to diminish the number of "Travelling Societies," and to increase the number of the stationary variety.

When the three years of accumulation have expired, the managers call in all the money, and give notice to the members who hold a feast. It is then determined at what date a theatrical exhibition shall be given, which is paid for by the accumulation of the assessments and the interest. If the members are natives of several different villages, a site may be chosen for the theatricals convenient for them all, but without being actually in any one of them. At other times the place is fixed by lot.

During the performance of the theatricals, generally three days or four, the members of the society are present, and may be said to be their own guests and their own hosts. For the essential part of the ceremony is the eating, without which nothing in China can make the smallest progress. The members frequently treat themselves to three excellent feasts each day, and in the intervals of eating and witnessing theatricals, they find time to do more or less worshipping of an image of the mountain goddess (T'ai Shan niang-niang) at a paper "mountain," which by a simple fiction is held to be, for all intents and purposes, the real Great Mountain. While there does not appear to be any deeply-seated conviction that there is greater merit in actually going to the real mountain than in worshipping at its paper representative at home, this almost inevitable feeling certainly does exist, and it expresses itself forcibly in nicknaming the stationary kind "squatting and fattening societies" (tun-piao hui). But while the Chinese are keenly alive to the inconsistencies and absurdities of their practices and professions, they are still more sensible of the delights of compliance with such customs as they happen to possess, without a too close scrutiny of "severe realities." The religious societies of the Chinese, faulty as they are from whatever point of view, do at least satisfy many social instincts of the people, and are the media by which an inconceivable amount of wealth is annually much worse than wasted. It is a notorious fact, that some of those which have the largest revenues and expenditures, are intimately connected with gambling practices.

Many large fairs, especially those held in the spring, which is a time of comparative leisure, are attended by thousands of persons whose real motive is to gamble with a freedom and on a scale impossible at home. In some towns where such fairs are held, the principal income of the inhabitants is derived from the rent of their houses to those who attend the fair, and no rents are so large as those received from persons whose occupation is mainly gambling. These are not necessarily professional gamblers, however, but simply country people who embrace this special opportunity to indulge their taste for risking their hard-earned money. In all such cases it is necessary to spend a certain sum upon the underlings of the nearest yamên, in order to secure immunity from arrest, but the profits to the keeper of the establishment (who generally does not gamble himself) are so great, that he can well afford all it costs. It is probably a safe estimate that as much money changes hands at some of the large fairs in the payment of gambling debts, as in the course of all the ordinary business arising from the trade with the tens of thousands of customers. In many places both men and women meet in the same apartments to gamble (a thing which would scarcely ever be tolerated at other times), and the passion is so consuming that even the clothes of the players are staked, the women making their appearance clad in several sets of trousers for this express purpose!

The routine acts of devotion to whatever god or goddess may be the object of worship are hurried through with, and both men and women spend the rest of their time struggling to conquer fate at the gaming-table. It is not without a certain propriety, therefore, that such fairs are styled "gambling fairs."

The "travelling" like the "sitting" society gathers in its money at the end of three years, and those who can arrange to do so, accompany the expedition which sets out soon after New Year for the Great Mountain. The expenses at the inns, as well as those of the carts employed, are defrayed from the common fund, but whatever purchases each member wishes to make must be paid for with his own money. On reaching their destination, another in the long series of feasts is held, an immense quantity of mock money is purchased and sent on in advance of the party, who are sure to find the six hundred steps of the sacred mount, (popularly supposed to be "forty li" from the base to the summit), a weariness to the flesh. At whatever point the mock money is burnt, a flag is raised to denote that this end has been accomplished. By the time the party of pilgrims have reached this spot, they are informed that the paper has already been consumed long ago, the wily priests taking care that much the larger portion is not wasted by being burnt, but only laid aside to be sold again to other confiding pilgrims.

If any contributor to the travelling society, or to any other of a like nature, should be unable to attend the procession to the mountain, or to go to the temple where worship is to be offered, his contribution is returned to him intact, but the interest he is supposed to devote to the virtuous object of the society, for he never sees any of it.

The countless secret sects of China, are all of them examples of the Chinese talent for coöperation in the alleged "practice of virtue." The general plan of procedure does not differ externally from that of a religious denomination in any Western land, except that there is an element of cloudiness about the basis upon which the whole superstructure rests, and great secrecy in the actual assembling at night. Masters and pupils, each in a graduated series, manuscript books containing doctrines, hymns which are recited or even composed to order, prayers, offerings, and ascetic observances are traits which many of these sects share in common with other forms of religion elsewhere. They have also definite assessments upon the members at fixed times without which, for lack of a motive power, no such society would long hold together.

XIII

COÖPERATION IN MARKETS AND FAIRS

In many parts of China the farmer comes much nearer to independence as regards producing what he needs, than any class of persons in Western lands. This is especially the case where cotton is raised, and where each family tries to make its own clothing from its own crops. But even with the minute and indefatigable industry of the Chinese, this ideal can be only imperfectly reached. No poor family has land enough to raise all that it requires, and every family not poor has a multitude of wants which must of necessity be supplied from without. Besides this, in any district most families have very little reserve capital, and must depend upon meeting their wants as they arise, by the use of such means as can be secured from day to day. The same comparative poverty makes it necessary for a considerable part of the population to dispose of some portion of its surplus products at frequent intervals, so as to turn it into the means of subsistence. The combined effect of these various causes is to make the Chinese dependent upon local markets to an extent which is not true of inhabitants of Occidental countries.

The establishment of any market, and even the mere existence of the class of buyers and of sellers, doubtless involves a certain amount of coöperation. But Chinese markets while not differing materially from those to be found in other lands, exhibit a higher degree of coöperation than any others of which we know. This coöperation is exhibited in the selection both of the places and of the times at which the markets shall be held. The density of population varies greatly in different provinces, but there are vast tracts in which villages are to be met at distances varying from a

153

quarter of a mile to two or three miles, and many of these villages contain hundreds, and some of them thousands of families.

At intervals of varying frequency, we hear of towns of still larger size than these called chên-tien, or market towns, and in them there is sure to be a regular fair. But fairs are not confined to the chên-tien, or the needs of the people would by no means be met. Many of the inferior villages also have a regular market, frequented by the neighbouring population, in a circle of greater or smaller radius according to circumstances. As a rule a village seems to be proud of its fair, and the natives of such a place are no doubt saved a vast amount of travel for the number of people who do not attend a fair is small.

We have met with one case of a village which once had a market, and gave it up in favour of another village, for the reason that the collection of such a miscellaneous assemblage was not for the advantage of the children and youth.

The market is under the supervision of headmen of the town, and some markets are called "official," because the headmen have communicated with the local magistrate, and have secured the issuing of a proclamation fixing the regulations under which business shall be transacted. This makes it easier to get redress for wrongs which may be committed by bad characters who abound at village markets in the direct ratio of the number of people assembled. Many of the larger markets bring together several thousand people, sometimes exceeding ten thousand in number, and among so many there are certain to be numerous gamblers, sharpers, thieves, and pick-pockets, against whom it behoves every one to be upon his guard. It occasionally happens that a feud arises between two sets of villages, as for example over an embankment which one of them makes to restrain the summer floods, which would thus be turned toward the territory of the other villages. In such cases it is not uncommon for the parties to the quarrel to refuse to attend each other's markets, and in that case new ones will be set up, with no reference to the needs of the territory, but with the sole purpose of breaking off all relations between neighbours.

In regions where animals are employed for farm-work, all the larger markets have attached to them "live-stock fairs," at which multitudes of beasts are constantly changing hands. It is common to find these live-stock fairs under a sort of official patronage, according to which the managers are allowed to levy a tax of perhaps one per cent. on the sales. Of this sum perhaps ten per cent. is required by the local Commissioner of Education (hsiao-li) for the purpose of supporting his establishment. The rest will be under the control of the village headmen, perhaps for the nominal purpose of paying the expenses of a free school, the funds for which not improbably find their way largely or wholly into the private treasuries of those who manage the public affairs of the village.

The times at which village markets are held vary greatly. In large cities there is a market every day, but in country places this would involve a waste of time. Sometimes the market takes place every other day, and sometimes on every day the numeral of which is a multiple of three. A more common arrangement however seems to be that which is based upon the division of the lunar month into thirty days. In this case "one market" signifies the space of five days, or the interval between two successive markets. It is in the establishment of these markets that coöperation is best illustrated. If a market is held every five days, it will occur six times every moon, for if the month happens to be a "small" one of twenty-nine days, the market that belongs on the thirtieth is held on the following day, which is the first of the next month. The various markets will be designated by the days on which they occur, as "One-Six," meaning the market which is held every first, sixth, eleventh, sixteenth, twenty-first, and twenty-sixth day of the moon. In like manner "Four-Nine," denotes the market attended on the fourth, ninth, fourteenth, nineteenth, twenty-fourth, twenty-ninth days, similarly with the rest. Every village will probably have a market within reach every day in the month, that is to say, every day in the year. In one direction for example is

155

to be found a "One-Six" market, in another "Two-Seven," in still others a "Three-Eight," a "Four-Nine," and a "Five-Ten." Some of these will be small markets, and some much larger, but the largest one will be attended by customers, especially wholesale dealers in cotton, cloth, etc., from great distances. The Chinese make nothing of walking to a market three, eight, or even ten miles away; for it is not a market only, but a kind of general exchange, where it is proverbially likely that any one will meet any one else.

Going To Market.

Chinese Market Scene.

Every village being thus surrounded with a ring of markets, each of these is also a cog in a wheel, playing into other wheels on each side of it. All those who attend a large market come to have a wide acquaintance with persons for great distances on each side of them, and the needs of all persons both buyers and sellers are adequately met.

The word which we have translated "market" (chi) denotes merely a gathering, and another character, (hui) is reserved for an assemblage of a much larger character, which is properly a fair. The number of persons who attend these fairs frequently rises to between ten and twenty thousand, giving a stranger the impression that the entire population of several counties must have been turned loose at once. Fairs are to be found in the largest Chinese cities, as well as in towns of every grade down even to small hamlets, though the proportion of towns and villages which support a fair is always a small one. It appears to be a general truth that by far the larger part of these large fairs owe their existence to the managers of some temple. The end in view is the accumulation of a revenue for the use of the temple, which is accomplished by levying certain taxes upon the traffic, and by the collection of a ground-rent. The latter is also a feature of the village market, the proprietor of each bit of ground appearing at each market to collect of the persons who have occupied his land, either a fixed amount, or a percentage upon their sale or supposed sales.

In the larger centres of population, it is common to find fairs held for a month or more at a time, and in some places there are several of these fairs every year, forming the centres of activity around which all the life of the place revolves. In such places the inhabitants make a good profit by renting buildings to the multitudes who come from a distance to sell and to buy, and where this is the case, when the fair is not in operation the city frequently appears to be nearly extinct. But trade no sooner begins, than countless thousands throng the lately almost deserted streets.

In order to make a fair a success, it is necessary that the managers should be men of enterprise and of sufficient business ability to deal with the many difficulties which are likely to arise. They exercise a certain supervision over everything, and are technically responsible for what goes wrong, though this responsibility they frequently evade. In order to attract a large attendance, it is generally necessary for fairs which are to last four days, to begin with a theatrical representation, which continues till the close. Sometimes, however, the players fail to appear, and in that case the whole fair may come to nothing. These large fairs are attended by merchants representing cities many hundred miles distant, and dealing in every article which is likely to attract customers.

As the means of transportation are very inadequate and locomotion is always slow and difficult, the merchants who go about from one fair to another for many months of the year, lead a life, or rather an existence, which is far from enviable. The half-month holiday with which the Chinese year begins is no sooner over than the large fairs begin also, and they continue with intermissions throughout the rest of the year. There is a brief interval for the wheat harvest, an event of the greatest importance to every class of the population, and the rainy season generally causes another interruption, often so serious a one as to upset all plans for two months or more.

The principal coöperative element in fairs lies in so arranging them as to dovetail into one another with least loss of time to the travelling merchants. The success generally attained is offset by many conspicuous failures, due to the Chinese thirst for gaining advantage over rivals, irrespective of the interests of others, which in matters involving coöperation, often results in disappointment. Thus, it is not uncommon to find that while the posters announcing a fair have been put up all through the country-side for an entire month, no one can tell when it is really to begin. That the day for beginning is "fixed" is a point of no consequence whatever, for with the exception of eclipses nothing in China is so "fixed" that it is not subject to alteration, and this exception may be thought to be due to the circumstance that eclipses are not under the supervision of the Chinese. We have known repeated instances in which persons who wished to attend a large fair, the date of which has been "fixed" for generations, have travelled many miles at great inconvenience, once and again, only to find that it was delayed owing to the fact that nobody had come, every one being apparently engaged in waiting for every one else. But infelicities like this are universal and constant in China, where punctuality is "a lost art."

XIV

COÖPERATIVE LOAN SOCIETIES

Among the most characteristic examples of Chinese capacity for combination, are Loan Societies, which seem everywhere to abound. The object of these organizations is the same as that of similar associations elsewhere, but it may be doubted whether the Chinese methods of procedure are not unique. As in everything else Chinese, with a general similarity, there is such divergence in detail, that it is sometimes very difficult for natives of one district, even to comprehend the rules of the Loan Societies of other and perhaps adjoining counties.

The reasons for the extensive organization of these societies, are those to which attention has been repeatedly called. Every Chinese has constant occasion to use money in sums which it is very difficult for him to command. The rate of interest is always so high, that a man who is compelled to borrow a considerable amount, upon which he must pay interest at two and a half, three, or even four per cent. a month, will not improbably be swamped by the endeavour to keep up with his creditors, a fact of which everyday experience furnishes countless examples. By distributing the payments over a long period, and by the introduction of an element of friendship into a merely commercial transaction, the Chinese is able to achieve the happy result of uniting business with pleasure. Of the measure of success attained we may be better able to judge, after an examination of the processes pursued.

The simplest of the many plans by which mutual loans are effected, is the contribution of a definite sum by each of the members of the society in rotation to some other one of their number. When all the rest have paid their assessment to the last man on the list, each one will have received back all that he put in and no more. The association is called in some places the "Club of the Seven Worthies" (Ch'i hsien hui). The technical name for any association of the kind in which coöperation is most conspicuous, is Shê. The man who is in need of money (Shê-chu) invites certain of his friends to coöperate with him, and in turn to invite some of their friends to do the same. When the requisite number has been secured, the members (Shê-yu), assemble and fix the order in which each shall have the use of the common fund. This would probably be decided by lot. Unless the amount in question is a very trifling one, every meeting of the members for business purposes will be accompanied with a feast attended by all the partners, and paid for either by the one for whose benefit the association was organized, or by the person whose turn it is to use the common fund.

At the first feast, given by the organizer of the association, each of the members attends provided with the sum agreed upon, let us suppose 10,000 cash, which is paid over to the headman, 60,000 cash in all, to be used by him, for a certain fixed period, say a year. The next year, the feast is given by the person who drew the second lot; the headman puts 10,000 cash into the treasury, and each of five other members the same sum, all of which is paid over to number three, who in like manner employs it for a year, when in the same way the fourth takes his turn. At the end of six years each of the seven members will have had a turn, each will have received 60,000 cash without interest, and each will have paid out 60,000 cash for which he has likewise received no interest. Each one will have been accommodated with the handling of a larger sum than he could have otherwise obtained, at the end each one has lost nothing in money, but has had six more or less excellent feasts, a matter from a Chinese point of view of some practical importance, however lightly it might be esteemed by a Westerner.

It would seem that the simple form of coöperative borrowing here described, is by no means so common as some of the various societies in which interest is paid, and it is not perhaps surprising that this should be the case. The Chinese are so much in the habit of paying an extortionate sum for the use of the money of others, that it doubtless appears to the average borrower that if he has exacted a high interest, he has made a better bargain than if he had received no interest at all, although he must eventually pay out just as much interest as he receives, and is demonstrably no better off at the final payment than if he had borrowed and lent, disregarding interest altogether.

The methods of societies which exact interest for loans, differ greatly in every detail, and there is evidently no limit to the variations which local custom may adopt in any particular district. In some regions the ordinary number of members appears to be sixteen as in the case just supposed. In others, the number rises to thirty or even more. Sometimes the meetings are held annually, in other districts the usual rule is semiannual meetings, in the second and eighth moons. In societies where the rate of interest is fixed, the only thing to be decided by lot, or by throwing dice, will be the order in which the members draw out the common fund. This may not improbably be determined at the first meeting, each member taking his turn in accordance with the excellence or otherwise of his throws with the dice. But if, as often happens, the interest is left open to competition, this competition may take place by a kind of auction, each one announcing orally what he is willing to pay for the use of the capital for one term, the highest bidder taking the precedence, but no member ever has a second turn. If the oral method of competition is not used, a still better plan may be adopted. This consists of prepared slips, like ballots, noting an offer of interest, deposited by each member in a box, the highest bidder getting the precedence, and in case of like amounts offered by different bidders a second ballot to decide who will add the most to his previous offer. It is easy to see that in this way, the interest to be paid might not be the same for any two loans, in which case there would seem to be inevitable some complexity in the accounts. But for the most part, the Chinese appear to take involved computations of this nature with surprising facility, especially considering the limited practice in mathematics which most of them have enjoyed.

For the sake of greater simplicity, we will take a case in which the interest for each period is assumed to be one-fifth of the principal, in which the number of members is ten, besides the organizer of the society, and in which the amount loaned by each member is 10,000 cash. It is also assumed that in this case the headman for whose benefit the lending was begun, does not repay the loan in money, but only in spreading at each meeting a feast of specially good quality. The interest is of the nature of a "bank discount," and is therefore collected in advance, the only certain way, it may be remarked, to collect it at all. Each man, it will be observed, with the exception of the first, actually receives only 8,000 cash, but repays to each one who follows him in drawing, a full 10,000. The result will be best seen in a tabulated form, as follows:

(The headman makes the feast only, but does not repay the loan.)

The headman receives from each member 10,000 cash (ten strings) 10 X 10 = 100.

Number	2	receives	9 X 8 =	...	72
"	3	"	8 X 8 =	64 + 10 =	74
"	4	"	7 X 8 =	56 + 20 =	76
"	5	"	6 X 8 =	48 + 30 =	78
"	6	"	5 X 8 =	40 + 40 =	70
"	7	"	4 X 8 =	32 + 50 =	82
"	8	"	3 X 8 =	24 + 60 =	84
"	9	"	2 X 8 =	16 + 70 =	86
"	10	"	1 X 8 =	8 + 80 =	88
"	11	"	9 X 10 =	...	90

In the following modification of the plan of loan, the headman pays back his loan, like the other members, and also provides each feast, which is regarded as his interest.

Headman	receives	10 X 10 strings	= 100
Number	2	" 9 X 8 = 72 + 10	= 82
" 3	"	8 X 8 = 64 + 20	= 84
" 4	"	7 X 8 = 56 + 30	= 86
" 5	"	6 X 8 = 48 + 40	= 88
" 6	"	5 X 8 = 40 + 50	= 90
" 7	"	4 X 8 = 32 + 60	= 92
" 8	"	3 X 8 = 24 + 70	= 94
" 9	"	2 X 8 = 16 + 80	= 96
" 10	"	1 X 8 = 8 + 90	= 98
" 11	"	10 X 10 =	100

In these examples it will be observed that the earlier each member draws his money, the less he gets on his investment. In the case last supposed, the final recipient, who has no interest to pay, but who receives interest from all but the headman, gets back all his money in a lump, with interest upon it. As already remarked, for the sake of simplicity we have disregarded the actual time for which the money is loaned, and for convenience have assumed a rate of interest which would probably be below the real one. It is evident that so far as financial considerations go, taken by themselves, it is for the advantage of the partners to come as late in the drawing as possible. But it is far from being the case that financial considerations are the only matters to be taken into account. The man who needs money, and who can never be sure of getting as much as he needs upon any better terms than these, will gladly take it as soon as he can get it, arranging the wedding for which he perhaps wishes to employ it, to suit the time of the loan.

Like other human contrivances, Chinese loan societies are to be judged by their results. The practical operation of these organizations often presents an instructive view of many aspects of Chinese life. The man for whose benefit the society is got together does not find that others are hungering and thirsting to do him a good turn, unless they clearly see their way to recover what they put in, with liberal interest. It is therefore often necessary to use a great deal of persuasion, to induce one to join, and especially to persuade him to bring in others. No one is willing to enter into a society of this kind unless it is reasonably certain that every member will meet every assessment, for if any individual fails to pay, everything is at a deadlock. To guard against this, it is customary to have security, or bondsmen, in some instances the headman acting as bail for all the rest. In case of failure on the part of any member to meet his payment, the headman is then required to pay the amount lacking, and this he is of course very unwilling to do, however freely he has engaged to do so. Troubles of this nature lead to many fights, and if this extreme measure is not resorted to, it is not at all unlikely that the person technically responsible will try the familiar method of begging off, striving to induce a creditor to accept a k'o-t'ou in place of cash. If sufficient pressure can be brought to bear in favour of any defaulting member, this plan may succeed in its object, as well as in breaking up the loan society.

Where the number is enlarged to more than a score, as in some districts, the probability that some one will fail to meet his obligations is greatly increased. It is also a fatal objection to these long loans, that before the whole term of years elapses, it is morally certain that something will occur to disturb the very unstable financial equilibrium of the members. For instance, the T'ai-p'ing rebellion, with its long train of sorrows, and the continual famines and floods of later years in Northern China, have tended to bring loan societies into discredit, because experience has shown that thousands of persons have put into them what could never be recovered. It is the almost unanimous testimony of the Chinese whom the writer has consulted on the subject, that in these days such societies fail to accomplish their uses, and are little better than a fraud. Whether a man loses by them, or not, will depend, however, mainly on his own skill in keeping out of those which are unsafe, regardless of the pressure which may be brought to bear upon him. Some men will tell you that they have been partners several times and have never lost their capital, or only lost it once, while others have a totally different account to give.

A Chinese whose easy-going disposition made him a valuable neighbour to those who wished to borrow without being at the inconvenience of repaying, stated that he had been six times a member of a loan society, and while once the capital had been doubled by a fortunate speculation, on each of the five other occasions he had lost all, or nearly all, put in. That such experiences are far from being uncommon, is testified by a current adage, to the effect that if a man has been in a loan society with another three separate times, if he has not been cheated, he has at least been robbed!

After the foregoing account of Coöperative Loan Societies was written, a suit was reported in the Hong Kong papers, which well serves to illustrate the legal difficulties which seem to puzzle not only the lawyers, but apparently the Judges also, for the case which was first heard in July, came on for another hearing upon appeal the next January, and was not decided until the following March. There were four plaintiffs and four defendants. It appeared that twelve men decided to form a Money Loan Association, one of them being trustee, and taking up the subscriptions. Each member undertook to pay $50 per month, by which a sum of $600 would be made up. Each month the members were to meet at a dinner, paid for by each of the members in turn, and at these dinners tenders were received for the fund of $600, the member offering the highest interest getting the "pool," less the amount of interest. After the association had run for eight months, the headman or trustee failed in business, disappeared, and the association came to an end.

The four persons who had paid money into the association for eight months, and who had received no benefit, sued the other four members who had ceased to pay their subscriptions after the failure in business of the trustee. The defence was that the only person responsible was this trustee, and that all the sums claimed had been paid to him by the defendants. The Acting Chief Justice, who heard the case, was of the opinion that the subscriptions not paid were due, and that the trustee had no authority from the other members to receive beforehand any contributions, and the Justice accordingly gave judgment for the plaintiffs.

The case was appealed, and counsel stated upon its coming up that it was appealed on a question of law. He related the circumstances of the case, and maintained that there was no contract between either of the plaintiffs and the four defendants jointly or severally, that they would pay a sum of $200. The only contract proved and shown, was a contract that each of the members would contribute to a common fund which he might not get in the first instance, but which he was certain to get some time. He therefore submitted that there was no contract at common law on which this action could be maintained, and that there was absolutely no means of deciding the issues in such a case.

To this statement, the opposing counsel replied by admitting that there was a certain amount of difficulty in working out the scheme as a whole, yet unless their Lordships held that these men were liable in this case, the prosecutors were practically deprived of any remedy at all. He submitted that this was against the whole intention of the association, which was in a certain sense for profit, for the mutual help of its members, and the common good of all. To hold that no action was maintainable individually, would be holding out a premium for dishonesty, because the man who got the first payment would then leave the Colony.

At this point the Justice remarked that this was what very often happened. In delivering his opinion, the Justice said that he thought the case was a claim for money lent, but it had been treated as a claim for the return of $50 from each of the defendants in respect of a money loan association. At the trial the defendants had denied that they had made any contract with the plaintiffs, and referred to the fact that certain meetings of the association had been held, and that the other meetings had not been regularly called in accordance with the articles of association. That being so, he held that there was no contract between the various members of the association, which would enable one member to sue another, and therefore he decided in favour of the appellants.

The Puisne Judge said that the contract entered into, was either one between the defendants and one of the plaintiffs, or else it was a mutual contract between the defendants, and the other members of the association. In the first case the plaintiffs could not recover, and if it was a mutual contract between all the members of the association, there ought to be a suit in equity to ascertain what were the various rights of the parties, and all the members of the association must be parties to that action. And so he also gave judgment in favour of the appellants, with costs. The money which had been paid into court, pending the appeal, would be paid out.

Whoever takes the trouble to follow these arguments, and the facts upon which they rest, ought to be convinced of several propositions: that it is very easy to make arrangements to pay out money to Chinese; that it is very easy not to get that money back again; that when there is a hitch in the intricate business of adjustment, it is not unlikely to take all the lawyers and Judges of a Crown Colony nine months to find out the law and equity, and that when the case has been decided it is difficult for an ordinary mortal to judge whether the decision was right or wrong!

XV

SOCIETIES FOR WATCHING THE CROPS

In a country where the poor are in such a majority as in China, and where the fields are altogether open, it is desirable if not necessary to have some plan by which property so unprotected can be effectively watched. In every orchard, as soon as the fruit begins to show the smallest sign of ripeness, the owner keeps some of his family on guard day and night, until the last apricot, plum or pear is removed from the trees. The darker and the more rainy the night, the more is vigilance required, so that a family with a bearing orchard is under the most absolute bondage to this property for a part of every year. During the months of July and August the fields are dotted with little booths some of them overrun with climbing vines, and each of these frail tenements is never for a moment deserted until the crops have all been removed. In some regions the traveller will observe these huts built upon a lofty staging so as to command a wide view, and they are often put up even in fields of sorghum, which would not seem likely to be stolen. But the lofty growth of this stalwart plant is itself a perfect protection to a thief, so that it is much more difficult to watch than crops far less elevated from the ground. Growing to an altitude of from ten to fifteen feet, it completely obscures the horizon, and practically obliterates all landmarks. So far as knowing where one goes, a traveller might as well be plunged into an African jungle. Even the natives of a region sometimes get lost within a few li of their own village on a cloudy day. The autumn crops of Shan-tung consist of the innumerable kinds of millet, sorghum, (which, though called "tall millet," has no affinity with real millet;) beans; Indian corn, or maize; peanuts; melons and squashes; sweet-potatoes and other vegetables (the others mostly in small patches); hemp; sesame; and especially cotton. There are many other items, but these are the chief.

Of all these diverse sorts of produce, there are hardly more than two which do not cause the owners anxiety, lest they be stolen from the field. The heads of sorghum and of millet are easily clipped off. Nothing is easier than rapidly to despoil a field of corn, or to dig sweet-potatoes. The latter, indeed, are not safe from the village dogs, which have learned by ages of experience that raw vegetable food is much better than no food at all. What requires the most unceasing vigilance, however, are the melon patches and the orchards. Of watermelons, especially, the Chinese are inordinately fond. Every field is fitted with a "lodge in a garden of cucumbers," and there is some one watching day and night. The same is true of the "fruit rows," familiarly called hang-tzü. Birds, insects, and man are the immitigable foes of him who has apples, pears, peaches, plums, cherries, apricots and grapes. If the orchard is of any size, there may be collusion between the thieves, who appear at both ends at once. Both sets cannot be pursued. The crows and the blue-jays are the worst bird robbers, but they can be scared off, especially with a gun. The human pilferers are not to be so easily dealt with. The farmer's hope is that seeing that some one is on guard they will go elsewhere, and steal from those not on guard. Hence everybody is obliged to stand guard over everything.

Where the population is densest, the extent to which this must be carried passes belief. In such regions about dusk an exodus sets forth from a village like that in the early morning to go to the fields to work. By every path the men, women, and even children stream forth. Light wooden beds, covered with a layer of the stiff sorghum stalk, are kept out in the fields for constant use. A few sorghum stalks are twisted together at the top, and a piece of old matting tacked on the sunny side, and under such a wretched shelter sits a toothless old woman all day and all night with alternations.

Crop-Watcher's Lodge.

Reaping Millet.

Very few farmers have their land all in one plot. A farm of not more than eighty Chinese acres may consist of from five to fifteen pieces lying on different sides of the village. And how do you contrive to "watch all these all night"? you inquire. "Oh we have to go from one to the other," you are told. In the case of cotton, the temptation to pick that of others is absolutely irresistible. The watchman sees some one at the end of the field meandering slowly along with a basket on his arm, picking cotton as he goes. The watchman yells, "Who are you?" and the figure moves along a little faster, but does not stop picking. If he disappears into the patch of some one else, that is success. But should the watchman become angry, as he certainly will, and should he pursue, as he is likely to do, and should he overtake, as is possible, then the trouble begins. Should the thief not get away in the scuffle, he ought to be taken before the village headmen and dealt with. If from another village, he probably will be tied up in the village temple, possibly beaten, and subsequently released upon payment of a fine. But the real difficulty is that many of the thieves are from the same village as the owners of the land the products of which they are appropriating. Not improbably they are "cousins" of the farmer himself. Perhaps they are his "uncles" or even his "grandfathers." If so, that complicates matters very much. Chinese ideas of meum and tuum are to our thought laxity itself under the most favourable conditions. But these conditions are the most unfavourable. The unity of the family is as that of a compound individual.

It is to afford some relief from these almost insupportable evils that societies for watching the crops have originated. They are by no means of universal occurrence, but like most other Chinese institutions, are to be met with in some districts, while others immediately adjoining may be wholly unacquainted with their working. We have known a District Magistrate in trying a case in which one of the defendants was a professional watcher of the crops, to be completely mystified by the term "crop-watcher" which had to be explained to him, as if to a foreigner, although he was himself a native of an adjacent province.

The villages which have entered into some one of the associations for the protection of their crops, generally proclaim this fact by painting or whitewashing upon the side of some conspicuous temple four characters (Kung k'an i p'o,) signifying that the fields are looked after in common. This proposition embodies a meaning which varies in different places. Sometimes it denotes that a certain number of persons are on guard each night, in which case the number (or some number which purports to be the real one) will perhaps be found posted on a temple wall with a view to striking awe into intending depredators (in case they should be persons of education), by showing how numerous are the chances of detection.

When a fixed number of persons is employed, the expense is shared by the village, being in fact a tax upon the land, paid in the direct ratio of the amount of land which each one owns. In other cases the arrangement for guarding standing crops is entered into by a single village, or more probably by a considerable number of contiguous villages. The details are agreed upon at a meeting called for the purpose in some temple convenient to all the villages, and the meeting is attended by representatives of each village interested. At this meeting are settled the steps to be taken in case of the arrest of offenders. This is a matter of supreme importance, being in fact the pivot upon which the whole machinery turns. If there is weakness here, the whole machine will be a failure.

It must be borne in mind that the reason for the organization of such a society as this is the fact that so many poor people everywhere exist, whose only resource is to steal. In the consultations preliminary to the organization of a crop-protecting league, the poor people of the various villages concerned have no voice, but they must be considered, for they will contrive to make themselves felt in many disagreeable ways. It will be agreed that any person owning land in any village belonging to the league is bound to seize and report any person whatever whom he may find stealing the crops of any person in any of these villages. But as this is the weakest point of all such agreements among the Chinese, it is further provided that if any person finds some one stealing and fails to seize and report the offender, and if the fact of this omission is ascertained, the person guilty of such omission shall be held to be himself guilty of the theft, and shall be fined as if he were the thief.

To provide an adequate tribunal to take cognizance of cases of this sort, the representatives of the several villages concerned, in public assembly nominate certain headmen from each village, who constitute a court before which offenders are to be brought, and by which fines are to be fixed. When a thief is captured he is brought to the village, and the men appointed for the purpose are summoned, who hear the report of the captors, and decide upon the fine. In cases of special importance the village gong may be beaten, so as to collect the headmen with the greater celerity. Much will depend upon what kind of a man the culprit is, and upon the status of the family to which the culprit belongs may be. There are some well-to-do people who are not above stealing the crops of others, and such persons are certain to be subjected to a heavy fine by way of "exemplary damages." The select-men who manage these cases have no regular way of punishing offenders but by the infliction of a fine, though culprits are undoubtedly sometimes tied up and beaten by exasperated neighbours, as the writer at one time happened to see for himself. But such cases must be relatively rare. The fines imposed must be paid immediately, and should this be refused or delayed, the penalty would be an accusation at the yamên of the District Magistrate, which being backed by all the principal men of the village, or of a group of villages, would be certain to issue in the punishment of the prisoner, as the Magistrate would be sure to assume that a prosecution of this nature was well grounded. The poorest man would have reason to dread being locked up in a cangue for a month or two at the busy time of harvest, when it is especially important for him to be at liberty.

The coloured resident of Georgia who complained that a black man had no chance in that State, being obliged "to work hard all day and steal all night in order to make an honest living," represented a class to be found in all parts of China, and a class which must be taken into account. Wherever arrangements are made for the protection of the crops from thieves, it is a necessary adjunct of the rules that the owners of the fields must follow the judicious plan of Boaz of ancient Bethlehem, who ordered his reapers not to be too careful to gather closely, that the gleaners might not glean in vain. Matters of this sort, even to the length of the stubble which shall be left in the fields, are not infrequently the subject of agreement and of regulation, for they are matters of large importance to many poor people.

In districts where the kao-liang (or sorghum) plant is cultivated it is common to strip off some of the lower leaves with a view, as one is told, to allowing the stalks "to breathe" more freely that the grain may ripen better. Where this practice prevails, the day on which the stripping of the leaves shall begin is sometimes strictly regulated by agreement, and no person, rich or poor, is allowed to anticipate the day. But on that day any one is at liberty to strip leaves from the fields of any one else, provided he does not go above the stipulated height on each plant. These leaves are much prized as food for animals. The day before the stripping of kao-liang leaves is to begin, warning is sounded on the village gong, and the next day all the people make this their main business.

Far more important than leaf-stripping is the regulation of the gleaning of cotton. In many parts of China, the cotton crop is the most valuable product of the soil, and it enjoys the distinction of being perhaps the only article raised in the empire which is to every man, woman and child an absolute necessity. As soon as the cotton-picking season sets in, women and children in the regions where this is the staple crop are absorbed in this fatiguing labour to the exclusion of almost everything else. With the first frost falls, the best of the season has passed, though the cotton balls continue to open for a long time afterward. It is considered to be the prerogative of the poor people to pick cotton wherever they can find it after a certain (or rather a very uncertain) date, and the determination of this date is settled in some districts by a proclamation of the Magistrate himself, for no lesser authority would be heeded. But in other regions this affair, like most others, is altogether relegated to local agreement, either of a single village, or a group of villages with each other. The day upon which it first becomes lawful to pick indiscriminately in any cotton field, a joyful one for the poor, is called "relaxation of punishment," because the fines are no longer to be enforced. At this time swarms of people are to be seen streaming to the fields, and many people go great distances from home, because the picking there is better. An acquaintance of the writer remarked that his wife had been gone from home for more than ten days gleaning in some region where the crops were better than nearer home, sleeping meantime in any doorway or cart-house from which she was not driven away.

It sometimes happens that the rich people attempt to exclude the poor from the large estates belonging to the former, but this is seldom successful, and can never be good policy. The writer once saw a dispute between the owner of a large cottonfield and many hundred poor women and children who were about to precipitate themselves upon the remnants of the crop. Even while the debate as to the proprieties of the case was in progress, a very large number of the poor people who cared much more for the cotton than for the proprieties, pressed on to gather what they might, leaving others to settle the question of abstract right as pleased themselves.

Reference has been repeatedly made to the fines imposed for a violation of the village laws or agreements, and it was remarked that the crucial point of the protection of crops, is found here. It is customary to employ the fines collected from such offenders for the purpose of hiring a theatrical company, which always proves to be a very expensive method of enjoying a surplus of money, since the incidental expenses of a theatrical representation, especially in the entertainment of guests, are often ten times greater than the sum paid to the players.

Spending the night in the fields during the harvest season, when the ground is generally saturated with moisture, constantly induces malaria, rheumatism and pneumonia, as well as many other ailments. But the necessity is imperative, and all risks must be disregarded, or there would be nothing to eat for a year. The quarrels which inevitably arise from crop pilfering and the other concomitants of an autumn harvest, give rise to serious feuds, as well as to devastating lawsuits, the money cost of which may be a thousand times the value of the property in question. But under such conditions every Chinese crop is gathered in year by year, and such have apparently been perpetuated from the earliest dawn of Chinese history.

XVI

VILLAGE AND CITY RAIN-MAKING

It is one of the eccentricities of the Chinese, that although they have developed elaborate philosophies, none of them have led them to confidence in the uniformity of nature. Polytheism has no basis for such a view. Thus it comes about that in an empire which is one of the most conspicuous examples of homogeneity the world has ever seen, neither the people nor their rulers have any fixed opinions as to the causes upon which the rain-fall depends. In the province of Shan-tung a great variety of beings real and imaginary are worshipped to cause the fall of water to adjust itself to the needs of the farmers. Among the divinities thus honoured are the Goddess of Mercy who in the south of China is generally regarded as male; the God of War; the Dragon God, or Lung Wang; and a Tai Wang, which is popularly supposed to be incarnated in a serpent, frequently a water-snake, but in default of that a common garter-snake will do just as well. Whenever one of these Tai Wangs is discovered, it is common to notify the nearest local official, and it is expected that he will go and worship it. Many years ago Li Hung Chang performed this service at Tientsin, where there is a very large temple to Tai Wang.

As if these incongruous adjuvants of nature were not enough, there are some who worship Yü Huang Shang Ti, or Pearly Emperor Supreme Ruler, and still others think they have warrant in offering sacrifice and worship to "Sun Ta Shêng," who is nothing more than an imaginary character in the novel known as "Travels to the West." Sun was originally a monkey hatched by a process of evolution out of a stone, but his exploits are so many and so striking that the popular mind has settled on him

179

as a suitable being to superintend the rain-fall. Yet his worship is apparently limited, and like that of all the divinities mentioned extremely irregular. The same village that worships the God of War now, may worship the Goddess of Mercy next time, perhaps on the principle of judicious rotation.

Besides all these, there is another and quite a different plan in extensive use. In the ancient but now ruined city of Han Tan Hsien, (in Western Chih-li) there is a temple on the premises of which there is a famous well, in which are a vast number of iron tablets. Whenever there is a scarcity of rain, it is almost always a last resort, after the District Magistrate has made the rounds of all the temples in and about his city, to post off an official messenger to Han Tan Hsien—a journey of several days—to get an iron tablet out of the well. The messenger takes an iron tablet from the city whence he starts on which is inscribed the date of the journey, and the name of the District which makes the petition, and on his arrival repairs to the Taoist temple, where for a certain sum he is provided with another iron tablet taken from the well, into which the tablet now brought is thrown.

On his return journey the messenger is supposed to eat nothing but bran, and to travel at the top of his speed day and night. His arrival is anxiously awaited. And now emerges a characteristic Chinese performance. The counties through which his route lies are not unlikely just as much in need of rain as the one which sends the messenger: the people of these districts not infrequently waylay the messenger temporarily, and "borrow" his tablet, which is thus "invited" to the other district, and the rain-fall will take place there, instead of in the one to which it ought to belong.

At first glance it certainly appears singular that so practical a people as the Chinese can put the least faith in mummeries of this sort, but the truth seems to be that very little actual faith is exercised, these performances only taking place in default of an acquaintance with the laws which govern the meteorology of the empire. Besides this, the months in which the most resort is had to such performances are the fifth and the sixth, and these are the ones in which the rain-fall is due. As a limit of some ten days is generally set for the efficacy of these petitions, it is extremely likely that the term will be coincident with a fall of rain, which fall will be credited to the petition; whereas the failure of the petition is set down to some wholly different reason.

An incident which occurred in one of the western counties of Shan-tung makes plain even to the most obtuse Chinese intellect the inconveniences of a wrong theory of the universe. A party of villagers with flags and a drum were on their way to a temple to pray for rain. They met a man leading a horse, on which was seated a married woman returning from one of the customary visits to her mother's family. She had a child in her arms, and the hired labourer leading the horse had on a wide straw hat. Now it is one of the eccentricities of the inaccurate views of those who pray for rain to non-existent monkeys and to garter-snakes, that they also entertain misconceptions as to the causes which hinder rain. Foreigners carrying umbrellas have been mobbed as the efficient cause of drought. The water-spouts of a new consulate in a treaty-port have been complained of as drawing off the moisture that was meant for the whole province. So in this case the big straw-hat of the rustic was resented as "contra-indicated"—as the physicians say—by the rain-prayers. The peasant was roared at, and a long pike-staff was thrust into his hat which was thrown from his head upon the horse, which being frightened pulled away and plunged ahead. The woman could not keep her seat, first dropping her child which was dashed to the ground and killed. The woman's foot caught in a stirrup and she was dragged for a long distance and when the horse was at length stopped she too was dead. She was pregnant, so that in one moment three lives had been sacrificed. The hired man ran on a little way to the woman's home, told his story, and as the men of the family happened to be at home, they all seized whatever implements they could find and ran after the rain-prayers, with whom they fought a fierce battle killing four or five of them outright. The case went into the District yamên, and what became of it then, we do not know.

Among the other eccentricities of rain-producing, is the borrowing of a god from one village for use in another. If he succeeds in getting rain he is taken back in honour; otherwise he is not unlikely to be left where he happened to be deposited when worshipped, the villagers—like a set of commissioners for educational examination—being solely influenced by "results." In other instances if the god does not show signs of appreciation of the need of rain, he may be taken out into the hot sun and left there to broil, as a hint to wake up and do his duty. A bunch of willows is thrust into his hand, because the willow is sensitive to the smallest moisture. It is a common saying in China that "when the Floods wash away the temple of Lung Wang (the Dragon King) it is a case of not knowing one's own folks." Yet this is what constantly happens.

It is more than forty years since the Yellow River changed its course to its present one, taking the bed of a small stream known as the Clear River and bringing with the turbid torrent devastation and utter ruin. During more than an entire generation Central Shan-tung has been cursed with "China's Sorrow," and even when the course was altered again in 1887, the Government spent fabulous sums, and at last brought the stream back again into its former bed—a feat which few foreigners who saw the new channel thought it possible to execute.

The next year the region was visited by a corps of Dutch engineers, who made an elaborate survey and published an exhaustive report, to which the Chinese Government paid no attention whatever. The plea at that time was lack of money, but the funds could have been had if the execution of the work had been put into foreign hands, than whom no more competent ones than the Dutch could have been found. But at the time when the Director General of the Yellow River—a title the humour of which is lost on the Chinese—memorialized the Throne on the necessity of employing foreign science for this otherwise hopeless task, his proposal was rebuked by the Empress Dowager as "premature and ostentatious!"

According to Chinese ideas the "Three Harmonies" are "Heaven, Earth, and Man." All three of them are at present out of sorts with each other. What is imperatively needed is a reconciliation, but this can never be had until the Chinese come to a more accurate appreciation of the limits of the powers of each of the triad. A new set of men would soon make a new earth, and then the heavens would be found to be well enough as they are. In the course of ten years enough water falls for the use of all, and not too much to be managed. But man must learn how to control it, and until he does so, "Heaven, earth and man" will never be in right relations.

XVII

THE VILLAGE HUNT

There are parts of the wide province of Shan-tung, in which there are great sheets of clear and deep water much frequented by water-fowl, especially in the autumn and in the winter. In any Western land these districts would be the paradise of hunters, but here the ducks and the geese go their several ways in "peace and tranquillity along the whole road," undisturbed by the gun of the sportsman or the pot-hunter. This is due to an old-time custom of the yamên in the Prefectural city contiguous to the largest marshes, of levying a squeeze on the results of the gunner's toil, a squeeze so comprehensive and virtually prohibitory in its action that water-fowl are practically out of the market altogether.

There is a record in the life of Dr. Medhurst, one of the pioneer missionaries in China, and father of Sir Walter Medhurst, sometime Her Majesty's Consul-General in Shanghai, of a trip which he and a companion made north from Shanghai along the coasts of Shan-tung. Their plan was to debark from the fishing junk in which they had taken passage, cut across from one headland to another and then rejoin their vessel to repeat the same process farther on. In this way they succeeded in penetrating to a few fishing villages and had conversation with a handful of people all along shore. With charming frankness the historian of this pioneer tour mentions that they nowhere saw any wild animals. We can readily believe him, for even at this advanced stage of extended exploration, the only wild animal that the most experienced traveller is likely to see is the hare, albeit there are sundry others such as weasels, a kind of ground-fox, and the like, which do not obtrude themselves to any extent in public.

184

It is said that in the little kingdom of Denmark the citizens have a winter sport which consists in a general and organized hunt for hares on the part of all the male population of a very extended territory, starting from a given point and working in a definite direction, under precise and carefully observed rules. At the close of the hunt there is a great feast to which all are welcomed, and the whole performance is one to which there is much anxious looking forward on the part of the young and vigorous country-folk. It is strange to meet with a custom of the same kind in China, but there is an ancient district in Shan-tung, known as P'ing-yüen, or Level-plains, where the Danish custom flourishes in full force, but minus the very important concluding feast. For where is the Chinese who would have the courage or indeed the means to welcome the countless swarms of his country-side to enjoy the pleasure of eating at somebody else's expense?

The whole arrangement of this combination hunt is in the hands of a few impecunious fellows who have the right of "protecting" merchants at the great fairs from imposition by other rascals, by means of levying a prophylactic black-mail of their own on a certain day at the principal market of the region. A man who has no single spear of hair on his head passes up and down the crowded lanes of the market, and calls out that on such and such a day there will be an attack by all the people of the "north district" on the hares. This notice is repeated with varied iteration, until the word is comprehended by all those within hearing, each one goes home and tells the rest of the village, and on the set day all are ready for the fray. The reason for having the notice circulated by a bald man exclusively is the eminently Chinese one that in the Mandarin dialect the word for Bald—T'u—and that for Hare are identical in sound. This circumstance once led to a very singular error on the part of a bright little child of certain foreigners living in Shan-tung. One of the employees of the establishment had been off somewhere on a donkey, and while he was leading it homeward the beast broke away and galloped off. A lad who was cutting grass in the neighbourhood saw the fleeing animal, rushed out and caught it, holding it till the rider came up. On their reaching home the dramatic story was told in the hearing of the lad, and the capture of the donkey was accredited to a little "T'u-tzŭ" or "Bald-boy." The foreign child heard the thrilling narrative which he duly retailed at the parental dinner-table, only he translated the name "T'u-tzŭ" as Hare, the only kind of t'u-tzŭ of which he had ever heard!

On the day appointed for the hare-hunt, almost the whole population of the district to be beaten up turn out to help in the sport. They often stand as thick together as soldiers in ranks. The frightened hares go from one side to the other of the wide-spreading ring, but as every one of the human assailants has a stick and many of them have two, the chances of escape for the hare are reduced below zero. It is a law of the game that whoever succeeds in seizing a hare must hold it aloft, and in a loud tone cry out, "I raise it" (chü), after which it is his, and no one can take it from him lawfully. Nevertheless, Chinese human nature is much like the article in other parts of the world, and the results are apt to be serious quarrels, fights, broken heads and limbs and perhaps lawsuits. But with that practical talent for which Chinese officials are distinguished, the Magistrates refuse to hear any case arising from these conditions, so that it is necessary to have them settled, as by far the majority of all Chinese law cases are, out of court by "peace-talkers."

How easy it is for quarrels to arise even among a most peaceable people like the Chinese, with or without a hare-hunt, is illustrated by an incident which occurred some years since, many of the actors in which are well known to the writer.

A few villagers were returning late on a moonlight night from a funeral in another village. Nearing their own hamlet, they came on two young fellows chopping down small trees of the kind called date (a jujube or rhamnus). They were getting ready clubs for the combined hare-hunt next day. On being hailed, the youths, who were trespassing on the territory of their neighbouring village, fled to their home pursued by the others. The latter returned to their own village and maliciously spread the report that the young men had been cutting pine trees from the clan graveyard. Although it was late at night a posse was soon raised to go to the other village (about a mile off) and demand satisfaction. The village was asleep, but some headmen were at last aroused who begged their visitors to postpone the matter till daylight, when the case would be looked into and the culprits punished, and any required satisfaction given.

To the reasonable request, only reviling was retorted, and the band returned to their own village filled with fury. A gong was beaten, every man in the village aroused and every male of fit age forced to accompany the mob armed with clubs, poles, etc., to attack the other village. The latter happened to have a mud wall and gates kept closed at night. So large a band made a great noise, and soon roused their antagonists by their abusive language. The village elders struggled to keep the gates closed, but they were overborne by the hot blood of the youth, who were resolved, since they must have it, to give their assailants all the satisfaction they wanted. The gates once opened, a furious battle ensued, and the women who clambered to the flat-house tops and struggled to see what was going on heard only the dull whacks of heavy blows. Several men were knocked senseless, and on the cry that they had been killed, the battle was renewed until the attacked were driven inside their village, each side having several men wounded, some of them severely. One old man had his skull beaten in with a carrying pole and was born home unconscious, in which condition he remained for a week or two.

The next morning the attacking village went out and chopped down three little pine-trees growing in their own cemetery (as "proof" of the injury done by the other party), and proceeded to the District city to enter a complaint. The other village of course did the same. The first village took with them the old man, unconscious, and apparently in a moribund condition. Each party had to arrange its yamên expenses before a step could be taken, and as the case was a serious one, these were heavy. The Magistrate dared not decide either way until it was seen whether the wounded recovered. An epileptic, half-witted boy captured by one side, who avowed his responsibility for the trouble (perhaps scared nearly to death) was cruelly beaten till he was half dead for so doing. The matter dragged on for a long time, and at length was decided on no principle either of law or of equity—as is the case with so many suits—each side settling its own debts, and neither side winning. The village attacked had squandered at the yamên 300 strings of cash, and the attacking party 500! The old man at last recovered, and peace reigned in Warsaw and its suburbs.

Now what was the motive for all this? Was there a feud between these villages? By no means, but exceptional amity, six or eight families being connected by marriage. Was there any special provocation? None whatever; all comprehensible motives led to a continuance of peace, but war and bloodshed followed just the same. Much may be accounted for by Chinese passion, but how can passion be suddenly made out of nothing? It is the current fashion to explain all phenomena, celestial and terrestrial, in terms of the development theory. Given heredity, education and environment and you have the man, and society. But it is questionable whether this classification is as exhaustive as it seems. At times another factor appears to be required. It is what Edgar Poe called the Imp of the Perverse.

XVIII

VILLAGE WEDDINGS AND FUNERALS

The Chinese share with the rest of the human race a desire to make a marriage ceremony an occasion of joy. One of the most frequent periphrases for a wedding, is the expression "joyful event." It is in China preëminently true that the highest forms of "joy," find expression in eating. While marriage feasts are no doubt to be found in all lands at all times, they are especially Oriental, and are characteristic of the Chinese.

Owing to the extent and the intricate ramifications of Chinese relationships, the number of persons who must be invited to a wedding is very large. In some regions it is customary for women only to contribute a "share" (fên-tsŭ) to a wedding, while the men give a present at that part of the ceremony when the bridegroom salutes the guests in turn with a prostration. As the name of each guest is called to be thus honoured, he hands over the amount of his offering. But in other places men and women contribute in the same way. Of two things, however, one may be confident; that nearly all those invited will be present either in person or by a representative; and that nearly every woman will be accompanied by children, who contribute nothing to the revenues, but add enormously to the expenses.

Marriage customs in China certainly vary widely, but of such a thing as being present at "the ceremony," but not at "the wedding breakfast," we have never heard. Indeed, it can scarcely be said that, in our sense of the word, there is any "ceremony." Whatever may be added or subtracted from the performances, the essence of a Chinese wedding seems to consist in the arrival of the bride at her future home. The "feast" is the main feature of the occasion. Sometimes the relatives are not invited at all upon the wedding day, but at a subsequent one; yet it is not the less true that when the guests do come, the "feast" is the centre and soul of the occasion.

If there is anything which the Chinese have reduced to an exact science, it is the business of eating. The sign of real friendship is to invite a man to a meal, and it is a proverbial saying that he who comes bearing a vessel of wine on his shoulder and leading a sheep, is the truly hospitable man, for he shows by his acts that his invitation is a real one. The great mass of the Chinese spend their days in a condition which is very remote from affluence, but the expenses of weddings and funerals in the mere matter of eating, are such as must, from the extent of such expenses and the frequency of the occasions upon which they are required, reduce any but a very affluent family to utter poverty.

Under the pressure of these inexorable circumstances, the Chinese have long ago hit upon an application of the share principle, by means of which wedding and funeral feasts become quite practicable, which would otherwise remain an utter impossibility. It can seldom be known with certainty how many guests will attend a wedding, or funeral, but the provision must be made upon the basis of the largest number likely to appear. Each guest, or rather each family, is not only expected, but by a rigid code of social etiquette required, as already mentioned, to contribute to the expenses of the occasion by a "share." This will sometimes be in food, but the general practice is to bring money, according to a scale which is perfectly understood by every one. The amount varies greatly in different places, from a trifling sum of the value of about five or six cents up to a quarter of a dollar or more, according to the degree of intimacy between the persons, and the ability of the guests to contribute. In some parts of China, the ordinary amount taken to such a feast seems to be twice as great as in others. Sometimes the standard is so well understood, that the phrase "a share" has a local meaning as definite as if, for example, the sum of 250 cash were expressly named.

In some places while the rate of "a share" for a funeral is 250 cash, that for a wedding is just double. This is because the food at a funeral is "plain" (su), while that for the wedding is of meat (hun) and much more expensive. It is not uncommon to find that "a share" for a person who comes from another city or district is two or three times that of a native of the place where the feast is given. To give only the same as a native would do would be considered for the person from a distance as a loss of "face"!

It is a characteristic example of Chinese procedure that the sums contributed upon occasions of this sort are in reality seldom what they profess to be. If local custom considers ninety-eight or ninety-six cash as a hundred, the temptation to put in a less number as a contribution is generally too strong to be resisted; the more so as in the confusion of receiving the numerous amounts, it is generally difficult to tell which particular string of cash was sent in by which persons, although the amounts are all entered in an "account," to be presently noticed.

Those householders who are very anxious to keep exact track of the relative honesty of the respective contributors, sometimes do so by having ready a long cord to which each successive sum of cash is tied by its string, after the sum is entered on the account. When the proceedings are ended, it will then be possible for the master of the house to go over the multitudinous strings of cash, ascertaining how much each one is short, and tracing it to its donor by its place on the cord, corresponding to the order of entry in the account-book. But this plan is not regarded with favour by the guests, and is not generally adopted, because it makes so much trouble. The advantage of it is that it enables the householder to pay off the debt to the family which gave short cash, at exactly the same rate, whenever they invite him to a wedding or a funeral. In some places it is well understood that though each guest contributes "a share" of 250 cash, it will take five "shares" to make 1,000, since every "hundred cash" is in reality only eighty.

It is the duty of the committee which looks after the finances, to take charge of all sums which may be brought by the guests, and to keep a record of the amount paid by each. This is a matter of great importance, as every such contribution occupies the double position of a repayment of some similar gift to the family of the giver, by the family which now receives the gift, and also of a precursor of similar return gifts in time to come. The amount which is sent by each person will depend upon the relations existing between the families, and especially upon the amount received by them on some former similar occasion. To disregard the unwritten code which demands from guests proportional contributions, is regarded as a grave offence against decorum, because of its serious consequences to the family concerned, in diminishing their receipts.

To attend a feast, but not to bring any contribution, either in money or in kind, seems to be practically unknown, though it constantly happens that the quantity of food which on certain occasions may be substituted for money, is less than half of what is eaten by the donor. This is especially the case when the giver is a woman, who, as already mentioned, is likely to bring one or more voracious children, who must be pacified by food at every stage of the performances, their capacities being apparently absolutely unlimited.

In cities and large towns, the business of managing a wedding or a funeral feast, is conducted much as it would be in any country of the West. A food shop contracts to deliver so many bowls of food of a definite quality and at a fixed price. Provision is also made for additional supplies should the number of guests be unexpectedly great. But if the feast is to be on a large scale, it is not unlikely that the cooking will be done on the premises by the professional caterers. It is usual to speak of an affair of this sort as embracing so many "feasts," a "feast" denoting not a single individual, as might be supposed, but the number who can sit at one table. This number, like everything Chinese, varies in different places. Sometimes it is eight, and the phrase, "eight fairy table" is the common designation of the articles of furniture required for the purpose.

In other regions, while all the tables are of the same size and shape as these, one side is left open for convenience in passing the food, and a "feast" signifies six persons only. When the feasts are provided by contract, the establishment also furnishes waiters, who convey the food to the guests, and to these waiters a small gratuity is given at the close.

The number of families who are within reach of facilities such as these, is but a small proportion of those who are obliged to arrange for feasts at weddings and funerals. For those to whom no such resource is open, there is no other way but to put the matter into the hands of certain experts, of great experience in such matters—a class of persons to be found everywhere. Every village or group of villages can furnish a professional cook, who devotes much of his time to the conduct of affairs of this sort. If he is a man of wide reputation, and employed by rich families, he will have a number of assistants who work under his direction, all of whom at the close of the feast will be rewarded with suitable gratuities.

The staff of persons into whose hands the business of arranging for a feast is committed, is divided into three departments or committees, the Stewards (chih fang), the Culinary Department (ch'u-fang), and Finance Department (chang-fang). Each of them is a check upon the other two, although in the smaller and less expensive affairs all three will naturally run together and be merged in a single head. The Stewards purchase such supplies as are supposed to be necessary, embracing the best which the local market affords.

In the northern part of China, the two items which prove the most expensive are wheaten bread-cakes (man-t'ou) and wine. If the accommodation of the dwelling admit of it, the articles which have been bought for the feast are placed in a separate apartment, under the exclusive charge of one of the stewards, by whose order alone can anything be paid out to the kitchen, on demand of the head cook. But in practice it is found that at this point there is always a serious leak, for many of the relatives and neighbours of the family which is to have the feast, will send over their children to the storeroom to "borrow" a few bread-cakes, or a few cups of wine. For a steward to refuse (as a foreigner would be likely to do), is to incur the ill-will of the family which wishes to "borrow," and the only advantage to the steward would be that he would be reviled, which no Chinese relishes. As a matter of practice therefore, it is customary to "give to him that asketh," and from him that would "borrow" not to turn away, even though, as the old English saying runs, "Broad thongs are cut out of other people's leather."

It not infrequently happens that the stewards who are in charge of the entertainment are smokers of opium, in which case the expenses are sure to be much heavier than otherwise. It has also come to be a custom in some regions, to furnish opium to the guests at weddings, and this may become an item of a very elastic nature. Besides this, a man who smokes opium is naturally incapacitated from taking even ordinary care of the stores under his charge. If he is himself a smoker, and if opium is one of the articles provided for the occasion, it will not be strange if all his opium-smoking comrades embrace the opportunity to visit him, when they must be invited to take a pipe—of course at the expense of the master of ceremonies.

The disappearance of wine and bread-cakes, on occasions of this sort, even before a single bowl of food has been set before a guest, suggests the evaporation of water on a hot summer day. It was reported to the writer, that on the occasion of a funeral in a neighbour's family, about sixty catties of wine vanished, without leaving behind any trace of its devious course.

The reason for such occurrences, which are of universal notoriety, is not that the stewards are not able to do that which they are set to do, nor is the explanation necessarily to be found in their indifference to the interests of the host. The real seat of the difficulty is, that every family sufficiently well-to-do to have a large feast is surrounded with a swarm of poor relatives, who have no other opportunities than these to make their connection of any service to themselves, and who on such occasions are determined not to be ignored. A poor family of the same surname as the host will stand at the door of the mansion where a great feast is in preparation, with bowls in hand, demanding that a share of the good things in course of being served shall be apportioned to them. Even if the master of the house should absolutely refuse his consent, and if the stewards should follow his directions and give nothing, it would be of no avail, for the poor family would raise such an uproar as practically to prevent further proceedings, and all the guests would take the part of the poor relatives, exhorting the host to give them what they asked.

The habit of levying tribute upon those who happen to be in a position to pay it, is, as already remarked, deeply rooted in Chinese life. To what this practice leads, may be seen in the extreme cases of which one now and then hears, such as the following, detailed to the writer by the principal sufferer. A man had a dispute with one of his uncles about a tree, the value of which did not amount to more than a dollar. As he was a person without force of character, and unable to get his rights, he was obliged to "eat loss." This enraged his wife to such an extent that she hung herself. It was now open to her husband to bring a suit at law, accusing the other party of "harrying to death" (pi ssŭ) the deceased wife. Perhaps this would have been the best plan for the injured husband, but "peace-talkers" persuaded him to compromise the matter for a money payment. The other party had a powerful advocate in a relative who was a notorious blackleg, expert in lawsuits, and who freely gave his advice. Even under these advantages, the middlemen into whose hands the matter was put, decided that the uncle should pay 30,000 cash to the family of the woman, as a contribution to the funeral, which was done.

It is not usual to make much parade over the funerals of suicides, unless the sum to be expended is exacted from those who are supposed to have impelled to the suicide. In this instance, half the amount paid would have been amply sufficient for the funeral and for all its expenses. The "family friends" of the husband, uncles, cousins, nephews, etc., took charge of the proceedings, which they contrived to drag out for more than a week, and when the funeral was over, the husband, whose crops had been that year totally destroyed by floods, ascertained that these "family friends" had not only made away with the 30,000 cash awarded as a fine, but that he was saddled with a debt of immediate urgency amounting to 20,000 more for bread-cakes and wine, which had been consumed (as alleged) by the "family friends" during the protracted negotiations. No clear accounts of the expenditure were to be had, and the only thing of which the poor husband was sure, was that he was practically ruined by his "family friends."

It is always taken for granted by the Chinese, that any family rich enough to spend a large amount of money on the funeral of a parent, will be mercilessly pillaged on that particular occasion. The reason for this is that, at such a time, the master of the house is (theoretically) overcome by grief, and ordinary propriety requires that he himself should take no part in the management of affairs, but should give his exclusive attention to the mourning rites. Even though he clearly perceives that everything is going wrong, he must act as if he were blind and deaf, and also dumb. Long practice has made the Chinese very expert in such an accomplishment, which, it is needless to say, for an Occidental would be difficult, not to say impossible. If the householder is a man for any reason generally unpopular, his disadvantages will be greatly increased, as is illustrated by the following case, narrated to the writer by a man who lived within two miles of the village in which the event occurred.

A wealthy man lost his father, and made preparations for an expensive funeral. He took a hundred strings of cash in a large farm-cart, and went to a market to buy swine to be slaughtered for the feast. On the way he was waylaid by a party of his own relatives, and robbed of all the money, in such a way as to render recovery of it hopeless. Having afterward bought four swine and an ox (a most generous provision for the feast), the arrangements were put into the hands of managers (tsung-li) as usual. These persons found themselves wholly unable to restrain the raids made upon the stores by "friends," neighbours and others, and the night before the funeral was to occur, thieves broke into the storeroom and carried off every scrap of meat, leaving nothing whatever for the feast. The managers were frightened and ran away. The feast was of necessity had with nothing but vegetables and was of a sort to bring the householder into disgrace. As a result he was afraid to try to have any more funerals, and there are at present on his premises two unburied coffins awaiting sepulture, perhaps by the next generation.

As soon as the "shares" have all been sent in and reckoned up, it is known how much the host is out of pocket by the affair, and this information is so far from being private that it is sometimes at once announced to the guests, and if the amount is a large one the host gets credit for doing business on an extensive scale, regardless of expense. This gives him a certain amount of honour among his neighbours, and honour of a kind which is particularly prized. Among poor families, where "face" is of much less consequence than cash, it is not uncommon to find the feasts on a scale of such extreme economy that the cost is very trifling, although the "shares" are as great as at much better entertainments. It occasionally happens that a family is able to reduce the expenses so that the contributions are large enough to cover them, and even to leave a margin. A man who has carried through an enterprise of this sort is regarded as worthy of a certain admiration; and not without reason, for the feat implies generalship of no mean order.

Another illustration of the application of coöperative principles is found in the organization of the men of a village into details, or reliefs, as bearers of the catafalque of a specified size, each having its own leader. Whenever a funeral is to take place, notice is sent to the head of the division whose turn it is to serve, and he calls upon the men of his detail in a regular order. If any one is not on hand to take his turn, he is subjected to a fine.

In country districts, the funeral catafalque, with its tremendous array of lacquered poles upon which it is borne, is often the property of a certain number of individuals, who are also ordinary farmers. On being summoned to take charge of a funeral, they often perform the service gratuitously for people living in their own village, but charging a definite sum for the rent of the materials, which sometimes represent a considerable capital. Wedding chairs are often owned and managed in the same way, of which the advantage is that an investment which it is so desirable for the community to have made, and which is too large for an individual, is made by a company, the members of which receive a small dividend on its cash outlay, and an acknowledgment in food, presents, etc., of the manual labour involved in serving those who invite their aid.

The principle is capable of indefinite expansion. The writer once lived in a Chinese village, where there was a "Bowl Association," owning 100 or 200 bowls which were rented to those who had occasion for a feast, at such a rate as to be remunerative to the owners, and at the same time more economical to the householder than the purchase of a great number of dishes for which on ordinary occasions he would have no use.

A Bridal Pair.

Temporary Funeral Pavilion.

Societies for the assistance of those who have funerals are of common occurrence, and are of many different kinds. There is special reason for the organization of such leagues (called pai-shê), since, while weddings may be postponed until suitable arrangements can be made, it is generally difficult, and sometimes impossible, to do the same with a funeral.

Sometimes each family belonging to the league pays into the common fund a monthly subscription of 100 cash a month. Each family so contributing is entitled upon occasion of the death of an adult member of the family (or perhaps the older generation only) to draw from this fund, say, 6,000 cash, to be used in defraying the expenses. If there is not so much money in the treasury as is called for by deaths in families of the members, the deficiency is made up by special taxes upon each member. According to a plan of this sort, a subscriber who drew out nothing for five years would have contributed the full amount to which he is entitled, without receiving anything in return. A mutual insurance company of this nature is probably entered into on account of the serious difficulty which most Chinese families experience in getting together ready money. From a financial point of view there may be nothing saved by the contribution, but practically it is found to be easier to raise 100 cash every month, than to get together 6,000 cash at any one time.

Another form of mutual assistance in the expenses of funerals is the following: A man whose parents are well advanced in life knows that he may at any time be called upon to spend upon the ceremonies at their death an amount which it will be difficult to raise. He therefore "invites an association" (ch'ing hui), each member of which is under obligation upon occasion of the death of a parent to contribute a fixed sum, say, 2,000 cash. The membership will thus be composed exclusively of those who have aged parents. The number of names may be forty, which would result, whenever a call shall be made, in the accumulation of 80,000 cash. With this sum a showy funeral can be paid for. It is customary to provide in the document which each signs, and which is deposited with the organizer of the association, that the funeral shall be conducted on a specified scale of expense, nor can the funds be diverted to any other use than for a funeral.

Whenever a member wishes for his own use to make a call for the quota from each member, he must previously find two bondsmen, who will be surety for him that he will continue to pay his share on demand, otherwise the other subscribers might be left in the lurch. Only those known to be able to meet their assessments would be likely to be invited to join such an association, and if for any reason a member should fail to furnish his quota, he would be heavily fined.

At each funeral, all the subscribers to the funeral fund are present ex officio, and it is not necessary for them to contribute any other share than that represented by the 2,000 cash of the assessment. Each member of the association appears in mourning costume, and wailing as would become a near relative of the deceased. The presence of so large a number of mourners in addition to those really near of kin, gives a great deal of "face" to the individual whose parent has died, and this is perhaps quite as attractive a feature of the arrangement as the financial assistance.

If it should happen that for a long time no one dies in the families of any subscribers to the funeral fund, it may be thought best to summon the members to a feast, at which the project is broached of making a call for a share to be used for a wedding, or some other purpose outside of the constitutional limits of the society. In any arrangement of this nature the feast is an indispensable concomitant of the proceedings. Without it nothing can begin, and without it nothing can end.

Associations of this nature are much more common in connection with funerals than with weddings, yet they are not unknown for the latter purpose. A family, for example, wishes to marry a son on a scale which the family resources will not warrant. It then resorts to an expedient, which is called "drawing friends by means of other friends." Let us suppose that it is desired to raise the sum of 100,000 cash. A hundred cards of invitation are prepared, ten of which are sent to ten friends of the family, who are invited to a preliminary feast. These friends receive the extra cards of invitation, and each one gives a card to nine other "friends" of his own, who agree to attend the wedding in question, each one bringing with him as a share a string of cash. By this means a family with little wealth and few connections is able suddenly to blossom out at a wedding with a hundred guests (many of whom nobody knows), and all expenses are provided for by the liberal contribution of the "friends," and of the friends of the "friends."

The only motive for the act, on the part of the original "friends" is friendship, and the gustatory joy of the wedding feast. The only motives for the friends of the "friends," are their friendship, and the same joyful feast. It is needless to observe that the 100,000 cash thus suddenly raised is a debt, which the family receiving it must repay in future contributions.

To a Westerner, it doubtless appears a preposterous proceeding to saddle a family with a liability of this sort, for the mere sake of a temporary display. But love of display is by no means confined to the Chinese, although doubtless they are satisfied with manifestations of it which to us are far from being attractive. It is a characteristic in the Chinese conduct of affairs, to make heavy drafts on the future in order to satisfy a present need. Many a family will sell all their land, and even pull down their house, to provide for a funeral of a parent, because to bury the deceased without a suitable display would be a loss of "face." And this irrational procedure is executed with an air of cheerfulness and of conscious virtue, which seems to say, "Behold me! I will do what is becoming at any personal inconvenience whatever!"

The elaborateness of a Chinese funeral may be roughly determined in advance by calculating the product of two factors, the age (especially the rank of the deceased by generations) and the social rank of the family. As soon as a death occurs the wailing begins, and at once, or possibly at sunset, the temple of the local-god is visited to make the announcement to him, accompanied with more wailing. Further exercises of this sort take place on "the third day," that is in some regions the next day, which is held to be to all intents "the third"! In case of an affair of great ceremony there will be special performances on every seventh day (a strange and apparently unique survival of the hebdominal division in China) for seven times, the funeral occurring on the forty-ninth day. During the whole of this period there is no quiet time for the distracted family. Perhaps both Buddhist and Taoist priests are chanting their Sacred Books in extemporized mat-shed pavilions of a tawdry splendour; for it is often considered safest in the dim uncertainty as to the best way to reach the regions of the blest, to take passage by both of these religious routes. Excruciating music rends the air from morn till eve, and bombs are detonating at frequent intervals to terrify malignant spirits, and to delight the swarms of village boys who riot in ecstasies during the whole procedure.

English-speaking peoples have been criticised for taking their pleasures sadly. The Chinese, on the contrary, often contrive to get through their mourning not without considerable enjoyment. Under no other mundane circumstances is so much to be had to eat on such easy terms. The adage says truly,

"When old folks die, the rest feed high."

The strain upon the exiguous resources of a single courtyard or set of yards in preparing food simultaneously for the guests, often numbering hundreds, is very great; yet the inevitable waiting, the crowding, the turmoil, and discomfort are all borne without a tenth of the complaint and resentment which a tithe of the same annoyances and provocations would probably cause the readers of these lines. In China there is no other way to bury the dead, and there never has been any other way. Ceremony is the very life of the Chinese race, and on no other occasion is ceremony so triumphantly tyrannical as at a Chinese funeral. Yet in the most showy pageantry there is likely to be an element of unutterable shabbiness. In city processions flags, banners, umbrellas, screens, and handsome wooden tablets shining with lacquer and glittering with gilt are carried in great numbers before and behind the coffin of notables, but the bearers are not infrequently dirty, ragged beggars, straggling along without aim and without order. Little or nothing of this is to be seen in the rural districts, but the confusion and disorderliness are omnipresent and inevitable. There is in the Chinese language no word meaning solemn, for there is no such thing as solemnity in the Chinese Empire.

White being the mourning colour, at a funeral swarms of people appear, some with a mere fillet about their head, others with square caps, and others with a more abundant display, up to those whose near relationship to the deceased requires that they be covered entirely with the coarse cloth which denotes the deepest depth of mourning, their feeble steps being supported by a short stick of willow upon which they ostentatiously lean, particularly at the numerous junctures when wailing is to take place. Generally speaking, the wearers of white are those who come within the "Five Degrees of Relationship" (wu fu), that is, all directly descended from one's grandfather's grandfather (the steps being indicated in Chinese by separate names for each generation, to wit, kao, tsêng, tsu, fu, and shên, viz., three generations of "grandfathers," my father, and myself). The family in mourning furnishes material for all the cloud of mourners, but if the married daughters are provided by their husband's family with a supply, this is a mark of special honour. Sometimes women are seen proudly carrying a huge bolt of wholly superfluous cloth on their arm all through a funeral, furnishing a public testimonial that their husbands or fathers-in-law have done the correct thing, thus giving the daughter-in-law a large supply of "face."

Since family graveyards are surrounded by planted fields, if a funeral happens to be held in the spring or early summer, it is inevitable that by the trampling of so many persons much damage should be done to growing crops. A space twenty feet wide or more would be required by the bearers of a catafalque, and if the funeral is a large one it will be followed all the way by a dense crowd. The unhappy owners of adjacent land sometimes provide themselves with shovels, and throw quantities of earth into the air so as to fall on the heads of the trespassers on their grain, as a protest (like all Chinese protests wholly futile) against the invasion of their rights.

Angry words and reviling are not infrequent concomitants of Chinese funerals, for the provocation is often grievous. To interfere with a funeral is a serious offence, but disputes sometimes arise between the participants. The writer once saw a coffin left for many days by the side of a public road because the bearers of the two coffins that were to have been buried together, differed as to which set should first leave the village, the disagreement terminating in a fight and an angry lawsuit, pending the settlement of which the dead man could not stir.

It is when the almost interminable feasts are at last over, and the loud cry is raised, "Take up the coffin," that the funeral's climax has arrived. Sixteen bearers, or some multiple of sixteen (and the more the better) wrestle with the huge and unwieldy burden of the ponderous coffin and the enormous catafalque supporting it. Only the bearers in the immediate front can see where they are going, so that it is necessary that a funeral director take charge of their motions, which he does by shrill shouts in a falsetto key ending in a piercing cry by no means unlike the scream of a catamount. To each of his directive yells the whole chorus of bearers responds with shouts resembling those of sailors heaving an anchor. These cries mingled with the ostentatious wails of the mourners piled into a whole caravan of village farm-carts, combine to produce a total effect as remote from our conception of what a funeral ought to be as can easily be imagined. When, by a slow and toilful progress, the family graveyard has been reached, the lowering of the coffin into the grave—sometimes a huge circular opening—is the culminating point of the many days of excitement. The cries of the director become shrieks, the responses are tumultuous and discordant, every one adding his own emendations according to his own point of view, and no one paying any attention to any one else. Thus, amid the explosion of more crackers and bombs, the fiercer wails of the mourners, the shouts of the bearers and the grave-diggers, and the buzz of the curious spectators, the Chinese is at last laid away to his long rest.

XIX

NEW YEAR IN CHINESE VILLAGES

If the foreigner who has lived in China long enough to take in its external phenomena, but not long enough to perceive the causes of them, were to explain to one of less knowledge his views as to the leading features of the change from one Chinese year to another as exhibited in the life of the Chinese, he would probably name (and with much plausibility) one or more of the following particulars.

DUMPLINGS

The customs of different parts of the wide empire doubtless vary, but probably there is no part of it in which either dumplings or some similar article are not inseparably associated with New Year's Day, in the same way as plum-pudding with an English Christmas, or roast-turkey and mince pie with a New England Thanksgiving. As compared with Western peoples the number of Chinese who are not obliged to practice self-denial either in the quantity or the quality of their food, and in both, is small. The diet of the vast mass of the nation is systematically and necessarily abstemious. Even in the case of farmers' families who are well enough off to afford the year round good food in abundance, we do not often see them indulging in such luxury. Or if the males of the elder generation indulge, the women and children of a younger generation are not allowed to do so. Hereditary economy in the item of food is a marked Chinese trait. To "eat good things" is a common phrase denoting the occurrence of a wedding, a funeral, or some occasion upon which "good things" cannot be dispensed with. To eat cakes of ordinary grain on New Year's Day, and not to get any dumplings at all, is proverbially worse than not to have any New Year.

Moreover, the keen joy with which every member of a Chinese family looks forward to the dietetic aspect of their New Year, the still keener joy with which every member is absorbed in devouring all he can get of the best there is to be got, and the scarcely less keen joy with which each one recalls the details of the menu when the family is once more launched upon the Sahara of ordinary fare—these are full of suggestion and instruction to Occidentals who habitually have so much to eat that they seldom secure the best sauce of gnawing hunger, and are more likely than not to be bored by being asked out to an elaborate dinner with many courses. The most robust imagination finds it impossible to conceive of a Chinese who should take this view of what always appeals to the finest feelings of his nature. There is therefore much reason in placing Dumplings in the forefront of a Chinese New Year.

REUNION

No feast-day in any Western land—the two previously mentioned not excepted—can at all compare with Chinese New Year, as regards powers of traction and attraction. We consider the gathering of families on these special occasions as theoretically desirable, and as practically useful. But we have this fatal disadvantage; our families divide and disperse, often to the ends of the earth, and a new home is soon made. Whole families cannot be transported long distances, especially at inclement seasons of the year, even if average dwellings would hold them all.

But in China, the family is already at home. It is only some of its male members who are absent, and they return to their ancestral abode, with the infallible instinct of the wild fowl to their southern haunts. If vast distances should make this physically impossible—as is the case with the countless Shan-hsi men scattered over the empire doing business as bankers, pawn-brokers, etc., or as happens with many from the northern provinces who go "outside the Great Wall,"—still the plan is to go home, perhaps one year in three, and the time selected is always at the close of the year.

A cat in a strange garret, a bird with a broken wing, a fish out of water are not more restless and unhappy than the average Chinese who cannot go home at New Year time. In addition to his personal deprivations, he has the certainty of being ridiculed not only by the persons with whom he is obliged to stay, but also by the people of his own village when he does go home. The Chinese dread ridicule, even more than they dread the loss of a good meal, and unless the circumstances are altogether exceptional, one can depend upon it that every Chinese can only be kept away from his home at New Year by circumstances over which he has no control. There is, therefore, good ground for regarding reunion as a leading feature of a Chinese New Year.

NEW CLOTHES

Whoever takes even a superficial view of the Chinese in their towns, cities and villages during the period from the first day of the first moon to the fifteenth of the same, will be struck with the display of new and bright-coloured garments. Every article of apparel, both of the men and of the women, and still more of the children, may be of any or all the colors of the rainbow. The Chinese do not seem to us to be conspicuous for what we call good taste, but rather at times to emulate the vagaries of the African savages, and never more so than at this time of holiday show. Combinations of colour which would cause Western ladies to shrug their shoulders, and to shiver with horror, appear to recommend themselves to the Chinese taste as the correct thing, and as good form. Bright green and blue, accompanied by deep scarlet, purple, lilac or orange, do not seem to "kill each other," as our modistes would shudderingly affirm, but they convey such evident and such universal pleasure to wearers and spectators alike, that it becomes plain to the most prejudiced foreigner, that here, at least, his standards do not apply. In consideration of the stress which the Chinese lay upon this feature of their great anniversary, we should be justified in assuming fine clothes as a main characteristic of the occasion.

RELIGIOUS RITES

The very first aspect in which Chinese New Year presents itself, no matter in what part of the world we happen to meet it, is that of noise. All night long, there is a bang! bang! bang! of firecrackers large and small, which, like other calamities, "come, not single spies, but in battalions." The root of all this is undoubtedly connected with religion, as in other similar performances all over the world. But though the explosion of gunpowder is the most prominent, it is far from being the most important act of New Year worship. There is the despatch of the last year's kitchen-god, generally on the twenty-third of the twelfth moon, and the installation of his successor at the close of the year. On the last evening of the year, there is the family gathering either at the ancestral temple, or should there not be one, in the dwelling-house, for the worship of the tablets of the past few generations of ancestors. In some parts of China ancestral tablets are comparatively rare among the farming and working people, and the place of them as regards the practical worship at New Year's eve, is taken by a large scroll, containing a portion of the family genealogy, which is hung up, and honoured with prostrations and the burning of incense. On the morning of the second day of the new first moon, perhaps at other times also, all the males of a suitable age go to the family or clan graveyard, and there make the customary offerings to the spirits of the departed. There has been considerable controversy among foreigners expert in Chinese affairs as to the true value of these various rites from a religious point of view, but there is no doubt on the part of any one that they constitute a most essential ingredient in a Chinese New Year, and that in the present temper of the Chinese race, a New Year without such rites is both inconceivable and impossible. We do well, therefore, to place Religious Rites prominently in our catalogue.

SOCIAL CEREMONIES

It requires but a slight acquaintance with the facts, however, to make us aware that while the ceremonies connected with the dead are important, they are soon disposed of once for all, and that they do not form a part of the permanent New Year landscape. It is quite otherwise with the social ceremonies connected with the living. The practice of New Year calls, as found in some Western lands is a very feeble parody of the Chinese usage. We call on whom we choose to call upon, when we choose to go. The Chinese pays his respects to those to whom he must pay his respects, at the time when it is his duty so to do and from this duty there is seldom any reprieve. For example, not to press into undue prominence local practices, which vary greatly, it may be the fashion for every one to be up long before daylight. After the family salutations have been concluded, all but the older generation of males set out to make the tour of the village, the representatives of each family entering the yard of every other family, and prostrating themselves to the elders who are at home to receive them. This business goes by priority in the genealogical table, as military and naval officers take rank from the date of their commissions. Early marriages on the part of some members of a collateral branch of a large clan, late marriages on the part of other branches, the adoption of heirs at any point, and other causes, constantly bring it about that the men oldest in years are by no means so in the order of the generation to which they belong. Thus we have the absurd spectacle of a man of seventy posing as a "nephew"—or, if worst comes to worst—as the "grandson" of a mere boy. One often hears a man in middle life complain of the fatigues of the New Year time, as he being of a "late generation," is obliged "to kotow to every child two feet long" whom he may happen to meet, as they are "older" than he, and in consequence of this inversion of "relative duties," the children are fresh as a rose, while the middle-aged man has lame knees for a week or two!

If the first day is devoted to one's native town or village, the succeeding ones are taken to pay calls of ceremony upon one's relatives living in other towns or villages, beginning with the mother's family, and branching into relationships the names of which few foreigners can remember, and which most cannot even comprehend. That all this social ceremony is upon the whole a good thing cannot be doubted, for it prevents many alienations, and heals in their early stages many cases of strained relations. Yet, to us such a formal and monotonous routine would prove insufferable.

To the Chinese, these visits are not only an important part of New Year, presumptively they are in real sense New Year itself. Every visit involves a "square meal," and (from the Chinese point of view) a good time. To omit them, would be not only to deprive oneself of much pleasure, it would be to commit a social crime, which would almost certainly give great offence.

NATIONAL LEISURE

Greater familiarity with the conditions and details of Chinese life lead us to wonder that so laborious a people find time for all this junketing and vain display. The marvel is indeed a permanent one, but it ceases to surprise us when we have once taken in the fact that the whole Chinese race have as a unit, practically agreed to deduct from the twelve available months, an entire half moon, from New Year till the Feast of Lanterns. Within this twenty-fourth part of the year, nothing shall be done which can be left undone. The outgo is to be put down to the expense account of the whole year, and the main purpose is to have a good time. This period thus becomes a safety-valve for the nation, which else might go distraught in all its otherwise ceaseless toils. If the Chinese did not as a rule, work so hard, they could not so heartily enjoy their long vacation. If they did not so heartily enjoy their vacation, they could not during the rest of the year work so well. We are therefore authorized, in arranging our table of contents of the Chinese New Year, to give large place to the almost complete cessation of productive industry. It is the epoch of national leisure.

GAMBLING

It is a venerable maxim that "Satan finds some mischief still, for idle hands to do." Probably no race that ever lived could resist the strain of such a sudden transition from constant industrial activity, to complete industrial inactivity, to be followed half a month later by the old routine and another year of bondage. They could not resist the strain, that is to say, without a corresponding reaction; neither can the Chinese. It is not in human nature to find consecutive enjoyment merely in the directions which have been named, without trying to go farther and to get more. This is precisely what the Chinese do, and they do it by the excitement of gambling. This, with opium smoking, is the greatest vice in China, and the most ruinous. But after all, taking the country districts through, the proportion of gamblers among the working classes, so far as we are aware, is limited, though vast sums are everywhere annually squandered in this way. But the remarkable thing is that at New Year's time all restrictions seem to be removed, and both men and women give themselves up to the absorbing excitement of cards, dominoes, etc., with money stakes of varying amount, and with no fear or even thought of future evil harvests. In the abstract, gambling is of course recognized as wrong and not to be indulged, as likely to lead to trouble. But at New Year's time "everybody does it," "it is only for amusement," and "there is nothing else to do,"—the latter an important fact to be taken account of at a time when even cooking is often prætermitted as much as possible. Merchants do not take down their shutters, but one can hear the clerks noisily gambling inside. Innkeepers will not open their front doors, but landlord and servants are all gambling together and will refuse to stop a game to feed your animals or get you a meal, telling you that it is no time to travel, and that business is business, and amusement amusement.

Old women and young women squatted on their mats or their k'angs, feverishly shuffle their cards and pay their little stakes, and all are having a good time.

That this state of things will not stop suddenly on the day after the Feast of Lanterns, is obvious. It often never stops at all, but goes on with a widening and lengthening trail of ruin, not ending even with the grave, but lasting to the third and fourth generation. Surely we are right in calling gambling a leading feature of a Chinese New Year. And yet after all, perhaps we have not got to the bottom of the matter.

DEBT-PAYING

However little attention he may pay to the Chinese calendar, every foreigner in China is sure to be reminded in a very effective way of the approach of the close of the Chinese year, long before the edge of the New Year is to be seen above the horizon. At some time during the twelfth moon, the "boy" makes his appearance, and with an unusual animation in his unanimated face, explains that owing to a combination of circumstances which seem to be to a large extent incapable of elucidation to us, he is obliged to request the advance of his wages for the current month, and also for the one to come. This may be contrary to rule, doubtless is so, but owing to the combination above alluded to, is an imperative necessity. Otherwise ruin impends. It is not long before a similar statement is made by the cook, with regard to his affairs, and by the various coolies as to theirs. In each case the necessity turns out upon investigation to be so real, and the pressure of the combination of circumstances so powerful, that we are, in a manner, forced to do violence to our own judgment, in order to avert the imminent ruin of those who are in our employ, and in whom we feel, perhaps, some interest. But it is a long time before it occurs to us to look into the matter more deeply than sufficiently to ascertain what everybody knew before, that Chinese New Year is preceded by a universal season of debt-paying from which no one is exempt. If we insist upon following up any specific case with a rigid examination into its remoter causes, we soon learn from the principal party such facts as appear to justify his assertion of an emergency, and also that there is nothing peculiar in his case, but that other people are in the same predicament. If these inquiries are carried far enough, and deep enough, they will bring to light the seven deadly sins of Chinese social financiering.

1. Everybody always needs to borrow. That the business of the world even in Western lands depends upon the borrowing of money, and that credit is the largest factor in trade, are positions which we do not for a moment forget. But Chinese borrowing is

of a different type from that with which the great expansion of modern commerce has made us familiar. We do not affirm that there are not Chinese who do not need the money of other people for the conduct of their affairs, but only that these people are so rare that they may as well be disregarded. The whole scale of Chinese living and the whole system of economics are of such a sort, that as a rule there is but a narrow margin of financial reserve. With all their practicality and skill in affairs, it is a constant source of wonder that so few Chinese ever have anything to fall back upon. One reason for this is the fact that it is very difficult for them to accumulate a reserve, and another equally potent is the fact that there is nothing which can be safely done with it pending its use. There are no savings-banks, and there are no investments which are safe. The only thing which can be done with ready money, is to lend it to those who need it, which is generally done with some reluctance, as the lender justly fears lest he should never again see either interest or principal. Whoever has a wedding in his family, is liable to have to borrow money to carry it through, and if it be a funeral the necessity will be still more urgent. He needs money to start in business, and he needs more to settle up at the end of the year, when, if their own accounts are to be trusted, nine Chinese out of ten who engage in business in a small way, find that they have "lost money"; though this often signifies that they have not realized so much as they had hoped. In short it is hard to find a Chinese to whom the loan of a sum of money at any time, would not be as welcome as "water to a fish in a dry rut." It is this all-prevailing need which smoothes the surface of the spot where the pit is to be dug.

2. Everybody is obliged to lend money. We have just remarked that the man who happens to have a little surplus cash does not like to lend it, lest he should never see it again. But there are various kinds and degrees of pressure which can be brought to bear upon the capitalist. One of these is connected with the solidarity of the Chinese family, or clan. If one of the members has money which he might lend and another is desperately in

need of it, the latter will get a member of the generation higher than that to which the capitalist belongs, to intercede for him. This may be done unwillingly, but it will probably be done. To a sufficient amount of pressure of this ancestral description, the capitalist will find it best to yield, though not improbably against his financial judgment. But every Chinese is from infancy accustomed to the idea that it is seldom easy to have one's own way in all things, and that when one cannot do as he would, he must do as he must. If the borrower does not belong to the same family or clan as the lender, the difficulty will be greater, but it may perhaps be overcome by the same description of pressure, by means of friends. A would-be borrower is often obliged to make a great many kotows before he can secure the favour of a loan (at an extortionately high rate of interest), but he is much aided in his efforts by the Chinese notion that when a certain amount of pressure has been brought to bear, a request must be granted, just as one of a pair of scales must go down if you put on enough weights. Thus it comes about that in all ranks of Chinese, the man who has, is the man who must be content to allow to share in his wealth (for a handsome remuneration).

3. From the foregoing propositions, it follows with inevitable certainty, that almost everybody owes some one else. There is never any occasion to ask a Chinese whether he owes money. The proper formula is, How much do you owe, and to whom, and what is the rate of interest?

4. No Chinese ever pays cash down, unless he is obliged to do so. To us this may appear a most eccentric habit, but it seems to be almost a law. The Chinese has learned by ages of experience, that he no sooner pays away money to satisfy one debt, than he needs that same money to liquidate other debts. In their own figuratively expressive phrase, a single cup of water is wanted in three or four places at once, and the supply is always as inadequate, as the classical "cup of water to put out the fire in a cart-load of fuel." Knowing this with a keenness of apprehension which it is difficult for us to appreciate, the Chinese holds on fast

to his cash till it is wrung from him by a force which overcomes his own tenacity of grip.

5. No Chinese ever pays a debt till he is dunned. To us this also seems a strange practice. Most of us have grown up with a fixed idea that as a debt must be paid, "if it were done when 'tis done, then 'twere well it were done quickly." The mind of a Chinese operates in quite a different way. His view is, "If it must be done, it were best done when it is done as deliberately as the case admits."

6. It seems also to be the rule, that no Chinese will pay his debts till he has been dunned a great number of times. Here again he is at the opposite pole from that which we occupy. We do not like to be dunned, and would rather make considerable sacrifices than to have needy persons dogging us for the collection of debts which we honestly owe, which we must ultimately pay, and not to arrange for the payment of which at once is more or less of a disgrace. By "we" we mean of course the average foreigner, for it is not to be denied that Western lands have their full proportion of impecunious and shameless rascals who "live off the interest of their debts," and who swindle all those whom they can. But the Chinese of whom we are speaking do not belong to this class. The mass of the Chinese people we believe to be honest, and they fully intend to pay all that they owe, but they do not intend to pay until they are ready to do so, and neither gods nor men can tell when that will be. It is a current saying that when a person has many debts he is no longer concerned about them, just as when one has many parasites he ceases to scratch!

7. In a large proportion of cases, the Chinese who pays a debt, pays but a part of it at a time. The rest he will try to get together in the "third month," "the ninth month," or at the "end of the next year." The practical outcome of these last three peculiarities is, that the twelfth moon of every Chinese year is a time of maximum activity all over the empire. One would suppose that a vast amount of work was being accomplished, but the facts are otherwise. One is reminded of the Witch in "Alice Behind the Looking-Glass," where the child was hurried along on a

broomstick at such a rate as to take her breath away. She thought she must be traversing illimitable space, but when this idea was communicated to the Witch, the latter only laughed, and replied that this was nothing at all, for they had to go like that to "keep up with things" and if they were really to get ahead to any extent, the rate of travel must be enormously faster than that! The racing around of the Chinese in their final moon, is just "to keep up with things." Every shop, no matter how trifling the sum total of its business, has its army of runners out, each "demanding debts," or rather endeavouring to do so; for to achieve it is no such easy matter. The debtor is himself a creditor, and he also will be occupied in the effort to call in the sums which are owing to him. Each separate individual is engaged in the task of trying to chase down the men who owe money to him, and compel them to pay up, and at the same time in trying to avoid the persons who are struggling to track him down and corkscrew from him the amount of his indebtedness to them? The dodges and subterfuges to which each is obliged to resort, increase in complexity and number with the advance of the season, until at the close of the month, the national activity is at fever heat. For if a debt is not secured then, it will go over till a new year, and no one knows what will be the status of a claim which has actually contrived to cheat the annual Day of Judgment. In spite of the excellent Chinese habit of making the close of a year a grand clearing-house for all debts, Chinese human nature is too much for Chinese custom, and there are many of these postponed debts which are a grief of mind to many a Chinese creditor.

The Chinese are at once the most practical and the most sentimental of the human race. New Year must not be violated by duns for debts, but the debt must be collected New Year though it be. For this reason one sometimes sees an urgent creditor going about early on the first day of the year carrying a lantern looking for his creditor. His artificial light shows that by a social fiction the sun has not yet risen, it is still yesterday and the debt can still be claimed!

We have but to imagine the application of the principles which we have named, to the whole Chinese empire, and we get new light upon the nature of the Chinese New Year festivities. They are a time of rejoicing, but there is no rejoicing so keen as that of a ruined debtor, who has succeeded by shrewd devices in avoiding the most relentless of his creditors and has thus postponed his ruin for at least another twelve months. For, once past the narrow strait at the end of the year, the debtor finds himself again in broad and peaceful waters, where he cannot be molested. Even should his creditors meet him on New Year's day, there could be no possibility of mentioning the fact of the previous day's disgraceful flight and concealment, or indeed of alluding to business at all, for this would not be "good form," and to the Chinese "Good Form" (otherwise known as Custom), is the chief national divinity.

An ingenious device by which to secure the desirable result that a family shall be sure to have a supply of the food most indispensable for a proper treatment of guests at the festive New Year season, is found in what are called New Year Societies. Each member of the society contributes a few hundred or perhaps a thousand cash a month for the first five months of the year, until the wheat harvest in June when wheat is at its lowest price, for example 1,200 cash for 100 catties or picul. During the five months which have elapsed, the money thus assessed upon the members has been put at interest, and has already accumulated a handsome income. As soon as the new wheat is in the market, the loans are all called in, and the treasurer takes the whole of the sum belonging to the association and invests it in wheat. This he keeps until the close of the year, by which time it is not at all unlikely that the price of the grain has doubled. He then exchanges the wheat, at the current rate, with some maker of bread-cakes (man-t'ou), and these are divided among the stockholders. In this way, each one gets not only the benefit of the interest on loans for five months, but also nearly or quite double the value of the wheat bought just after harvest. Sometimes the monthly payments are continued throughout the year, and the sum is then expended in a lump for bread-cakes, wheat, cotton, or whatever each family most needs for the New Year season. In societies of this kind, the rate of interest is sure to be at least three per cent. per month, and perhaps four per cent. The amounts borrowed are usually small, and each borrower must have a security from among the contributors to the fund. In case payment is not forthcoming at the due date, the next step is to raise an uproar, and if possible to collect the debt by force. The inevitable and universal uncertainty and difficulty attending the collection of any money on loan, give emphasis to the adage that "where the profit is large, the risk is correspondingly great."

Extortionate as are the ordinary rates of Chinese interest, ranging from twenty-four to forty eight or more per cent. per annum, there are other ways than direct loans, by which even greater profits may be gathered. The passion for gambling seems to be all-pervasive among the Chinese, and it is perhaps a greater bar to the prosperity of the common people than any other habit of their lives. Many of the phenomena of Chinese coöperation are associated with gambling practices, from which the profit to those who manage the finances is very great. In all cases where there is money to loan, it is possible to employ it for gaming, under the direction of the managers, or trustees. Those who are in the habit of gambling do not stop when their supply of money fails, but draw upon the bank of the loan association at terms which are agreed upon, but which differ according to circumstances. In an emergency, it might happen that a person whose fortune had failed him, would be obliged to borrow of the bank, say 800 cash, which in a short time he must replace with 1,000. At the end of the year when the accounts are made up and the money paid in, it is equally divided among the contributors of the society, whether they may have used the capital for gambling or not. In case they have borrowed a part of the capital and are not able to repay it, their debt is set against their contribution, and they lose their investment.

XX

THE VILLAGE BULLY

No adequate understanding of the life of the Chinese is possible without some comprehension of the place therein of the bully, and conversely it might almost be said that a just apprehension of the character and functions of the Chinese bully is equivalent to a comprehension of Chinese society.

So far as we know, the Chinese bully is a character peculiar to China. By this it is not of course meant that other lands do not have and have not always had their bullies, but that the mode in which Chinese bullies exert their power is unique. It depends largely upon the peculiar characteristics of the Chinese race, prominent among which is the desire for peace, and a reluctance to engage in a quarrel. The traits of a bully among a savage and warlike people such as our ancestors once were, and of a bully among such a quiet folk as the Chinese, are inherently different.

The Chinese have many terms to designate the individual whom we have termed a bully, among which one of the most common is that which means literally "bare-stick" (kuang-kun), in allusion to the fact that those who are most frequently bullies are generally those who have no property to lose. But the general term is applicable to any one who plays the part, whatever his social condition may be, and it is in this sense that we shall employ it.

In considering the social functions of the bully, it is necessary to distinguish him from several classes of persons, to any one of which he may belong, but from each one of which he may be different. These four classes are,—first, headmen of the village (called also, as we have already remarked, by many other names);

223

second, intermediaries (not "middlemen" in the technical sense, but those who as peace-talkers, intervene in the affairs of others) etc.; third, beggars; and lastly thieves.

In China next in importance after the division of human beings into two sexes, is another classification which every Chinese instinctively adopts. According to this arrangement, all members of society are rated according to their probable behaviour under bad treatment, just as the chemist considers all substances in the light of their capacity for combination with other elements.

In the popular speech of the people, every Chinese villager is said to be either "lao-shih" or not "lao-shih." The words "lao-shih" mean literally "old and solid," or in a derived sense gentle, tractable, from which again arises a third signification of stupid, and gullible. The highest degree of this latter quality is expressed in the phrase "ssü-lao-shih," which literally denotes one who is "dead-stupid"; that is, one who can be imposed upon to any extent. Such a one, in a common adage, is compared to the toes on an old woman's feet, which have been suppressed all their life, without any power of asserting themselves.

The village bully is, (as we used to be taught of vulgar fractions) of three kinds, simple, compound, and complex. The simple bully is a unit by himself, managing his own affairs with his own resources. The compound bully calls to his aid the power of numbers, and the mysterious and almost irresistible talent for combination inherent in the Chinese. The complex bully is not a bully merely, but has some business or profession, in the management of which he is materially aided by the fact that he is a man to be feared.

In his simplest form, a Chinese bully is a man of a more or less violent temper and strong passions, who is resolved never to "eat loss," and under all circumstances to give as good (or as bad) as he gets. Fortunately for the peace of society, the overwhelming majority of the Chinese belong to the "lao-shih" variety. In order to secure the reputation of being not "lao-shih," a shrewd villager will sometimes adopt the expedient, not unknown to other lands, of wearing his clothes in a loose and rowdy-like fashion, talking in a boisterous tone, and resenting contradiction or any overt lack of compliance with his opinions.

His cap is worn studiedly awry; his outer garment instead of being decorously fastened, is left purposely unlooped; his abundant hair is braided into a loose cue apparently as thick as his arm, the plaiting beginning several inches away from the head: the end of the cue is generally coiled about his neck or over his head (a gross breach of Chinese etiquette), as if to show that he thirsts for a fight. His outer leggings are not improbably so tied as to display a lining which is more expensive than the outside; and his shoes are invariably worn down at the heel, perhaps to make an ostentatious display of a silk embroidered heel to the cotton stocking—a touch of splendour adapted to strike awe into the rustic beholder. In a time of intense excitement over alleged kidnapping of children, we have known a man to be apprehended in open court and examined as a bad character, because the colour of his clothes was unusual.

By persistently following out his peculiar lines of action, he will not unlikely succeed in diffusing the impression that he is a dangerous man to interfere with, and will in consequence be let severely alone. A cat of even a small experience will not improbably manifest considerable hesitation before attempting to swallow a lizard. It is evident, therefore, that if any small reptile is obliged to associate with cats, the art of simulating a lizard is a valuable one. The grade of bully of which we are now speaking is in all Chinese society too common to attract much notice, and he can be avoided by letting him alone. His weapons, like the walls of Chinese cities, are defensive only.

Much more to be dreaded is the bully who will not let others alone, but who is always inserting himself into their affairs with a view to extracting some benefit for himself. The most dangerous type of these men is the one who makes very little ado, but whose acts are ruinous to those whom he wishes to injure. Such a one is aptly likened to a dog which bites without showing his teeth.

The tactics which such a man adopts to establish his claim to the rank of "village king," are the same with which we are only too familiar in other lands, and which an advancing civilization has not yet succeeded in rendering wholly obsolete. If there is no overt act which he sees his way to commit, he can always pick a quarrel by reviling, which is regarded as throwing down a glove of defiance. Not to notice such a challenge is from a Chinese standpoint almost impossible. "To be reviled and to feel no pain," this is the Chinese ideal of shamelessness. Nothing is rarer than to find a Chinese who has been reviled, and who, when he was strong enough to demand an apology, has allowed the matter to drop.

The intricate constitution of Chinese society is such that there is a great variety of acts which, while they may not be directly hostile, must be understood in the light of a challenge. If for example a bully has let it be known that he is determined that a theatrical representation shall take place the next autumn in his village, for some one to oppose it might not improbably be such an act of hostility as to amount to a challenge. The bully must then see that the theatre is engaged, or his "face" is lost, which one may be sure will never happen as long as he is able to prevent it.

There is always about one of these village bullies a general atmosphere of menace, as if he were thirsting for an opportunity to issue an ultimatum. He often does so, in a singularly vague manner, the significance of which is, however, perfectly well understood. If A is the bully, and B is known to oppose him, then A publicly states that if B does so and so, A will not put up with it (pu suan t'a, literally, "will not take the account," but insinuating a dark hint as to consequences). If B takes the hint and quietly retires, there is peace, but otherwise there is war.

One of the qualifications which is very convenient for the village bully, although not absolutely indispensable, is physical strength. One of the nicknames of the local bully as just remarked, is that of village king. Among those whose forte is violence, the king must be a man who has inherent power, "the man who can," for it is impossible to say at what moment all his strength will be needed in some fight.

It is in view of this consideration, that it is very common for young fellows who wish to distinguish themselves among their comrades, to take systematic lessons in "fist-and-foot," that is, in gymnastics. A high degree of skill in wrestling, and the ability (as alleged) to deliver such a blow with the fist as shall knock out a brick from a wall a foot thick, are in many circumstances valuable accomplishments.

The writer is well acquainted with a young man who enjoyed the reputation of being the strongest person in his village. Being sent on an errand to a distant city, he had occasion to pass through a smaller city some forty li from his home, where he was not known. Here a number of bullies, who happened to be gathered in front of the district yamên, struck with his rusticity, stopped him, and demanded who he was and where he was going. His replies to their inquiries not being sufficiently prompt to give satisfaction, he was set upon by several men, who attacked him simultaneously. Here his "fist-and-foot" skill was of great service; for though two men were on top of him, he was able to seize the ankle of one of them and to give it such a fearful twist as almost to dislocate the joint, whereupon his assailants, howling with pain, were only too glad to release him. At a later date the matter was looked into, and at the feast which the attacking party was compelled to give, by way of apology, one of those present hobbled around in a particularly feeble manner, and freely expressed the opinion that upon this occasion he had mistaken his man!

In the numerous cases in which persons are imposed upon by a bully who is too much for them, their earliest thoughts are how it may be practicable to collect a band of men, expert in the "fist-and-foot" practices, and make an attack upon the aggressive party, by which means he may be suppressed. The writer once met a man whose home is in a village noted as the headquarters of a daring and unscrupulous band of thieves. Having been robbed by them with no prospect of any redress through legal channels, this man collected a band of athletes and attacked the thieves in the vicinity of the village where they made their home, so belabouring them that the band removed its headquarters elsewhere.

It is a useful, but by no means a necessary qualification of the bully, that he should be a poor man, with nothing to lose. Poverty in China is often a synonym for the most abject misery and want. The entire possessions of great numbers of the people would not amount in value to five dollars, and thousands of persons never know whence the next meal is to come. Such persons would in European countries constitute what are called "the dangerous classes." In China, unless their distress is extreme, they do not mass themselves, and they seldom wage war against society as a whole. But individuals of this type may, if they have other requisite abilities, become "village kings," and order the course of current events much according to their own will.

Such persons, in the figurative language of the Chinese, are called "barefoot men," in allusion to their destitute condition, and it is a common saying that "the barefoot man (otherwise known as 'mud-legs') is not afraid of him who has stockings on his feet," for the former can at once retreat into the mud, where the latter dare not follow. In other words, the barefoot man is able to hold in terror the man who has property to lose, by an open or an implicit threat of vengeance, against which the man of property cannot safeguard himself.

The forms which this vengeance will take vary according to circumstances. One of the most common is that of incendiary fires, which, in a thickly inhabited village, where there is often a large accumulation of fuel stacked up, is a mode of attack particularly to be dreaded. It is always easy to set a fire, but difficult and frequently impossible to extinguish it. We have known numberless instances of this sort, in which, despite all diligence, no one was ever detected in setting the fire. The terror which such fires inspire is so great, that the man who is thought to be specially liable to them may be marked and avoided for that reason alone. It is considered unsafe to have anything to do with him, much less to aid him in extinguishing his fires. In one case of this sort, the same individual was repeatedly visited with incendiary fires, and on the last occasion all his carts were totally destroyed, nothing remaining but the tires of the wheels. It was afterward found that strong leather straps had been used to bind the wheels to the framework of the shed in which they were kept, so that any attempt to drag the carts out was certain to fail.

Another method by which the bully signifies his dissatisfaction with his enemy, is by injuring his crops. In a country where the farms are subdivided into mere fragments, every farmer's land is contiguous to that of a great number of other persons. As already mentioned a large farm will often consist of scores of different pieces of ground, which have been bought as opportunity offered. When the land is planted, and again when the harvest is gathered, excellent opportunity is afforded for disputes. The little bushes which serve as boundaries of the fields of different owners, in regions where stone posts are too expensive, are readily destroyed or removed, and in any case the boundaries are more or less inexact, leaving room for uncertainty as to the precise point at which one piece of ground ends and another begins.

It is in such situations as this that the bully is at his best. It is well understood that he will suffer no loss, and that whoever happens to be his neighbour, will literally have "a hard row to hoe." There are sometimes sections of ground, such as those belonging to public uses, river embankments, the land of certain temples, and the like, which no one but a bully could cultivate at all, because the crops must be defended against invasion from all quarters, and only a bully can furnish the necessary skill and ferocity to protect himself.

In his essay on Lord Clive, Macaulay mentions the circumstance which was still remembered in Shropshire, that in his boyish days the great Indian soldier "formed all the idle lads of the town into a kind of predatory army, and compelled the shopkeepers to submit to a tribute of apples and half-pence, in consideration of which he guaranteed the security of the windows." Young Robert Clive had hit upon the precise principle by which the Chinese bully maintains himself in perpetual rule, a principle indeed as old as the race:

"The good old rule, the simple plan
That those should take who have the power,
And those should keep who can."

The means of enforcing these exactions is always at hand, and is expressed in one fateful and compound noun, law-suit. The bully who understands his business is well acquainted with every one at the district yamên, and is in fact one of their best customers, or rather the man who brings them their custom. The yamên is the spider's web, and the bully is the large insect which drives the flies into the net, where it will go ill with them ere they escape.

If his adversary is rich, the bully may adopt the plan of leaving a bag of smuggled salt in the doorway of the rich man, at the same time taking care to have a "salt inspector" ready to seize the salt, and bring an accusation against the man of means as a defier of the law. The "salt inspectors" are themselves smugglers, selected for their expertness in the art, and like all other underlings in Chinese official life they are quite free from the trammels of any sort of conscience. From a suit of this kind no rich man would be likely to escape without the sacrifice of many thousand strings of cash, being not improbably forced to furnish the funds for repairing a city wall, for rebuilding a temple, or some other public work. The capacity to conduct successfully a lawsuit is in China what it must have been in Bagdad during the time of the Caliph Haroun Al Raschid to wear the Cap of Darkness and Shoes of Swiftness. Such agencies defy all foes except those similarly equipped. And as in the Arabian Nights there are many stories of magicians warring with magicians who also "did so with their enchantments," in like manner when Chinese bullies meet in a legal fight at a yamên, it is a battle of giants.

Entrance to a Yamen.

Chinese Court of Justice.

The most expert of all this dreaded class is the bully who is also a literary man, perhaps a hsiu-ts'ai, or Bachelor of Arts, and who thus has a special prestige of his own, securing him a hearing where others would fail of it, guaranteeing him immunity from beating in open court, to which others are liable, and enabling him to prepare accusations for himself or others, and to be certain of the bearing of these documents upon the case in hand.

These advantages are so great, that it is not uncommon to find persons who make no secret of the fact that their main motive in submitting to the toils requisite to gain the lowest literary degree, is that they may be able, during the rest of their lives, to make use of this leverage as a means of raising themselves and of harming their neighbours. Any Chinese bully is greatly to be feared, but none is so formidable as the literary bully.

One other type of Chinese bully must not fail of mention, for it is in some respects the most unique of all, to wit the female bully. Her traits are, mutatis mutandis, the same as those of the individuals already mentioned, but her mere existence is so great a departure from our ordinary conceptions of Chinese social life, that it needs a word of explanation. She is simply an evolution of her surroundings. Skill in speech, physical violence in act, and an executive talent are her endowments, and her usefulness to the perennially hungry "wolves and tigers" of the yamên is such that she is called their draught-horse to draw victims. Like her male compatriots, she is able from her value to the underlings of the yamên to conduct a lawsuit of her own, without any of those numberless and vexatious expenses which suck out the lifeblood of ordinary victims. This makes her a terrible, if not an invulnerable, foe, and those who are wise will beware of her. According to a Chinese proverb, a woman is more to be dreaded in such cases than a graduate of the second degree. It is a saying of a certain humorous philosopher, that "one hornet can break up a whole camp-meeting, when he feels well." How much mischief one Chinese bully can accomplish in an average lifetime, it is impossible to estimate.

While the government of China appears to have elements of extreme stability, it is at the same time often practically weak in the very points where it most needs strength, namely, in its capacity to put forth powerful and sudden efforts. Whenever any uprising of the people takes place, there is generally nothing to prevent its gaining a great momentum, owing to the incapacity of the local authorities to cope with it. The same phenomenon is seen in any personal affray between single individuals. There are no police to arrest the one who commits a breach of the peace, and it is only by the intervention of third parties, friendly to the principals, that order is restored. But if either of the parties is able to bring a large force to bear upon the person whom he attacks, he is almost certain to be victorious.

It is at this point that the organisation of the followers of the bully proves a formidable foe to the peace of Chinese society. Let us suppose that a man has a violent personal quarrel with an enemy. An outbreak of their feud occurs at a great fair, such as abound at almost all seasons of the year. One of the men is intimate with another man who is a professional bully and who has within call a number of associates who can be depended upon in an emergency. The man who knows the bully goes to him and tells him of the grievance and asks his help. The bully lets it be known among his comrades that a friend is in need of assistance, and that their services will be called for. The party assembled goes to that section of the fair-ground where congregate the dealers in sticks used for supports for awnings, etc., and each man "borrows" a stout sapling, promising to return it later. With this lawless band, like the forces of Robin Hood, the bully sets upon his victim and wins an easy victory. None of the spectators will interfere in a brawl of this sort, for the consequences might be most serious. It does not follow that there is any regular organization among the rough members of the dangerous classes who are assembled, except that they are ready to unite in anything which promises the joy of battle, and a probable reward in the shape of a complimentary feast.

Cases of this sort, which are by no means of infrequent occurrence, exhibit the weakness of the Chinese government, but they also exhibit its strength. If the millions of China were not satisfied with the existing rule, nothing would be easier than for them to unite and overthrow it. But the security of the government is based mainly upon the well-understood and well-ascertained fact that the people as a whole have no wish to overturn the system under which they live, as well as upon the equally indisputable fact that, with the Chinese, effective combination is an exceedingly difficult matter.

The assemblage of bands of men under the virtual direction of a leader is a menace to the peace of the whole region in which they live, and it is not strange that Magistrates of such Districts live a life which is not to be envied. As plunder is often the real object of these combinations, the yamên of the Magistrate is as likely to be the point of attack as any other place, which makes it necessary that the official shall provide himself with trained athletes, who shall be able to meet and repel assaults made at night. Cases are occasionally reported in the Peking Gazette, where in spite of this precaution the yamên was robbed, and the seal actually carried off, to the ruin of the Magistrate, upon whom perhaps the people are glad to be revenged.

The existence of such small and lawless forces in the midst of Chinese social life, quiet and orderly as that life ordinarily is, renders it certain that outbreaks will continually occur. But these attacks are not all from one side. There are in Chinese many proverbial sayings referring to the tiger, which have a metaphorical significance, and really denote the person whom we have named the bully, who is regarded as a social tiger. One of these sayings is to the effect that a tiger who has wounded too many men, is liable to fall into a mountain ravine. This means that the bully who has made enemies of too many people will at last himself fall into trouble, and then his enemies will be able to have their revenge upon him.

Cases of this sort are constantly occurring, and often result in one or more murders, which must be reported, and which are sometimes narrated in detail in the Peking Gazette. It is not uncommon to hear of instances in which bullies have been attacked by large bands of men, many of them formerly the victims of the bully. Sometimes he is kidnapped, and sometimes he is killed outright. The method by which the village wars and clan fights of the Fu-kien and Kuang-tung provinces are conducted, probably bears a close analogy to these proceedings. They appear to be trials of strength between neighbouring rivals, conducted upon the plan of warfare during the middle ages in which the feudal system reigned. The local Magistrates take care not to interfere too soon or too far, lest it be the worse for them. When the fight is over the officers put in an appearance, arrests are made, and the machinery of government recovers from its temporary paralysis.

We have spoken of the literary bully as one of those most to be dreaded in China. But there is another qualification which a bully may possess, either with or without that of learning, which makes him an almost irresistible enemy. If he belongs to a family, one or more members of which are in official life and have a certain degree of power with the official class, such a man is a dangerous foe. Instances are constantly coming to light, not only in the native papers of China but also in memorials in the Peking Gazette (to which we have so frequently had occasion to refer), showing how difficult, or rather how altogether hopeless, it is to deal with such offenders. Even in cases of the most wanton murder, there is always some way by which the matter can be adjusted, and there is no assurance that the influential culprit gets any real punishment at all.

The following instance which occurred more than a generation ago, in a District near to that in which the writer lived for a long time, illustrates the kind of proceedings to which reference is made.

During the eighteenth century there lived in that County a family named Lu, one of the members of which attained to the lofty eminence of Ko Lao, or Grand Secretary. A family of this class, especially if it should be the only one of the sort in the District, exerts a commanding influence, and it is necessary for the local Magistrate to conduct himself discreetly, in order not to win the ill-will of such a powerful corporation. It is well if he is able to collect from them even the ordinary land-tax, which all the soil of the empire is supposed to pay.

It is related of this family that, upon one occasion having been ordered by the District Magistrate to collect this tax, the local constable was unable to do as he was told. Having been repeatedly beaten for his delinquencies in this respect, he presented himself at the entrance of the premises of his wealthy neighbour, and with earnest prostrations begged the gatekeeper to intercede for him, and get the tax paid.

The elderly widow who was the manager of the establishment, having been informed of this plea, ordered her cart harnessed, and proceeded to the District Magistrate's yamên, for an interview. The official perhaps entertained a wild hope that she had come to settle up her arrears of taxes, and even planned to borrow a sum of money of her, but she soon dispelled this idea, by telling him in so many words that she herself required a "loan" of a certain number of thousands of tæls, which the Magistrate was obliged to promise to get for her, at the earliest possible moment. As she rose to take her leave, she remarked incidentally that her gatekeeper had been much annoyed by some of the yamên underlings who hung about the premises under pretence of wanting a grain-tax, adding that she should expect to hear no more of such proceedings in future!

Upon another occasion, while the Ko Lao himself was alive, a complaint was made to the District Magistrate that a son of the Ko Lao had a maidservant, who was virtually imprisoned in the family mansion. She was originally hired having been betrothed, but although it was time for her to be married, her employer refused to let her go. The Magistrate sent for the son of the Ko Lao, made known the charge, and desired the release of the person detained. He even went to the length of beating the attendant of the Lu family, who had accompanied his master, the latter being himself too lofty a subject for punishment. The son went to his home in a towering rage, and wrote a letter to his father in Peking, detailing the circumstances. Soon after this, the Magistrate received the news of his promotion from the grade of Sub-prefect to that of Prefect, in the province of Ssŭ-ch'uan.

The journey to a new post is often a most serious matter for an official, and where, as in this case, he has the entire empire to cross, the trouble and expense are very great. He had no sooner reached this distant post, than he received a notification that he was promoted to another in the province of Yün-nan, again involving an expensive and tedious journey. When he had at length taken up the duties of this office it was only to be informed that he was promoted afresh to the high rank of Tao-t'ai in a region beyond the Great Wall. He now began to perceive the significance of this strange series of events, and wholly unable either to bear the ills which he already had, or to support the prospect of perhaps greater ones yet to come, he "swallowed gold," and thus escaped further promotion and ruin!

XXI

VILLAGE HEADMEN

Many of the phenomena of village life which we shall have occasion to notice, are instances of the Chinese talent for coöperation.

Perhaps no more important exemplification of this principle is to be found in Chinese society than that embodied in the local self-government of the small communities of which the greater part of the empire is composed. The management of the village is in the hands of the people themselves. At first this condition of affairs is liable to be mistaken for a pure democracy, but very slight inquiry is sufficient to make it evident that while all matters of local concern are theoretically managed by the people, in practice the burden falls not upon the people as a whole, but upon the shoulders of a few persons, who in different places are called by different titles and whose functions differ as much as their designations.

The apparent dead-level uniformity of China is found upon investigation to be subject to surprising variations, not only in parts of the empire remote from one another, but in those which are separated by but a short distance. On this account it is difficult to generalize in regard to the government of villages in general, but easy to describe that of some villages, with the explanation that elsewhere the same results may be attained by means slightly different, or by the same means under different names.

Every Chinese village is a little principality by itself, although it is not uncommon for two or more which are contiguous and perhaps otherwise linked together, to manage their affairs in unison, and perhaps by the same set of persons. These headmen are sometimes styled village elders (hsiang chang, or hsiang lao), and sometimes they are termed merely managers (shou shih jên). The theory in regard to these persons is that they are chosen, or rather nominated, by their fellow-townsmen, and confirmed in their position by the District Magistrate. In some regions this is actually done, and for the good conduct of the headmen in their office the leading land-owners are required to become a security.

The designation "village elders" might be understood to denote that the persons who bear it are the oldest men in the village, but this is not necessarily the case. Neither are they necessarily the wealthiest men, although it is probable that every family of property will be in some way represented among them. They are not necessarily men of literary attainments, although this may be the case with a few.

In those regions where the method of selection is most loose, the number of headmen has no necessary relation to the size of the village; the position is not hereditary, neither is there any fixed time of service. A man may act in this capacity at one time, and refuse or neglect to do so at another time. Where this plan prevails, the headmen are not formally chosen, nor formally deposed. They drop into their places—or perhaps climb into them—by a kind of natural selection. The qualities which fit a villager to act as headman are the same which contribute to success in any line of business. He must be a practical person who has some native ability, acquainted with the ways of the world, as well as able and willing to devote upon occasion an indefinite amount of time and attention to the affairs which may be put in his charge.

The duties and functions of the headmen are numerous. They may be classified as those which have relation to the government of the District, those which relate to the village as such, and those which concern private individuals, and are brought to the notice of the headmen as being the persons best able to manage them.

Of the affairs which concern the government, the most important is the imperial land or grain-tax, the nature of which and the mode of collecting which vary greatly. Calls are constantly made by the local officials for government transportation, provision for the entertainment of officers on government business, materials for the repairs of the banks of rivers, work on river-banks, patrols for the Imperial roads at the season of year when travel is at its maximum, and many other similar objects.

The medium through whom the District Magistrate communicates with the village, is the "local constable," (called the ti-fang or ti-pao,) and this individual has necessarily intimate relations with the headmen, who constitute the executive board, through which alone definite action is taken.

Among affairs which relate to a village as such, are to be named the construction and repair of the wall (if it has one), and the care of the gates (if they are closed at night), the establishment and supervision of fairs and markets, the engagement of theatrical companies, the organized watching of the crops, together with the punishment of persons detected in violating the rules which have been agreed upon, the building and repair of temples, the sinking of wells for the use of the village, or the cleaning of those which are already in use, and a great variety of other similar duties, depending upon the situation of the village and its traditions and circumstances.

It is a noteworthy fact that the government of China, while in theory more or less despotic, places no practical restrictions upon the right of free assemblage by the people for the consideration of their own affairs. The people of any village can if they choose meet every day in the year. There is no government censor present, and no restriction upon liberty of debate. The people can say what they like, and the local Magistrate neither knows nor cares what is said. The government has other security for itself than espionage, and by a system of graded responsibility, is able to hold all its subjects under strict control. But should insurrection break out, these popular rights might be extinguished in a moment, a fact of which all the people are perfectly well aware.

The methods of Chinese management being what they are, it

is not surprising that those who are in the position of headmen find it, or rather make it to their advantage to stay in it. The ways in which this comes about are numerous.

There is in every village an unceasing supply of matters which do not belong to the public, but which must be adjusted by some man or men who are in the habit of transacting business, and who not only know what is to be done but how to do it. There are always Chinese who like to engage in these affairs, such as the adjustment of domestic quarrels, differences between neighbours, and the like. The headmen of the village will be certain to be frequently called upon for services of this sort.

But such labours, onerous as they often are, will be acknowledged only by the thanks of those interested, and a participation in the inevitable final feast. It is quite otherwise with such public matters as the collection of material for public uses, and the disbursement of public funds. Every village has numerous enterprises which involve the handling of money, and these enterprises must be in the hands of those competent to take charge of them.

There is not in such cases that constant struggle between the "ins" and the "outs," which is seen in lands where the democracy is of a more flagrant type than in China. Yet even in China such contests do sometimes occur. We know of one village in which the public business had for a long time been monopolized by a band of men who had subjected themselves to the criticisms of those who, although younger, felt sure that they were not on that account the less capable. The result of the criticisms was that the incumbents withdrew from their places, leaving them to those who offered the criticisms, a method of adjustment which is known to be practiced in the government of the empire.

But it is probable that cases of such easy victory are relatively rare, for the reason that the "ins" have every opportunity to keep themselves in their position and they are for the most part not at all sensitive to criticism, being quite content to reap the substantial benefits of their position, and to leave the talking to spectators. In the ordinary matters of routine, it is easy for them to find abundant precedents for almost any irregularity, and to the Chinese precedents are most precious, as marking out the natural limits of human action.

In many villages but a small portion of the population can read well enough to inspect accounts, and many of those whose knowledge is equal to this strain upon it, have no practical familiarity with public business, with which they have never had any opportunity to become acquainted.

Many who clearly recognize the evils attending the methods in which the business of their village is managed, do not for two excellent reasons make any protest. In the first place, to do so would raise a storm about their heads, which they have no wish to encounter. Even if the movement should prove completely successful, and the present incumbents should all be removed from their places, it would be difficult, not to say impossible, to find others who would manage matters upon any plan essentially different. A change would be simply the removal of a well-fed swarm of flies, to make way for a set much more hungry, a substitution against which the fox in the fable wisely remonstrated. The Chinese wholly agree with the sagacious fox.

The course which matters take when complaint is really made, may be understood by an illustrative example with which the writer is acquainted. During one of the years in which the Yellow River made destructive breaks in central Shan-tung, an order was issued that all the counties in the province accessible to the river should furnish a certain quota of millet stalks to be used in the repair of the river-banks. These stalks were to be paid for in ready money by the government agents. But as some of the counties were situated more than two days' journey from the river-banks, the amount received for the stalks did not cover the cost of the feed of men and animals for so long a journey. Besides this, the government officials had a ready means by which to exercise complete control over those who brought the stalks, by refusing to take over the material or to weigh it until such time as the officials might be ready. By this means, both men and teams were kept on expense, so that at last the persons who hauled stalks were only too glad to be allowed to depart without any pay at all for the loads which they had brought.

Abuses of this sort were said to be exceedingly common at that time, although on subsequent occasions we have been assured by those who have taken stalks to river-embankment, that full pay in good money was invariably given. In the village to which we refer, the business of providing and delivering the stalks was put by the District Magistrate into the hands of an elderly headman, a literary graduate. This man naturally called about him some of his former pupils, who did the practical part of the work. They took stalks three times to the place of deposit, and received in payment about 70,000 cash. Taking advantage of the general uncertainty which prevailed in regard to payments, these managers rendered no accounts to the village, but proceeded to appropriate a certain part of their receipts to their own use.

Matters continued in this way for more than a year, when some of those who were dissatisfied, called a public meeting in a village temple, and demanded a clear account of receipts and expenses, which for reasons well understood, it was impossible to give. Finding that the affair was becoming serious, the graduate got some residents of the same village to "talk peace" to the excited villagers. Their argument was this: "If we press this matter, and take it before the District Magistrate, the old graduate, who is really altogether innocent, will lose his button and will be disgraced. The others concerned will all be beaten, and this will engender hatred and feuds which will last for generations." The middlemen then proposed that by way of settlement a feast should be prepared by the graduate, at which a representative of every surname in the village should be present, and this plan being adopted, because nothing else was feasible, the matter was buried in compulsory oblivion. This is a type of a large class of cases.

In many villages, there are those who are never so happy as when they are in a disturbance with others, and such men will be a thorn in the side of any "board of aldermen" to whose councils admission is not to be had. It is very common indeed to hear of lawsuits arising about village temples, and there is good reason to believe that it is exceptional to meet with a large ancestral temple, in connection with which quarrels have not arisen and perhaps lawsuits been prosecuted.

In some districts the temples are built rather from a general impulse to do as others do than from any sense of the need of such structures, which become a perpetual tax on the revenues of the people and a source of dispute. In such regions it is a common thing to meet with temples from which the priests have been ousted, or which they have voluntarily abandoned, finding the place too hot for them.

In one instance of this description, which occurred near the writer's home, a certain prominent headman set on foot a lawsuit which drove several priests from a Buddhist monastery, and left only one priest where before there had been many. After the priests had left, this headman kindly took charge of the temple lands, and absorbed the entire income himself to the exclusion of the priest, dispensing altogether with rendering any account whatever for the proceeds. Even the cart and the harness which belong to the temple, are in this man's yard as if they were his own.

Intelligent men of this village, when asked why some of them do not protest against this usurpation, always make the same reply: "Who wants to stir up a lawsuit, out of which he will gain nothing but loss? It is certainly no affair of mine." This particular village is scarcely a type of the average, but it is a very fair sample of the more flagrant cases in which a small knot of men fasten themselves upon a Chinese community, by the same process by which many years ago the Tweed ring saddled themselves upon the city of New York. If any objection is made to their procedure, the ring inquire disdainfully, in the language of Mr. Tweed, "What are you going to do about it?" And all the people hasten to reply, "Oh, nothing at all. It is all right as it is."

An instance of the facility with which trouble may arise in

village affairs was afforded in this same town, during one of the years in which heavy rains threatened the lands of the village. A part of these lands were situated in a region subject to inundation, and the rest on higher ground. As soon as the danger of a flood became apparent, the village headmen ordered relays of men to work on a bank, which was made of whatever soil was at hand, and in order to strengthen this bank, the standing millet was pulled up by the roots, and buried in the earthwork. Those whose crops were thus ruined, had for this loss no redress whatever. It is held that the exigency of a public need justifies any injury of this kind, the persons who benefit by the sacrifice, always largely in the majority, having no disposition to make up the incidental losses. Some days after this occurred, the headmen went about collecting a definite assessment from each acre of land in the village, for the purpose of paying for the labour upon the bank previously made. They visited the house of one of the men whose crops had been destroyed, at a time when he chanced to be away from home and were met by his son, who not only manifested no awe of the village authorities, but expressed his indignation at the destruction of the family crops, and declared that instead of being called upon to contribute to the cost of the ruin which had been wrought, his family ought to be reimbursed for their own losses. However compatible such a view may appear with abstract justice, to the minds of the village headmen this was nothing less than rank treason of the most dangerous type.

When the head of the family returned, it was to find that the headmen had already left the village on their way to the District city, to enter a complaint against him, as one who refused to pay his just dues to the defence of the village. A lawsuit begun upon such a basis meant nothing less than a calamity greater than any flood that was likely to overtake him, so the distracted father hastened to pursue the headmen with offers of adjustment, made through third parties. By dint of an immense amount of talking, the headmen were induced to return to the village, without entering the city and making a formal complaint.

245

The father of the offending lad then appealed to certain friends living in another village, to come and intercede for him with the outraged guardians of the welfare of his own village. In the course of the next forenoon, the persons who had been entrusted with this difficult task, made their way to the village, and had interviews with some of the headmen. It was impossible to get all of these men together at any one time, but one set was first seen, and then another, until the matter had been thoroughly discussed in all its bearings. These conferences, including plans of adjustment offered, modified, rejected, amended, and afterward brought up again and again, actually consumed the whole day, and all the next night until the crowing of the cocks announced the dawn, and it was not until daylight on the second day, that the weary and disgusted "middlemen" returned to their own village, having at last succeeded in securing a reduction of the proposed fine, which was to have been an exemplary one, to a merely nominal amount.

This instance is a type of countless cases everywhere in which the evil forces of Chinese society effect a coöperation of their own, seriously modifying all other social phenomena, and leading to results of great importance.

PART II

Village Family Life

XXII

VILLAGE BOYS AND MEN

There is a passage in one of the oldest Chinese Classics, the Book of Odes, which, in describing the palace of an ancient king, shows in a striking light the relative estimation at that remote time put upon boys and upon girls. After speaking of the dreams of the king, the poet adds a couple of stanzas, which, according to Dr. Legge's translation, are as follows:

> Sons shall be born to him; they will be put to sleep on couches;
> They will be clothed in robes; they will have sceptres to play with;
> Their cry will be loud.
> They will be (hereafter) resplendent with red knee-covers,
> The (future) king, the princes of the land.
> Daughters will be born to him. They will be put to sleep on the ground;
> They will be clothed with wrappers; they will have tiles to play with.
> It will be theirs neither to do wrong nor to do good.
> Only about the spirits and the food will they have to think,
> And to cause no sorrow to their parents.

From the sentiment of this poem alone it would be easy to determine the Chinese of to-day to be lineal descendants of their ancient ancestors.

The early years of a Chinese boy are spent in what, viewed from the experience of a decade later, must appear to him a condition of supreme happiness. He is welcomed to the household with a wild delight, to which it is wholly impossible for an Occidental to do any justice. He begins life on the theory that whatever he wants, that he must have; this theory is also the one acted upon

249

by those who have him in charge, to an extent which seems to us, who occupy the position of impartial critics, truly amazing. A Chinese mother is the literal slave of her children. If they cry, they must be coddled, most probably carried about, and at whatever expense, if it is possible to prevent such a terrible state of things. They must not be allowed to cry continuously. In this respect, at least, it does not appear that there is much distinction between the treatment of boys and girls.

The names given to Chinese children, like those of the babies of North American Indians, are frequently suggested by whatever happens first to attract the father's attention, such as Basket, Cart, etc. Each year of the cycle of twelve has an animal which "belongs to" it, as Dog, Cat, Chicken, Tiger, Horse or Monkey, and all these names are constantly employed. If when the child is born an old grandmother happens to be three score and ten, he is not improbably dubbed "Seventy." Many have no other appellation than a numerical one such as Three, Five, or Six, to the hopeless confusion of an inquirer. If the child seems to be of a good constitution he may receive the title of Stone, or Solid. Should he be plump, he is likely to be styled Little Fat One; if dark coloured, Little Black One. Bad Temper, and Little Idiot are common, and if all the previous children have died, the last one may go by the name of Great Repairs.

When the parents are peculiarly fearful lest an only boy should be made away with by malicious spirits, they often call him by a girl's name in order to deceive the powers of evil, and thus beat them at their own game. Another plan with the same end in view is a nominal adoption into another family, where the children spend at least a portion of their time, the spirits being thus hopelessly perplexed as to which family really owns the child! Slave Girl, and Old Woman are names sometimes given to boys under these conditions. A man who had more girls than he desired, called one of them Enough Hawks (Kou Ying), while another little maid was outfitted with the happy title "Ought-to-have-been-a-Boy" (Kai Tzŭ). Girls are frequently named for birds, fruits, and flowers.

All the preceding are "milk-names," or "small names," which strangers must be careful even should they know them, never to employ. No greater insult can be put upon an adult Chinese than to revile him in public by his "small name"—a by no means infrequent occurrence—which seems to convey the implication that the reviler knows all about his antecedents and holds them in supreme contempt.

It is a highly convenient arrangement of Chinese family nomenclature, that the names of each member of the same generation (within certain defined degrees of cousinship) furnish a clue to his relationship to the rest. Thus, if a man's surname is Wang, his family name (which can be either two characters or one) may be compounded with the character denoting Spring, in which case one brother might be called Wang Spring-Flowers, the next Wang Spring-Fragrance, a third Wang Spring-Fields, and so universally for that generation as far away among the cousins as the Spring influence penetrates. These family names are theoretically recorded in carefully kept registers, and must not be repeated in later generations, or only after the lapse of a due number of generations. Memorials sometimes appear in the Peking Gazette from high officials asking permission to have a family name altered, since a repeated title has inadvertently been taken.

This use of the same characters in Chinese family names has often been compared to the Anglo-Saxon habit of bestowing upon brothers names of which one syllable is constant, as Edward, Edwin, Edmund, Edgar, etc.

Besides the name, there is the "style," often much more in use than any other designation, which may be bestowed upon the owner by a friend. It is common by a respectful familiarity to prefix to the first character of the style, the honourific "Old," (Lao) making still another title. Thus supposing Mr. Wang Spring-Fragrance has the style of Illustrious Virtue, his common appellation may be Wang Old Illustrious, his other names being used as alternatives. The result of all this is that a single Chinese not infrequently appears to be three and sometimes four, since students have also their examination names, differing, strange to say, from any which they have hitherto borne. The confusion attending the addressing of Chinese letters in correspondence would be intolerable to an Occidental.

Aside from the ambiguities already mentioned, it sometimes appears to the writer of a letter a happy expedient to employ a title on the back of his epistle, known only to himself and to the recipient, to the great bewilderment of the persons through whose hands the missive may pass. We have seen a Chinese teacher invited to inspect the address of a letter of this sort, the destination of which neither he nor any one else could decide. Yet it subsequently turned out that the epistle was meant for his own son! With all this labyrinth of future complexity the village boy is very little concerned, often passing through life without any name at all to speak of.

In this connection it is worth noting that the foreigner in China suffers from a chronic embarrassment as to how to address a Chinese. There is in the language no term answering to our Mister or Master, the nearest equivalent being the words Elder-born or Seignor (Hsien-shêng). The expression properly connotes a Teacher in reality or by courtesy, and although applied indiscriminately to blind men (even if they should be beggars) will not serve for general use. Honourific terms abound, but in the rural regions these are not in use, and are but dimly comprehensible. On the principle that "Within the four seas all are brethren," it is the Chinese habit to assume the existence of a relationship, so that the passing stranger may appropriately call out to one whom he has never seen before: "Great elder-brother may I borrow your light and inquire whether this is the right road to Peking?" Should the person addressed be an old man, the title would be changed to Uncle or Grandfather. The fact that the term for an older uncle differs from that for a younger one, embarrasses the foreigner by forcing upon him a decision of the difficult question which one to use, for deciding which point he often has absolutely no data.

A Chinese married woman has literally no name at all, but only two surnames, her husband's and her father's, so that when these chance to be common ones, it is impossible by this means to discriminate one woman from another. If Chinese women are to be addressed by strangers at all, there is even more embarrassment than in the case of men. In some regions the term Elder-sister-in-law (sao-tzŭ) serves indiscriminately for any woman, but in others Aunt (la-niang) must be used, while in yet others nothing is appropriate but Grandmother (nai-nai) which elsewhere would be equivalent to Old Granny. When there happen to be three generations of women in the same family to dub them all "Grandmother" (especially if one of them is a girl in her teens just married) is flagrantly absurd. Beggars at the other gates clamour to have their "Aunts" bestow a little food, and the phrase Old Lady (lao T'ai-t'ai) is in constant use for any woman past middle life.

The age at which a boy is too large to be carried is a very indefinite one, and it is common to see distracted mothers staggering with their little goat-feet under the weight of children half their own size, lugging their offspring about for the reason that "they would not stand it" to be put down. A preparatory discipline of this nature is not adapted to teach children independence, self-control, or any useful lessons, and the result is such as might have been expected. But the Chinese child is an eminently practical being, and he finds by experience that, when there are half a dozen children smaller than himself, the period of his own supreme rule has passed away, and has passed away never to return. To this altered condition he soon learns to adapt himself.

Of that sympathy for childhood as such, which is so distinguishing a part of our modern civilization, an average Chinese father has no conception whatever. By this is not meant that he is not fond of his children, for the reverse is most palpably true. But he has no capacity for entering into the life of a child, and comprehending it. His fondness for his children is the result of the paternal instinct, and is not an intelligent and sympathetic appreciation of the mind of a child. He not only has no conception of such a thing, but he would not be able to understand what is meant by it, if the possibility of such sympathy were pointed out. The invariable reply to all suggestions, looking toward such sympathy coming from a foreigner, seems to be, "Why, he is only a mere child!" It is by the slow moulding forces of maturing life alone that the boy is expected to learn the lessons of life, and these lessons he must learn largely—though not altogether—by himself.

To most Chinese children, there is very little that is attractive in their own homes. The instinct of self-preservation does of course lead them to fly thither, as soon as they meet with any repulse from without, but this instinct they share with animals.

Chinese courtyards are almost invariably very contracted, and allow little scope for enterprising youth to indulge in any but the most crude and simple forms of amusement. The Chinese lad generally has but few toys, and those of the simplest and most clumsy description. At certain festivals, especially in the cities, one sees the children loaded down with all varieties of playthings often of a flimsy and highly inexpensive character. In the country the same phenomenon is observed wherever there has been a large fair, at which the provision for the children is always on a scale commensurate with their known wants. But of these articles made of earth, paper, bits of cloth, clay, reeds, sugar, and other perishable substances, nothing will be left when the next moon shall have completed its orbit. In regions where bamboo is to be had, there are a few more serviceable and less fragile articles constructed expressly for the children, and such articles doubtless have a longer lease of life.

That Chinese parents should take occasion to have a romp with their children, or even to engage with them in any game whatever, is, so far as we have observed, a thing wholly outside of the range of their wildest imagination. Children have very few games which can be played in the house, and the time which is to our little ones the cream of the whole day, that namely in which they can gather "around the evening lamp," is to the Chinese a period of dismal obscurity. By the dim light of a small and ill-trimmed wick, dipped into a few spoonfuls of crude vegetable oil, the evening's occupations are carried on as best they may be; but to a foreigner a Chinese home is at such times most ideally comfortless, especially if the season be winter. No wonder that those members of the family who can do so, are glad to crawl upon the more or less perfectly warmed k'ang, and wrap themselves in their wadded bedclothes. During the portion of his existence in which the father and the mother of the Chinese child most gladly forsake him, kind Morpheus takes him up, and claims him for his own.

The outdoor games of Chinese children are mostly of a tame and uninteresting type. Tossing bits of earth at a mark, playing shuttlecock with his toes and heels, striking a small stick sharpened at the ends so as to make it jump into a "city," a species of "fox and geese," a kind of "cat's-cradle," a variety of "jack-stones,"—these are among the most popular juvenile amusements in the rural regions with which we happen to be acquainted. Chinese cities have allurements of their own, some of which do not differ essentially from those found in other parts of the world than China. But even in the country, where restrictions are at a minimum, Chinese lads do not appear to take kindly to anything which involves much exercise. One does not ordinarily see them running races, as foreign boys of the same age cannot fail to do, and their jumping and climbing are of the most elementary sort. We have never heard of a crow which was so injudicious as to build its nest in a spot where it would be visible to the eye of an Anglo-Saxon boy, unless the owner of the eye had previously made a long journey with it to a distance from all human habitations. But Chinese crows build their huge nests in all sorts of trees, in and about every Chinese village. It is not

255

uncommon to see an old poplar with ten or twelve of these huge nests of sticks, which are undisturbed from year to year and from generation to generation.

The writer once counted twenty-four such nests in a single moderate sized elm, and this in the suburbs of a Chinese city. Buddhist teachings in regard to the sacredness of animal life do not suffice to account for the singular inviolability which crows' nests enjoy in China. In the spring they are sometimes defended with the query; "How would you like to have your house pulled down?" But in a region where every stick of fuel is precious, what sacredness can attach to a bushel or two of large twigs, when the crows have visibly done using them? Neither does superstition in regard to ill-luck arising from demolition of the nests of crows explain their security, although at first sight this may seem to be the case. Extensive inquiries have satisfied us that the true explanation is simply the natural one, that the Chinese boy is afraid to climb so high as a crow's-nest. "What if he should fall?" says every one when applied to for information on the point, and it is this unanswered and unanswerable question which seems to protect young Chinese crows from age to age.

The Chinese boy can seldom get access to running water; that is to say, the proportion of Chinese who can do so is infinitesimal. Most of them have no lakes, rivers, or ponds in which they can plunge and learn to swim, or in which they can fish. The village mud-hole is the nearest approach to the joys of a "watering-place" to which Chinese children can ordinarily aspire. These excavations are the hole whence the material for the village houses was originally dug. During the summer time these pits, many of them as large as a dry-dock, are filled to the brim with dirty water, and at such times they are sure to be surrounded by groups of children clad in the costume of the garden of Eden, enjoying one of the few luxuries of their mundane existence. When the boys are too large to indulge in this amusement, there is much reason to fear that most of them have taken their last bath, no matter to what age their lives may be prolonged!

Chinese Punch and Judy.

The Village Story-Teller.

If he cannot fish, neither can the Chinese boy go a-hunting, for in the most populous parts of the plains, of which so large a portion of the empire is composed, there is nothing to hunt. A few small birds, and the common hare, seem to constitute the objects most frequently shot, but except in the case of the limited number of those who make a business of securing such game to sell as a means of support, there are very few persons who devote their energies to any form of hunting. Indeed, the instinct which is said to lead the average Englishman to remark "It is a fine day, let us go and kill something," is totally lacking in the Chinese.

In those relatively limited parts of the empire where ice forms to a sufficient thickness to bear the weight of human beings, one does see considerable frolicking upon frozen rivers and ponds. But the propulsion of the ice-sleds with passengers is a matter of business with those boatmen who during the season of navigation have no other means of earning a living. Chinese children do not take to them as our boys do to sleds, and even if they wish to do so, their parents would never dream of furnishing the children with such an ice-sled simply for amusement. To earn one, as a boy at home earns a sled or a pair of skates, by doing extra work, by picking up old iron, and other similar expedients, would be for a Chinese lad an impossibility.

If the amusements of the Chinese lad are relatively scanty and uninteresting, there is one feature of his life which is a fixed fact, and upon which nothing is allowed to intrude. This is his work. The number of Chinese children within any given area is literally incalculable, but it may be safely laid down as a general truth, that by far the larger part of these children are for the greater part of their time made to do some useful work. There is scarcely any handicraft in which even the very smallest children cannot be utilized, and it is for this reason in part that hereditary occupations are so commonly the rule. The child bred up to one mode of physical activity is fitted for that, if he is fitted for nothing else. If he is the son of a farmer, there is a very small portion of the year during which there is not some definite work for him to do, by way of assisting in the cultivation of the land. This is no doubt true of farming everywhere, but the unfailing industry of the Chinese and the heavy pressure of the common poverty give to this fact an emphasis not so strongly felt in other lands.

But even if the work on the land were all done, which is never the case until the winter has actually set in, there are two occupations at which the children may be set at any time, and at which more myriads of young persons are probably employed, than in any other portion of the planet. These two employments are gathering fuel and collecting manure. In a land where the expense of transportation forbids the use of coal in places distant even a few miles from the mouth of the pit, it is necessary to depend upon what comes from the soil in any particular place, for fuel to cook the food and furnish such warmth as can be got. Not a stalk, not a twig, not a leaf is wasted. Even at the best, the products of a field ill suffice in the item of fuel for the wants of those who own it. The Chinese habit of constantly drinking hot water, which must be furnished afresh as often as it cools and for each chance comer, consumes a vast amount of fuel over and above what would be strictly required for the preparation of food. The collection and storage of the fuel supply is an affair second in importance only to the gathering of the crops. But in every village, a considerable although varying proportion of the population is to be found who own no land. These people pick up a precarious living as they can, by working for others who have land, but their remuneration is slight, and often wholly insufficient for the food supply of the many mouths clamouring to be filled.

Farm labourers can be hired by the year in Shan-tung, for a sum equal to not more than five dollars in gold, with food but no perquisites. If the year has an intercalary month the labourer sometimes gets less than two cents a day. When refugees from regions flooded by the Yellow River abound, workmen can be obtained at merely nominal wages.

The writer has known an able-bodied boy engaged for a year for a sum equal to about a dollar and a half (gold). In another case a lad was offered about a dollar for a year's toil, and was required to find some one as security that he would not abscond!

For the fuel wherewith to cook the exiguous supplies of this uncertain food, the family is wholly dependent upon what the children can scratch together. Any intermission of this labour is scarcely less a check upon the means of existence, than the interruption of the work of the bread-winner himself. In this dismal struggle for a basket full of leaves and weeds, the children of China expend annually incomputable millenniums of work.

In the midst of such a barren wilderness as constitutes the life of most Chinese children, anything which breaks the dull monotony is welcomed with keen joy. The feast-days, the annual or semiannual fairs held at some neighbouring town, an occasional theatrical exhibition, the humbler Punch and Judy performance, the peripatetic story-teller, the unfailing succession of weddings and funerals, and most of all the half-month holiday at New Year all serve as happy reliefs to the unceasing grind of daily toil.

There is one incident in the life of the Chinese lad, which assumes in his eyes some degree of importance, to which most Occidental boys are strangers. This is the ceremony of donning the cap, in other words of becoming a man and his marriage. The age at which this takes place is far from being a fixed one, but is often in the vicinity of sixteen. The customs observed vary widely, in some rural districts they frequently consist in nothing more exciting than the playing by a band of music in the evening before his marriage, and a visit on the part of the young man to each house in the village where he makes his prostration, much as at New Year, and is henceforth to be considered a full-grown man, and is protected to some extent from snubs because he is "only a child."

The more conspicuous part of the affair, however, is the wedding. This proceeding is based upon principles so radically different from those to which we are accustomed, that it is generally hard for a Westerner to become reconciled either to the Chinese theory or to the practice. To us, marriage seems suitable for persons who have attained, not merely years of puberty, but a certain maturity of development compatible with the new relations which they now assume. We regard the man and wife as the basis and centre of a new family, and there is ancient and adequate authority for the doctrine that they should leave father and mother. In China it is altogether otherwise. The boy and girl who are married are not a new family, but the latest branch in a tall family tree, independent of which they have no corporate existence.

It is by no means uncommon for boys to be married at the age of ten, although this is regarded as a trifle premature. The physical, intellectual, or moral development of the parties concerned has nothing whatever to do with the matter of their marriage, which is an affair controlled by wholly different considerations. Sometimes it is hastened because an old grandmother is in feeble health and insists upon seeing the main business of life done up before she is called away. Sometimes the motive is to settle the division of a piece of property so that it shall be impossible for the elder heirs to retreat from the settlement. Quite as often the real motive for hastening the wedding is the felt need in the boy's family of an additional servant, which need will be supplied by the introduction of a new bride. It is for this reason that so many Chinese women are older than their husbands. When they are betrothed, the bigger they are the better, because they can do all the more work.

To a Chinese, there is no more sense of incongruity in marrying a little slip of a boy, simply because he is young, and perhaps not more than half the size of his bride, than there would be in playing checkers with buttons, and then crowning the first button that happened to get to the king-row. What signified whether the button is a small one or a large one, since it has reached the last row, and has now a set of moves of its own, a fact which must be recognized by doubling itself. It is not otherwise with the Chinese boy. He is a double button, it is true, but he is nothing but a button still, and a small one, and is only an insignificant part of a wide and complicated game.

During the celebration of a Chinese wedding it does not strike the spectator that the bridegroom is the centre of interest, and the bride is so only for the time being, and in consequence of the curiosity which is felt to see what sort of a bargain the family has made in getting her. The young man is ordered out of the apartment where he has been kept in ambush—according to the custom in some regions—like an ox for the sacrifice. He is to fall upon his knees at a word of command, and kotow with intermittent sequence to a great variety of persons, until his knees are stiff and his legs lame. His eyes are fixed upon the ground, as if in deepest humility, and the most awkward Chinese youth will perform the details of this trying ordeal with a natural grace, with which the most well-bred Occidental youth could scarcely hope to vie, and which he assuredly could not hope to surpass.

When the complicated protracted ceremonies are all over, our young lad is, it is true, a married man, but he is not the "head" of any family, not even of his own. He is still under the same control of his father as before, his bride is under the control of the mother-in-law, to a degree which it is difficult for us to comprehend. If the youthful husband is trying to learn to compose essays, his marriage does not at all interrupt his educational enterprise and as soon as the ceremonies are over he goes on just as before. If he is dull, and cannot make the "seven empty particles"—the terror of the inexpert Chinese essayist—fit into his laborious sentences to the satisfaction of his teacher, he is not unlikely to be beaten over the head for his lack of critical acumen, and can then go weeping home to have his wife stick a black gummy plaster over the area of his chastisement. We have known a Chinese boy who had the dropsy in an aggravated form but who could not be persuaded to take a single dose of medicine that was at all bitter. If he was pressed to do so by his fond mother, he either fell into a passion, or cried. If he was not allowed to eat two whole watermelons at a time his tactics were the same, a domestic scene either of violent temper, or of dismal howling grief. He was merely prolonging into youth the plan universally adopted in the childhood of Chinese children. Yet this sensitive infant of seventeen had been married for several years, and leaves a widow to mourn the circumstance that drugs, dropsy, and watermelons, have blighted her existence.

It is far from being an infrequent circumstance for boys who have been married early, on occasion of some grievance, to run crying to their mothers for comfort as they have been in the habit of doing, and to be met with the chilling inquiry: "Why do you come to me? If you want anything, go to Her!"

By a strange exception to the otherwise almost uniform prudishness of Chinese practice, on the occasion of a wedding it is common—although by no means universal—for guests to take the liberty of going into the apartment set apart for the married pair, inspecting the bride as if she were an animal just purchased at a market, openly expressing whatever criticisms may occur. In this as in everything else customs differ greatly, but the phrase "playing pranks in the bridal room" (nao tung-fang) testifies to the frequency of the occurrence. In the year 1893, a native newspaper of Canton reported a case in which the bride was actually killed in this way, by having cold water poured on her, the perpetrators being fined $200 for "consolation money," and all the costs of remarrying.

It is a postulate of Chinese ethics that no branch of any family should be allowed to be without its living representative, in order that the ancestral rites may be duly performed. As it constantly happens that there are no sons, it becomes necessary to adopt those of other brothers, or failing these the grandson of an uncle, or the great-grandson of a granduncle. Sons thus adopted are on the same footing as if they were own children, and cannot be displaced by such sons born later. The universality of these adoptions often makes it difficult to ascertain with precision the real relationship of a man to others of his family. Sometimes he continues to call his real father by that title, and sometimes he terms the uncle who has adopted him his "father" and his own father "uncle." Again, he may be nominally adopted by an uncle, but continue to live with his own parents as before. The adoption of relatives is expressed by the general term "crossing over," (kuo) and it is a sufficiently important feature of Chinese life to serve as the subject for a treatise rather than for a paragraph. It enters into the warp and woof of all Chinese family life, which cannot be comprehended without taking into account the substratum upon which the universal practice rests. While it is rooted in ancestral worship it is kept alive among even the poorest classes in the social scale by their very poverty. If a man has no heir he can be compelled to adopt some one of the numerous candidates who are thirsting to enter into prospective possession of even a small holding. But whoever is thus adopted becomes responsible for the funeral expenses of the one who adopts him. Innumerable lawsuits arise out of these complex conditions.

If there are no suitable persons for adoption among the family or clan of the adopter, he is often obliged to content himself with the son of his sisters, or even the grandchildren of his aunts. To our thought one "nephew" is as good as another, but it is otherwise with a Chinese, to whom the children of his sister (being of a different surname) are much farther off than those of his brothers. Besides this, on occasion of the death of the adopter, the position of a sister's son is liable to be very insecure. Rather than take such an heir many Chinese will pick up a mere stranger, but in this case he can be easily got rid of should he turn out unsatisfactory. Outsiders thus adopted although they may be as filial and in every way as satisfactory as an own son, never escape the stigma of being only "picked up," and this taint lasts to distant generations. A man told the writer that he was wholly without influence in the village where he was born, since his grandfather had been adopted as a stranger.

There is still another method of securing a son which is far less common than we should expect it to be. This is that of finding a suitable husband for a daughter, and then adopting him as a son. By this means the parents are enabled to have the services of an own daughter all their lives—a rare privilege in China, and an adopted heir of this kind is certainly much more closely bound to the family than any other of a different family would be likely to be. But there are not many clans which do not have a number of candidates available for an adoptive vacancy. It would be necessary to conciliate whoever was entitled to adoption by dividing the property with him, which, in the case of those with but small resources, would be tantamount to perpetual pauperism. For this reason most cases of "calling a son-in-law" occur in families where there are no sons of brothers or cousins available.

As a rule every Chinese is as wide awake to opportunities for laying claim to the property of some one else, as a cat apparently asleep is to seize an injudiciously venturesome bird. The writer is acquainted with a man who had adopted a son-in-law in legal form, but who at the funeral of his own father was surprised to see a large band of strangers enter his courtyard clad in mourning, and set up a simultaneous wail for their "Uncle," "Grandfather," etc., according to the alleged relationship. Upon inquiry he learned that they came from a village at some distance, and bearing the same surname as the deceased had determined to claim kinship with him in order to fall heirs to the property which consisted of but little more than enough to support a moderate sized family. The result was a lawsuit in which the pretenders being unable to produce any family register to the purpose, were severely beaten by the District Magistrate as a penalty for their presumption.

One is constantly surprised in China to hear that a Chinese whose name he knows perfectly well, has taken an entirely different surname, so that Mr. Wang Spring-Flowers suddenly appears as Mr. Ma Illustrious-Virtue. This is called "reverting to the original name," and may be due to any one of a great variety of causes. Even while these lines are being committed to paper, a friend of the writer has called to mention the experiences through which he has recently passed, a résumé of which may throw a little light on the Chinese theory and practice of adoption. This man is the second of four brothers, the eldest of whom was adopted into a somewhat distant branch of the family, and has three sons. Number two has two sons, the youngest of whom is adopted by number three, who has none of his own. Number four died some time ago without a son. The funeral has never been held, and the body has been encoffined awaiting a favourable time, that is to say, a period of financial prosperity. Number four owed to a grain-shop in which numbers two and three are interested, several hundred strings of cash. To pay up this debt and to have a proper funeral, would require the sale of all the forty acres of land, so that the right of adoption has not seemed worth contesting. But of late a son of number one has set up a claim to this inheritance, and it is this which has been in active dispute for a period of twelve days. To adjust the matter, "peace-talkers" have been summoned to the number of thirty-eight, many of them literary graduates. There have been angry disputes between them and some of the members of the family, and an actual fight. The "peace-talkers" were reviled, and took revenge by beating the son of number one who was in fault. This involved fresh complications, which had just been settled by a final feast.

During the course of the intricate controversies the eight and thirty men had by no means omitted to eat and drink (one of the leading functions of "peace-talkers" and for the sake of which many quarrels are purposely stirred up, and many more kept unsettled for long periods). They consumed in all seventy catties of wine, and a hundred more of bread-cakes, and the total cost to number two is about two hundred and thirty strings of cash, one hundred of which are paid by number two to number one's family as "consolation money." Yet in this whole matter the financial interest of number two is absolutely nil!

Another of the many devices which the Chinese have chosen for perpetuating a branch of the family which might otherwise become extinct, is to have a single individual represent two branches. Thus suppose there are two brothers only one of whom has a son, he may be married to two wives, one for each branch.

The establishment must be a double one, and he will probably be obliged to divide his time equally between his partners, even having to change all his clothing in going from one house to the other. It is needless to remark that the jealousies thus provoked are such as would destroy any home.

If there is very little sentiment connected with the introduction of a daughter-in-law into a family, on the part of the husband's family at least, there is often not much more on the occasion of her death. But this is generally regretted, if for no other reason, on account of the trouble and expense involved. Perhaps there is no single particular in which the Orient and the Occident differ more widely than in the utter disregard of Orientals for what we understand by privacy and for quiet. The lack of the latter is indeed often vaguely felt, but as it is a blessing known only by the imaginative faculty and never from experience, its absence has none of the intolerable features which we should associate with it. The moment that any Chinese is ill, the first step is to send in every direction to notify all sorts and grades of relatives, many of whom will feel it their stern duty to drop whatever they are doing, no matter what its importance, to go, and "take a look." This inspection not infrequently extends for days and sometimes for weeks, when the presence of the relative has not the smallest relation to the care of the sick person, except as a hinderance by adding to the throng that hover over the patient, each with his endless questions as to how he feels now, and each with fertile suggestions as to articles of food vying with one another in preposterousness. Few of us would not welcome death as a relief from the experiences incident to serious illness under Chinese conditions, but under these conditions all Chinese are born, live, and die.

If a sick person is considered to be beyond the possibility of recovery, the next step is to "put on the clothes," that is, those in which he is to be buried, a process which involves pulling him about to an extent which it is distressing to contemplate. In the case of old men there are sometimes angry disputes about the property in the immediate presence of death, and in that of wives—especially younger ones—if there is any considerable property, it will not be strange if the house is visited by relays of go-betweens intent upon proposing an eligible successor to the one about to depart, so as to be certain to forestall other offers. These negotiations may take place in the immediate presence of the dying woman, perhaps two or more strangers striving at the same time to get a hearing with their rival proposals!

The writer is acquainted with a family in which this took place, and one of the offers was accepted, but the sick woman contrived not to die after all! The agreement, however, was valid, and the prospectively stricken husband thus found himself provided with two lawful wives, each of whom subsequently bore him sons. Strange to say the family life is in this instance a comparatively peaceful one. Should a wife die, it is often a short time before the marriage of the next one takes place, an interval regulated not by sentiment, but by the difficulty of raising funds. Soon after the wedding may come the funeral of the predecessor.

In theory a Chinese lad becomes of age at sixteen, but as a practical thing he is not his own master while any of the generation above him within the five degrees of relationship remain on the mundane stage. To what extent these relatives will carry their interference with his affairs, will depend to a large extent upon their disposition, and to some extent upon his own. In some households there is a great amount of freedom, while in others life is a weariness and an incessant vexation because Chinese social arrangements effectually thwart Nature's design in giving each human being a separate personality, which in China is too often simply merged in the common stock, leaving a man a free agent only in name.

Taking it in an all around survey there is very little in the life of the village boy to excite one's envy. As we have already seen, he generally learns well two valuable lessons, and the thoroughness with which they are mastered does much to atone for the great defects of his training in other regards. He learns obedience and respect for authority, and he learns to be industrious. In most cases, the latter quality is the condition of his continued existence and those who refuse to submit to the inexorable law, are disposed of by that law, to the great advantage of the survivors. But of intellectual independence, he has not the faintest conception or even a capacity of comprehension. He does as others do, and neither knows nor can imagine any other way. If he is educated, his mind is like a subsoil pipe, filled with all the drainage which has ever run through the ground. A part of this drainage originally came, it is true, from the skies, but it has been considerably altered in its constituents since that time; and a much larger part is a wholly human secretion, painfully lacking in chemical purity. In any case this is the content of his mind, and it is all of its content.

If, on the other hand, the Chinese youth is uneducated, his mind is like an open ditch, partly vacant, and partly full of whatever is flowing or blowing over the surface. He is not indeed destitute of humility; in fact he has a most depressing amount of it. He knows that he knows nothing, that he never did, never shall, never can know anything, and also that it makes very little difference what he knows. He has a blind respect for learning, but no idea of gathering any crumbs thereof for himself. The long, broad, black and hopeless shadow of practical Confucianism is over him. It means a high degree of intellectual cultivation for the few, who are necessarily narrow and often bigoted, and for the many it means a lifetime of intellectual stagnation.

XXIII

CHINESE COUNTRY GIRLS AND WOMEN

The Chinese are as practical a people as ever had a national existence, and we know of no reason to suppose that the Chinese ever had the least doubt that a substantial equality of the sexes in point of numbers is a condition of the continued propagation of the race. Certainly no race was ever more careful to keep itself propagated, or has ever met with greater success in the undertaking. Yet the Chinese are almost the only people boasting an ancient and developed civilization who despise their own daughters who are married into the families of others, and are by that process lost to their own because according to ancient custom they can offer no sacrifices for their parents when the latter are dead. It is for this reason that the popular saying declares that the most ideally excellent daughter (literally a daughter with the virtues of the eighteen Lo-hans) is not equal to a splay-footed son. This sentiment is endorsed by all Chinese consciously and unconsciously, in a manner to show that it is interwoven with the very fibres of their being. Its ultimate root is the same as that of so many other human opinions, pure selfishness.

The Chinese girl when she makes her first appearance in the world is very likely to be unwelcome, though this is by no means invariably the case. The ratio in which fortune-tellers allot happiness is generally about five sons to two daughters. "Whatsoever is more than these cometh of evil." With theories like those of the Chinese about the unavailability of daughters for the performance of ancestral rites, and with the Chinese nature as it is, it is not to be wondered at that the great pressure of poverty leads to the crime of infanticide upon an enormous scale. For aught that appears, this has always been the case. It is not that the Chinese conscience does not recognize the murder of girl babies as wrong, but that the temptation to such murder, especially the temptation to the disappointed and often abused mother, is too strong to be resisted by any motives which have the opportunity to act upon her.

Much has already been done by those who have had most opportunity to learn the facts, toward exhibiting the real practice of the Chinese in the matter of destroying female infants. Yet no more can be safely predicated than that this is a crime which to some extent everywhere prevails, and in some places to such a degree as seriously to affect the proportion of the sexes. It seems to be most common in the maritime provinces of the southern part of China, in some districts of which it is by the Chinese themselves regarded as a terrible and a threatening evil. Native tract societies publish books exhorting the people against the practice, and magistrates occasionally issue proclamations forbidding it, but it is evident that the nature of the offence is such that no laws can touch it, and nothing short of the elevation of the mothers themselves to a far higher point of view than they now occupy, can have any permanent effect upon Chinese female infanticide.

Next to the destruction of the lives of female infants, the Chinese practice most revolting to our Western ideas is the sale of their daughters, at all periods from infancy up to a marriageable age. The usages of different parts of the empire vary widely, but the sale of girls, like infanticide, seems to flourish most in the maritime provinces of the south, where it is conducted as openly as any other traffic. That the parents are generally impelled to this extreme step simply by the pressure of poverty we are quite ready to believe. Yet the knowledge that the girl must be separated from her family at a later period, and that this parting is irrevocable, must tend to reconcile many Chinese parents to an anticipation, by a few years, of the inevitable. Of the miseries which girls who have been thus sold are likely to endure, it is unnecessary to speak in detail, but enough is known on the subject to lead us to regard the practice with horror. If the parents do not feel able to keep their daughter until she is old enough to be married, and yet do not wish to sell her, Chinese custom has invented another expedient, which is a compromise between the two. This is the well-known "rearing-marriage," by which the girl is made over to the family into which she is to be married, and is by that family brought up, and married whenever their convenience dictates. There are manifest and grave objections to this practice, but there can be no doubt that it is far better than the custom of child marriages, which lead to so much wretchedness in India. In some instances the relations with the family of the girl are wholly broken off, when she is taken for a "rearing-marriage," and in all cases it is regarded as a confession of poverty and weakness, which places the girl's family at much more than their usual disadvantage, at best sufficiently great. When a girl is brought up in the family the son of which is to become her future husband, it is of course wholly out of the question that the parties should not have the fullest opportunities to become acquainted with each other's disposition, however they may be forbidden by usage to speak to one another. There is and can be very little sentiment about Chinese matches, but anything which tends to make the parties to one of these matches better able to adapt themselves to the inevitable friction of after life, cannot fail to have its advantages. Whether the parties to a "rearing-marriage" are or are not on the whole happier than those married in the ordinary way, is a question which no Chinese would be likely to ask, for the reason that he has no associations connecting marriage with happiness, but rather the reverse, and if the question is proposed by a foreigner, he is not likely to be made much the wiser by the replies which he receives.

The practice of binding the feet of Chinese girls is familiar to all who have the smallest knowledge of China, and requires but the barest mention. It is almost universal throughout China, yet with some conspicuous exceptions, as among the Hakkas of the south, an exception for which it is not easy to account. The custom forcibly illustrates some of the innate traits of Chinese character, especially the readiness to endure great and prolonged suffering in attaining to a standard, merely for the sake of appearances. There is no other non-religious custom peculiar to the Chinese which is so utterly opposed to the natural instincts of mankind, and yet which is at the same time so dear to the Chinese, and which would be given up with more reluctance.

It is well known that the greatest emperor who ever sat upon the throne of China dared not risk his authority in an attempt to put down this custom, although his father had successfully imposed upon the Chinese race the wearing of the queue as a badge of subjection. A quarter of a millennium of Tartar rule seems to have done absolutely nothing toward modifying the practice of foot-binding in favour of the more rational one of the governing race, except to a limited extent in the capital itself. But a few li away from Peking, the old habits hold their iron sway. The only impulse toward reform of this useless and cruel custom originated with foreigners in China, and was long in making itself felt, which it is now, especially in the central part of the empire, beginning to be.

The observations which may be made with regard to the industry of Chinese boys, are equally applicable—mutatis mutandis—to Chinese girls. In all lands and in all climes, "woman's work is never done," and this is most especially true of China, where machinery has not yet expelled the primitive processes of what is literally manufacture, or work by the hand. The care of silk-worms, and the picking, spinning, and weaving of cotton, are largely the labour of women, to which the girls are introduced at a very early age. The sewing for a Chinese family is a serious matter, especially as the number of families who can afford to hire help in this line is a very trifling proportion. But aside from this employment, in which a Chinese girl who expects to be acceptable to the family of her mother-in-law must be expert, girls can also be made useful in almost any line of home work to which the father may be devoted. In the country districts all over the empire, boys and girls alike are sent out to scratch together as much fuel as possible, for the preparation of the food, and this continues in the case of the girls until they are too large to go to any distance from home. It is not an unmeaning appellation, which is given to girls generally, that of ya-t'ou, or "slave-girl," used just as we should say "daughter." To a foreigner, this sounds much like the term "nigger" applied to black men, but to the Chinese there is a fitness in the designation, which they refuse to surrender.

With the exception of such limited raids as she may have been able to make in early childhood, and occasional visits to relatives, most Chinese girls never go anywhere to speak of, and live what is literally the existence of a frog in a well.[2] Tens of thousands of them have never been two miles away from the village in which they happened to be born, with the occasional exception of the visit to the mother's family just mentioned, where they are not improbably regarded as terrible beings who cannot be exterminated, but who are to be as much as possible repressed. If the nieces on the mother's side are numerous, as is often the case, there is some reason for dread of the visits, on the part of the bread-winners, for no Chinese mother can be dissociated from her flock of children, whose appetites are invariably several horse-power strong, and who, like their elders, are all excessively fond of enjoying the pleasure of eating at some one else's expense.

Women Preparing Food.

On the Way to the Feast.

It is when the married daughters of a large family have all returned to their parents to spend a few days or weeks, that the most dramatic scenes of childhood occur. Self-control and unselfishness have not been a feature in the culture of any one of the numerous cousins thus brought together in a cluster which frequently resembles those on the inside of a beehive. Each of the young generation has the keenest instinct for getting as much of the best of what is to be had as any one else, and if possible more. This leads to occasional "scenes of confusion, and creature complaints," in which each small participant publishes his or her version of the particular squabble in piercing tones, which soon summon the whole establishment to the scene of action. Judicious parents would punish the children all round for their complicity in such a quarrel, which is most often based upon alleged or supposed inequalities in distribution of food. But Chinese parents are seldom judicious, and the most that can be expected is that the mother will call off her child or children, and "yell" it, or them. "Yelling" a person is the act of proclaiming in a loud and piercing voice the disapprobation on the part of the "yeller" of the conduct of the "yellee," often accompanied by reviling language, and frequently also with promises to "beat" and "kill" the said "yellee" in the event of further provocation. These remarks are interpreted by the "yellee" as a hint to stop, a feat which is at length accomplished after a period of more or less spasmodic and convulsive recrimination.

But if, as often happens, each of the mothers feels called upon from a high sense of duty to take a firm stand for the rights of her offspring, the case becomes much more serious. Each of the mothers will then scream simultaneously, to the accompaniment of the wails, yells, and reviling of the whole half-dozen or more of her posterity, while above the general clamour may be distinctly caught the shrill shrieks of the grandmother, whose views, whatever difficulty they may have in getting themselves heard, must eventually prevail when peace once more reigns in the domestic teapot. After one of these family cyclones, the atmosphere gradually becomes cleared again, and things go on as before; but we have known a particularly spirited married daughter, who exhibited her dissatisfaction with the terms of settlement of a dispute of this sort by refusing to speak to her sisters for some days together.

With the humdrum routine of her life at home, the occasional visits to relatives, and now and then a large fair or a theatrical exhibition, the Chinese girl grows to be what we should call a "young schoolgirl," by which time all her friends begin to be very uneasy about her. This uneasiness, we need scarcely remark, has not the smallest connection with her intellectual nature, which, so far as any culture which it receives is concerned, might as well be non-existent. Unless her father happens to be a schoolmaster, and at home with nothing to do, he never thinks of teaching his daughter to read. Even in the case of boys, this would be exceptional and irregular, but in the case of girls it is felt to be preposterous. And why? asks the incredulous foreigner. It will take the average Chinese a long time to explain the nature of his objection, and when he does so he will not have stated the whole of the case, nor have gone to the root of the matter. The real difficulty is that to educate a girl is like weeding the field of some other man. It is like putting a gold chain around the neck of some one else's puppy, which may at any moment be whistled off, and then what will have become of the chain? It is a proverbially mean man in China, who, when marrying his daughter, wants to be paid for the food he has wasted upon her up to the date of marriage. But the expression illustrates clearly one of the underlying assumptions of Chinese society, that it is the body of the girl for which the parents are responsible, and not the mind. To almost any Chinese it would probably appear a self-evident proposition that to spend time, strength, and much more money in educating the daughter-in-law of some one else is a sheer waste. But, you say to him, she is your daughter. "Not after she is married," he replies; "she is theirs, let them educate her themselves if they want her educated." "Why should I teach her how to read, write and reckon, when it will never do me any good?" With which utilitarian inquiry, the education of most Chinese girls has been banished from human thought for the space of some millenniums.

The anxiety which all her friends begin to feel about a Chinese girl, as soon as she attains any considerable size, is exhibited in the inquiries which are made about her whenever she happens to be spoken of. These inquiries do not concern her character or her domestic accomplishments, much less her intellectual capacity—of which she has, theoretically, none to speak of—but they may all be summed up in the single phrase, "Is she said?" meaning by the term "said" "betrothed." If the reply should be in the negative, the intelligence is received in much the same way as we should receive the information that a foreign child had been allowed to grow to the age of sixteen without having been taught anything whatever out of books. "Why?" we should say, "what is the explanation age of this strange neglect?" The instinctive feeling of a Chinese in regard to a girl is that she should be betrothed as soon as possible. This is one of the many points in regard to which it is almost impossible for the Chinese and the Anglo-Saxon to come to terms. To the latter the betrothal of a mere child, scarcely in her teens, is a piece of absolute barbarity.

As soon as a Chinese girl is once betrothed, she is placed in different relations to the universe generally. She is no longer allowed such freedom as hitherto, although that may have been little enough. She cannot go anywhere, because it would be "inconvenient." She might be seen by some member of the family into which she is to marry, than which it is hardly possible to think of anything more horrible. "Why?" the irrepressible Occidental inquires; and is quenched by the information that "it would not be proper."

The imminent risk that the girl might in some unguarded moment be actually seen by the family of the future mother-in-law is a reason why so few engagements for girls are made in the town in which the girl lives, an arrangement which would seem to be for the convenience of all parties in a great variety of ways. It would put a stop to the constant deceptions practiced by the middle-women, or professional match-makers, whose only object is to carry through whatever match has been proposed, in order to reap the percentage which will accrue to the agent. It would do away with the waste of time and money involved in transporting brides from one of their homes to the other, often at great inconvenience and loss. It would make the interchange of little courtesies between the families easy and frequent. But for all these advantages the Chinese do not seem to care, and the most frequent explanation of the neglect of them is that there would be the risk already mentioned. When these two families are such as would in the ordinary course of events be likely to meet, nothing is more amusing to a foreigner than to watch the struggles which are made to avert such a catastrophe. One is reminded of some of our childhood's games, in which one party is "poison" and the other party is liable to be "poisoned" and must at all hazards keep out of the way. The only difference between the cases is that in the Chinese game, each party is afraid of being "poisoned," and will struggle to prevent it. There is one set of circumstances, however, in which, despite their utmost efforts, Fate is too much both for the poisoners and the poisoned. If during the betrothal a death of an older person takes place in the family of the mother-in-law, it is generally thought necessary that the girl (who is considered as already "belonging" to that family) should be present and should perform the same reverence to the coffin of the deceased as if she had been already married. She is (theoretically) their daughter; why should she not come and lament like the rest?[3] If it is possible to arrange it, however, the marriage will be hastened, in the event of a death of a person belonging to an older generation, even if a later date had been previously set.

To a foreigner, the Chinese habit of early engagements appears to have no single redeeming feature. It hampers both families with no apparent corresponding advantages, if indeed there are advantages of any kind. It assumes, what is far from certain, and often not at all likely, that the relative position of the two families will continue to be the same. This assumption is contradicted by universal experience. Time and change happen to all, and the insecurity of human affairs is nowhere more manifest than in the tenure of Chinese property. Families are going up and coming down all the time. It is a well-settled principle in China that matches should be between those who are in the same general circumstances. Disregard of this rule is sure to bring trouble. But if early betrothals are the practice, the chances of material alteration in the condition of each of the families are greatly increased. When he is engaged, the character of the boy, upon which so much of a bride's happiness is to depend, has not perhaps been formed. Even if it has been formed, it is generally next to impossible for the girl's family to learn anything authentic as to what the character is, though to all appearance it would be so easy for them to ascertain by latent methods. But as a rule, it would appear that they do not concern themselves much about the matter after the engagement is proposed and accepted, and at no time do they give it a hundredth part of the investigation which it seems to us to warrant. If the boy becomes a gambler, a profligate, or dissipated in any other way, there is no retreat for the family of the girl, no matter to what extremities they may be driven. Chinese violation of the most ordinary rules of prudence and common sense in the matter of the betrothal of their daughters is, to a Westerner, previous to experience and observation, almost incredible.

A Chinese marriage engagement begins when the red cards have been interchanged, ratifying the agreement. These are in some districts formidable documents, almost as large as a crib-blanket, and are very important as evidence in case of future trouble. It is very rare to hear of the breaking of a marriage engagement in China, though such instances do doubtless occur. In a case of this sort the card of the boy's family had been delivered to the other family, at which point the transaction is considered to be definitely closed. But an uncle of the betrothed girl, although younger than the father of the girl, created a disturbance and refused to allow the engagement to stand. This made the matter very serious, but as the younger brother was inflexible, there was no help for it but to send the red acceptance card back by the middleman who brought it. This also was a delicate matter, but a Chinese is seldom at a loss for expedients when a disagreeable thing must be done. He selected a time when all the male members of the boy's family were in the wheatfield, and then threw the card declining the match into the yard of the family of the boy, and went his way. None of the women of the family could read, and it was not until the men returned that it was discovered what the document was. The result was a lawsuit of portentous proportions, in which an accusation was brought against both the father of the girl and against the middleman. This case was finally adjusted by a money payment.

The delivery of the red cards is, as we have remarked, the beginning of the engagement, the culmination being the arrival of the bride in her chair at the home of her husband. The date of this event is generally dependent upon the pleasure of the boy's family. Whatever accessories the wedding may have, the arrival of the bride is the de facto completion of the contract. This becomes evident in the case of second marriages, where there is often, and even proverbially, no ceremony of any sort which must be observed. The Chinese imperial calendar designates the days which are the most felicitous for weddings, and it constantly happens that on these particular days there will be what the Chinese term "red festivities" in almost every village. This is one of the many instances in which Chinese superstitions are financially expensive. On "lucky days" the hire of sedan-chairs rises with the great demand, while those who disregard luck are able to get better service at a lower price. There is a tradition of a winter in the early part of this century when on a "fortunate day" many brides were being carried to their new homes during the progress of a tremendous snowstorm which blinded the bearers and obliterated the roads. Some of the brides were frozen to death, and many were taken to the wrong places. On the other hand in a blistering summer, cases have been known where the bride was found to be dead when the chair was deposited at the husband's home. The same bridal sedan-chair may be used many times. In regions where it is the custom to have all weddings in the forenoon, second marriages are put off until the afternoon, or even postponed until the evening, marking their minor importance.

That the only essential feature of a Chinese wedding is the delivery of the bride at her husband's home, is strikingly shown in those not very uncommon instances in which a Chinese is married without himself being present at all. It is usually considered a very ill omen to change the date set for a wedding, especially to postpone it. Yet it sometimes happens that the young man is at a distance from home, and fails to return in time. Or the bridegroom may be a scholar, and find that the date of an important examination coincides with the day set for his wedding. In such a case he will probably choose "business before pleasure" and the bride will be "taken delivery of" by older members of his family, without disturbing his own literary ambitions.

Of the details of Chinese weddings we do not intend to speak. There are wide variations of usage in almost all particulars, though the general plan is doubtless much the same. The variations appertain, not to the ceremonies of the wedding alone, but to all the proceedings from beginning to end. It is supposed that the explanation of the singular and sometimes apparently unaccountable variation in these and other usages, found all over China, may be due to the persistent survival of customs which have been handed down from the time of the Divided Kingdoms. But very considerable differences in usage are to be met with in regions not far apart, and which were never a part of different kingdoms. The saying runs, "Customs vary every ten li," which seems at times to be a literal truth.

In the south of China, as we have already remarked, the transfer of money, at the engagement of a daughter, from the parents of the boy to those of the girl, assumes for all practical purposes the aspect of a purchase, which, pure and simple, it often is. But in other parts of China we never hear of such a transaction, but only of a dowry from the bride's family, much in the manner of Western lands at times. Vast sums are undoubtedly squandered by the very wealthy Chinese at the weddings of their daughters, and it is a common adage that to such expenditures there is no limit. But in weddings in the ordinary walks of life, to which all but a small fraction of the people belong, the impression which will be made upon the observant foreigner will generally be that there is a great amount of shabby gentility, a thin veneer of display beneath which it is easy to see the real texture.

In this as in everything relating to Chinese usages it is impossible to make general statements which shall at the same time be accurate. There are regions in northern China where the money exacted from the family of the future bridegroom is so considerable, that what remains after the real bridal outfit has been purchased is a positive source of profit to the father. There are also other districts where local custom requires the bridegroom's family to give very little or even nothing at all for dowry, but exacts heavily from the bride's family. There must be a large supply of clothing, and bedding; even when at her own home the young married woman must sew for her husband's family, and the one which furnishes the bride is subject to a constant series of petty exactions.

The bridal chair is often itself a fit emblem of a Chinese wedding. Looked at from a distance, it appears to be of the most gorgeous description, but on a nearer view it is frequently perceived to be a most unattractive framework covered with a gaudy set of trappings sometimes much worn and evidently the worse for wear. In some cases there is a double framework, the outer of which can be lifted entirely off, being too clumsy to be got into a courtyard. The inner chair can be carried through the narrow doors of any Chinese yard, or, if required, into the house itself.

The bride is no sooner out of the chair than the process of dismantling the bridal chair begins, in the immediate sight of all the guests, and as a matter of course. The Chinese is not a victim of sentiment, and he fails to see anything incongruous in these proceedings. It not infrequently happens that the resplendent garment worn by the bride is hired for the occasion, a fact of which the guests present are not likely to be ignorant. We once saw a garment of this sort which the bride had just taken off, delivered to the headman in charge of the bridal chair and of the accompanying paraphernalia. Upon examining it to make sure that it was in as good condition as when it was hired, this man found, or professed to find, a grease-spot upon it, which not only attracted his attention but excited his wrath. He began to talk in loud and excited tones, waxing more and more furious until the guests were all called away from their other occupations to listen to the dispute. Yet the foreign spectator was probably the only person present to whom it occurred that this was an untimely and unseemly proceeding, out of harmony with the time and the circumstances.

The arrival of a first baby is, in the life of a Chinese wife, a very different event from the like occurrence in the life of a wife in Occidental lands. If the child is a boy, the joy of the whole household is of course great, but if on the contrary it is a girl, the depression of the spirits of the entire establishment is equally marked. In such a case, the young wife is often treated with coldness, and not infrequently with harshness, even if, as sometimes happens, she is not actually beaten for her lack of discretion in not producing a son. If she has had several daughters in succession, especially if she has borne no son or none which has lived, her life cannot be a pleasant one.

There is a story of a certain noble English lord, who had more daughters than any other member of the aristocracy. When on the Continent travelling, he walked out one day with six of his daughters. Some one who saw him, remarked to a companion, "Poor man." The noble lord overheard the observation, and turning to the person who made it, replied, "Not so 'poor' as you think; I have six more at home!" It is questionable whether any Chinese could be found who would not sympathize with the comment of the bystander, or who would agree with the reply of the father. Indeed, we have serious doubts whether, among all the innumerable myriads of this race, there ever lived a Chinese who had twelve daughters living at once.

It is one of the postulates of Chinese propriety that however much a wife may continue to visit at the maternal home, (and on this point the usages in some regions are very liberal), her children must all be born at their father's house. This is a rule of such unbending rigour that a breach of it is considered a deep disgrace, and in the effort to avoid it women will sometimes submit to extreme inconveniences, and run the most serious risks, not infrequently, it is said, meeting in consequence with painful and humiliating accidents. To the Occidental question as to the reason for this powerful prejudice against a confinement at a mother's home, the Chinese are able to give no better reply than an affirmation that, if such an event should happen, the mother's family may be expected to become very poor. This superstition is so strong that in some localities, if such an event has happened, it is customary for the family of the husband to harness a team to a plough, and, proceeding to the home of the girl's parents, plough up their courtyard. The son-in-law must also cook a kettle full of millet or rice for his mother-in-law, by which means the dire extremity of poverty may be avoided. Perhaps, after all, the idea at the bottom of these singular performances is merely the thoroughly Chinese one that, if a married daughter and her children are to come upon her mother's family for their support, poverty will be the certain result, a view which has in it some reason.

A description of the ceremonious superstitions common among the Chinese on occasion of the birth of a child, especially of a son, and most especially of a firstborn son, would fill a volume. These are far more rigorously observed in the southern part of the empire than at the north, and more in cities than in the country village, where many of these customs may be wholly unknown.

There is the highest Chinese classical authority for the proposition that if a mother is really anxious to do the best that she can for her infant, although she may not succeed perfectly, she will not come far short of success. There is equally trustworthy Occidental medical authority for the statement that, as applied to Chinese women, this proposition is a gross error. Undoubtedly superstition directly or indirectly destroys the lives of many Chinese children. But this cause, which is complex in its operations, is probably much less efficient for evil than the utter lack, on the part of the parents, of the instinct of conformity to the most obvious of Nature's laws.

The newborn infant is laid upon the k'ang where it is sometimes warmly covered, and sometimes exposed to excessive changes of temperature. Many children continue to nurse at the breast for a series of years, and whenever they cry this is the sole method of effectually quieting them, even though they be thus fed an hundred times a day. When the baby is large enough to eat miscellaneous food, there is almost no restraint either upon the kind or the quantity. He is allowed to swallow unripe fruits and melons to almost any extent, and raw sweet-potatoes or turnips are gnawed on by very small infants in arms.

When children are able to run about they are likely to be constantly nibbling at something, often sucking their father's tobacco pipe, sometimes producing serious weakening of the system and atrophy. In Shan hsi mere babies learn to smoke opium, which thus becomes at once a natural and an invincible appetite.

Taking into account the conditions of their early life, it is by no means improbable that more than half the whole number of Chinese infants die before they are two years old. This result is greatly promoted by many of those superstitions which sometimes have more than the force of law. Thus in some regions there is an absolute interdict on seeing either mother or child until forty days shall have elapsed from its birth. During this critical period myriads of young lives disappear almost without the knowledge of near neighbours. Similar bans are laid upon the period of some of the most common and most fatal of infantile diseases, such as measles, diphtheria, and smallpox, the mortality frequently attending which is enormous.

Multitudes of Chinese children die in fits, the causes of which are sufficiently obvious to foreigners who see the carelessness with which Chinese children are handled. We have known a Chinese mother, in a moment of dissatisfaction, to throw her young and naked infant out of doors into a snowbank. Another cut off one of her baby's fingers with a pair of dull shears, to save it from fits, and was rewarded by seeing it die in convulsions. Such a practice is said to be not uncommon. "Who would have supposed that it would have done so?" her mother remarked to a foreigner. But even if the young mother were endowed with the best of judgment, it would still be impossible for her to secure proper care for her children, for the reason that she is herself only a "child"[4] and in her management of her children, as in other affairs, is wholly subject to the dictation of her mother-in-law, as well as to the caprices of a platoon of aunts, grandmothers, etc., with whom nearly all Chinese courtyards swarm.

The severe labour entailed upon Chinese women in the drudgery of caring for large families, assisting in gathering the crops, and other outside toils, and the great drafts made upon their physical vitality by bearing and nursing so many children, amply suffice to account for the nearly universally observed fact that these women grow old rapidly. A Chinese bride, handsome at the age of eighteen, will be faded at thirty, and at fifty wrinkled and ugly.

It has been already remarked that the life of the Chinese village woman is an apt illustration of the inherent impossibility that woman's work should ever be done. Before her own children have ceased to be a constant care by day and by night, grandchildren have not improbably made their appearance, giving the grandmother little peace or rest. The mere preparation of the food for so many in the single kettle which must serve for everything, is a heavy task incessantly repeated. All articles of apparel, including shoes, are literally manufactured or done by hand, and so likewise is the supply of bedding or wadded quilts which like the wadded garments must be ripped open from time to time, cleaned and renewed.

Women and girls take their share of watching the orchards and the melon patches, etc., by day, and sometimes by night as well. When the wheat harvest comes on, all the available women of the family are helping to gather it, and in the autumn harvest likewise every threshing-floor abounds with them, and their countless children. In cotton growing districts the women and girls are busy a large part of the time in the fields, and often earn the only pin-money which they ever see by picking cotton for others.

The preparation of this indispensable staple for use occupies the hands of millions of Chinese women, from its collection in the field—a most laborious work since the plant grows so low— to its appearance as garments, and its final disappearance as flat padding to be used in shoe-soles. The ginning, the "scutching" or separation of fibres, the spinning, the cording, the winding and starching, and especially the weaving are all hard and tiresome work, and that too without end in sight while life lasts. In some regions every family owns a loom (one of the clumsy machines exiled from the West a century ago) and it is not uncommon for the members of a family to take turns, the husband weaving until midnight, when the wife takes up the task till daylight, (often in cellars two-thirds underground, damp, unventilated, and unwholesome). Even so it is frequently difficult to keep the wolf away from the door. Within the past few years the competition of machine twisted cotton yarns is severely felt in the cotton regions of China, and many who just managed to exist in former days are now perpetually on the edge of starvation. This is the "seamy side" of "progress."

The fact that Chinese girls are married so young, and that they have not been taught those lessons of self-control which it is so important for them to learn, suffices to demonstrate the absolute necessity for the existence of the Chinese mother-in-law as an element in the family. A Chinese married woman must address her mother-in-law as "mother," but for precision is allowed to refer to her as "mother-in-law mother." A Chinese woman calling on a foreign lady asked the latter (in the presence of her husband) about her family in the homeland. The lady mentioned that she had "a mother-in-law," upon which the Chinese woman in an awed whisper pointing to the foreign gentleman, inquired: "Won't he beat you for saying that?"

A great deal is heard of the tyranny and cruelty of these mothers-in-law, and there is a firm basis of fact for all that is so often said upon that point. But it must at the same time be borne in mind that without her the Chinese family would go to utter ruin. The father-in-law is not only unfitted to take the control which belongs to his wife, even were he at home all the time which would seldom be the case, but propriety forbids him to do any such thing, even were he able. In families where a mother-in-law is lacking, there are not unlikely to be much greater evils than the worst mother-in-law. Abuse of the daughter-in-law is so common a circumstance, that unless it be especially flagrant, it attracts very little attention.

It would be wholly incorrect to represent this as the normal or the inevitable condition to which Chinese brides are reduced, but it is not too much to affirm that no bride has any adequate security against such abuse. It assumes all varieties of forms, from incessant scolding up to the most cruel treatment. If it is carried to an extreme pitch, the mother's family will interfere, not legally, for that they cannot do, but by brute force. In a typical case of this sort, where the daughter-in-law had been repeatedly and shamefully abused by the family of her husband, which had been remonstrated with in vain by the family of the girl, the latter family mustered a large force, went to the house of the mother-in-law, destroyed the furniture, beat the other family severely, and dragged the old mother-in-law out into the street, where she was left screaming with what strength remained to her, and covered with blood, in which condition she was seen by foreigners. These proceedings are designed as a practical protest against tyranny and an intimation that sauce for a young goose may be in like manner sauce for an older one also. One would suppose that the only outcome of such a disturbance as this would be a long and bitter lawsuit, wasting the property of each of the parties, and perhaps reducing them to ruin. But with that eminent practicality which characterizes the Chinese, the girl was carried off to the home of her parents, "peace-talkers" intervened, and the girl was returned to her husband's home upon the promise of better treatment. This would probably be secured, just in proportion to the ability of the girl's family to enforce it.

In another case reported to the writer, similar in its nature to the one just mentioned, the girl was sent to her husband, after "peace-talkers" had adjusted the affair, and was locked up by the mother-in-law in a small room with only one meal a day. Within a year she had hanged herself.

It is not the ignorant and the uneducated only who thus take the law into their own hands on behalf of injured daughters. We have heard of a case in which the father of the girl who drowned herself was a literary graduate. He raised a band of men, went to the home of his son-in-law, and pulled down the gate-house to the premises, and some of the buildings. In the resulting lawsuit he was severely reproved by the District Magistrate, who told him that he had no right to assume to avenge his own wrongs, and that he was only saved from a beating in court by his literary degree.

A still more striking example was offered by an official of the third rank, whose daughter's wrongs moved him to raise an armed band and make an attack upon the house of the son-in-law. This proved to be strong and not easily taken, upon which the angry Tao-t'ai contented himself with reviling the whole family at the top of his voice, exactly as a coolie would have done. Wrongs which can only be met with such acts as this, on the part of those who are the most conservative members of Chinese society, must be very real and very grievous. In the very numerous cases in which a daughter-in-law is driven to suicide by the treatment which she receives, the subsequent proceedings will depend mainly upon the number and standing of her relatives. The first thing is to notify the family of the deceased that she has died, for without their presence the funeral cannot take place, or if it should take place the body would have to be exhumed, to satisfy her friends that the death was a natural one, and not due to violence, which is always likely to be suspected. A Chinese in the employ of the writer, was summoned one day to see his married daughter in another village, who was said to be "not very well." When the father arrived, he found her hanging by her girdle to a beam!

In cases of this sort, a lawsuit is exceptional. There are several powerful considerations which act as deterrents from such a step as sending in an accusation. It is almost always next to impossible to prove the case of the girl's family, for the reason that the opposite party can always so represent the matter as to throw the blame on the girl. In one such instance, the husband brought into court a very small woman's shoe, explaining that he had scolded his wife for wearing so small a one, which unfitted her for work. He alleged that she then reviled him, for which he struck her (of which there were marks), whereupon she drowned herself. To a defence like this, it is impossible for the girl's family to make any reply whatever. The accusation is not brought against the husband, but against the father-in-law, for practically the law does not interfere between husband and wife. It is only necessary for the husband to admit the fact of having beaten his wife, alleging as a reason that she was "unfilial" to his parents, to screen himself completely. We have heard of a suit where in reply to a claim of this sort, the brother of the girl testified that she had been beaten previous to the alleged "unfilial" conduct. This seemed to make the magistrate angry, and he ordered the brother to receive several hundred blows for his testimony, and decided that the husband's family should only be required to provide a cheap willow-wood coffin for the deceased.

Another even more efficient cause deterring from such lawsuits, is the necessity of holding an inquest over the girl's body. This is conducted with the utmost publicity, upon the Oriental plan of letting the public see how the matter really stands. A threshing floor is turned into an official arena, a set of mat-sheds are put up, and the whole village soon swarms with yamên-runners. The corpse of the deceased is laid uncovered on a mat exposed to the sight of every one, before and during the inquest. In order to avoid the shame of such exposure, and the great expense, the most bitter enemies are often willing enough to put the matter in the hands of "peace-talkers." These represent the village of each of the principals, and they meet to agree upon the terms of settlement. These terms will depend altogether upon the wealth or otherwise of the family of the mother-in-law. If this family is a rich one, the opposite party always insist upon bleeding it to the utmost practicable extent. Every detail of the funeral is arranged to be as expensive to the family as possible. There must be a cypress-wood coffin, of a specified size and thickness, a certain variety of funeral clothes, often far in excess of what the coffin could by any possibility contain, and some of them made perhaps of silk or satin. A definite amount is required to be spent in hiring Buddhist or Taoist priests, or both, to read masses at the funeral. It is considered disgraceful to compound with the family of the mother-in-law, by receiving a money payment, instead of exacting all this funeral show, but doubtless such compositions are sometimes made. As a business arrangement merely, it is evidently more to the interest of all parties to pay the girl's relatives say two hundred strings of cash, rather than to expend a thousand strings on a funeral which can do no one any good. But Chinese sensitiveness to public sentiment is so extreme, that such settlements for a mere transfer of cash must be comparatively rare.

The wedding outfit of a bride is often very extensive, but in case of her suicide none of it goes back to her family. We have heard from eyewitnesses of many cases in which huge piles of clothing which had been required for the funeral of such a suicide from the family of the mother-in-law, have been burnt in a vast heap at the grave. We know of one instance in which all the wedding outfit, which had been a large one, wardrobes, tables, mirrors, ornaments, etc., was taken out upon the street and destroyed in the presence of the girl's family. The motive to this is of course revenge, but the ultimate effect of such proceedings is to act as an imperfect check upon the behaviour of the mother-in-law and her family toward the daughter-in-law, for whom while she lives the laws of the land have no protection.

When the funeral actually takes place, under conditions such as we have described, there is great danger that despite the exertions of the "peace-talkers" from both sides, the dispute may break out anew. At sight of the girl's livid face, the result of death by strangulation, it will not be strange if, excited by the spectacle, her family cry out "Let her be avenged! Let her be avenged!" To keep the women of the girl's family quiet at such a time, is beyond the power of any collection of "peace-talkers," however numerous and respectable. If the respective parties are restrained from mutual reviling and from a fight, the funeral is regarded as a successful one. The girl's family complain of everything, the coffin, the clothing, the ornaments for the corpse, and all the appointments generally. But they are soothed by the comforting reminder that the dead are dead, and cannot be brought to life, and also that the resources of the family of the mother-in-law have been utterly exhausted, the last acre of land mortgaged to raise money for the funeral, and that they are loaded besides with a millstone of debt.

It is an ancient observation that one-half the world does not know how the other half lives. It is quite possible to dwell among the Chinese for a long time without becoming practically acquainted with their modes of settling those difficulties to which their form of civilization makes them especially liable.

The best way to study phenomena of this sort is through

concrete cases. A single instance, well considered in all its bearings, may be a window which will let in more light than a volume of abstract statements. Whoever is disposed to enter into such studies will find in China the material ready to his hand, and it will not be strange if it is forced upon his attention whether he desires to contemplate it or not, as happened in the following highly illustrative case. Many years ago a Chinese teacher in the writer's employ had leave of absence for a definite period, but when that period had expired he failed to make his appearance. This is so common, or rather so almost universal an occurrence in China, that it might have passed with only a temporary notice, but for the explanation which the teacher afterward gave of his inability to return, an explanation which appeared to be so peculiar that he was requested to reduce it to the form of a written statement, of which the following is a synopsis.

An elder sister of the teacher was married to a very poor man in a village called the "Tower of the Li Family," an insignificant hamlet consisting of only four families. In a year of great famine (1878), both the sister and her husband died, leaving three sons, all married. Of these the second died, and his widow remarried. The wife of the elder nephew of the teacher also died, and this nephew married for his second wife a widow, who had a daughter of her own, twelve years of age. This widow enjoyed the not very assuring reputation of having beaten her former mother-in-law, and also of having caused the death of her first husband. The wife of the third nephew was a quarrelsome woman, and the two sisters-in-law were always at sword's points, especially as all four of the adults and their four children shared the house and land together.

In the month of August of that year the third nephew started for a distant market, with a boat-load of watermelons. On leaving he ordered his wife to fetch his winter garments, which she refused to do, upon which they had a fight, and he left. The next day was cold and rainy. The elder nephew was sitting in a neighbour's house, and heard his wife engaged in a violent quarrel with her sister-in-law, but he did not even rise to look into the merits of the case, and no other neighbour intervened to exhort to peace. The younger sister-in-law left the house in a fury, and from that time she disappeared. About noon her continued absence became alarming to the elder brother, who searched for her till dark, and then sent word to her mother's family at a village called "The Little Camp" two li distant. This family, upon hearing of the disappearance of their daughter, raised a company of ten or a dozen persons, went over to the "Tower of the Li Family," entered the yard, and smashed all the water-jars and other pottery-ware which they could. "Peace-talkers" emerged, and succeeded in preventing the attacking party from entering the house, or the damage would have been still greater.

After they had gone, the "Lord-of-bitterness" (i. e., the elder brother) begged his friends to interfere and "talk peace," for as he was a resident of a small village, he could not for a moment stand before the men of "The Little Camp," which is a large village. These latter belonged to one of the numerous small sects which are styled "black-doors," or secret societies. In these societies there is often a class of persons called "Seers" or "Bright-eyes" (ming-yen), who profess to be able to tell what progress the pupils have made in their learning of the doctrine. Sometimes, as in this instance, they also undertake the functions of fortune-tellers. To the Bright-eye of their sect, the Little Campers applied for information as to what had become of the missing woman. In response they learnt that she had been beaten to death and buried in the yard of the "Lord-of-bitterness." Upon hearing this, the family of the murdered woman went to every door in their village, making a kotow at each door, a common and significant mode of imploring their help. Thus a large force was raised, which went to the "Tower of the Li Family," armed with spades to dig up the body. Warned of their coming, all the male residents of this latter village fled, the family of the "Lord-of-bitterness" taking refuge at the village in the house of the local constable who had charge of several villages. The teacher in question, being a near relative of the "Lord-of-bitterness," and a man of intelligence and pleasant manners, was asked to look after the house of his nephew, which he did. Owing to his presence and his politeness, no further damage was then done to the property, but the whole yard was dug over to find the body. On the failure of this quest, the Bright-eye modified the former announcement by the revelation that the body was outside the yard, but not more than thirty paces distant. The search was kept up with spades and picks by day and by night for a week. After repeated attempts had been made by the Lord-of bitterness to get the matter adjusted, and after the other party had refused to listen to any terms, the latter lodged an accusation in the District Magistrate's yamên. The Magistrate heard the case twice, but each time the family of the missing woman behaved in such an unreasonable and violent manner that the official dismissed their case, merely ordering the local constable to enlist more peace-talkers, and make the parties come to some agreement.

It happened that about that time another case somewhat resembling this had occurred in that neighbourhood, in which a woman was suspected of having drowned herself. On this account a sharp watch was kept at the ferry of the District city, some miles lower down the river, for any floating body.

About the time of the Magistrate's decision, a woman's body appeared abreast of the ferry and was identified as that of the missing woman from the Li Family Tower. The official held an inquest, in which all parties made diligent search for wounds, but none being found the Magistrate compelled the family of the woman to affix their thumb marks to a paper recognizing this fact. He ordered the Lord-of-bitterness to buy a good coffin, clothes, and prepare other appointments for a showy funeral, including chanting by Buddhist priests, and to have the body taken to his house. He also instructed the constable once more to secure peace-talkers, to arrange the details and to hold the funeral.

But the Little Campers proved to be the most obstinate of mortals, and would not only listen to no reason, but drove the peace-talkers from their village with reviling language, never so exasperating to a Chinese as when employed against those who are sacrificing their interests for those of the public. At this juncture the husband of the drowned woman returned from the watermelon market, went himself to the home of his late wife, and expostulated with her family and also urged peace through still other third parties. But the Little Campers insisted upon funeral paraphernalia which would have cost 10,000 strings of cash.

One more effort at compromise was made, by the visit of an uncle of the teacher who was guarding the house of the Lord-of-bitterness, to the Little Campers. The latter now altered their demands to a payment of 800 strings of cash, which by much chaffering was eventually reduced to 400. The Lord-of-bitterness offered 250 strings, but this was rejected with disdain.

Upon the failure of these numerous negotiations, the local constable presented another complaint to the Magistrate, reciting the facts in the repeated refusal, on the part of the family of the woman, to come to any terms. The Magistrate, recognizing the case as one in which the relatives were resolved to make the utmost possible capital out of a dead body, ordered eight men from his own yamên to go on that very day and attend the funeral, in order to insure that there should be no breach of peace. These yamên-runners, after the customary Chinese manner, hoped to be bribed to do as they were ordered and did not go to the place at all. The Lord-of-bitterness and all his neighbours continued in obscurity, but in the interval the men from the Little Camp again gathered their hosts, and made four more visits to the premises at the Li Family Tower, breaking everything which they could lay their hands upon. The next day the yamên-runners arrived, and the Lord-of-bitterness, now thoroughly exasperated, succeeded in collecting a force of several hundred men from other villages, intending at all hazards to hold the funeral and also to have a general fight, if need arose. But the men of the Little Camp failed to put in an appearance at this time, and the funeral accordingly at last took place. The friends of the woman, however, obstinately refused to consider the matter as settled, at which point the curtain falls, with a plentiful promise of future lawsuits, fights, and ruin.

The reader who is sufficiently interested in the inner-working of the life of the Chinese to follow the tangled thread of a tale like this, is rewarded by the perception of several important facts. It is an axiom in China that the family of the married daughter holds its head down, while the family of the man whom she has married holds its head up. But in case of the violent death of the married woman all this is reversed, and by a natural process of reaction the family of the married woman becomes a fierce and formidable antagonist.

Principles such as these have but to be put in issue between two large villages, or families, and we have the well-known clan fights of southern China, in all their perennial bitterness and intensity. One of the weakest parts of the Chinese social fabric is the insecurity of the life and happiness of woman, but no structure is stronger than its weakest part, and Chinese society is no exception to this law. Every year thousands upon thousands of Chinese wives commit suicide, tens of thousands of other persons are thereby involved in serious trouble, hundreds of thousands of yet others are dragged in as co-partners in the difficulty, and millions of dollars are expended in extravagant funerals and ruinous lawsuits. And all this is the outcome of the Confucian theory that a wife has no rights which a husband is bound to respect. The law affords her no protection while she lives, and such justice as she is able with difficulty to exact is strictly a post mortem concession.

The reality of the evils of the Chinese system of marriages is evidenced by the extreme expedients to which unmarried girls sometimes resort, to avoid matrimony. Chinese newspapers not infrequently contain references to organized societies of young maidens, who solemnly vow never to wed. The following paragraphs are translated from a Chinese newspaper called the Shih Pao:

SUICIDE AS A VIRTUE.

There is a prevailing custom in a district called Shun-tê in the Canton province, among female society to form different kinds of sisterhoods such as "All pure" sisterhoods, "Never-to-be-married" sisterhoods, etc. Each sisterhood consists of about ten young maidens who swear vows to heaven never to get married, as they regard marriages as something horrid, believing that their married lives would be miserable and unholy; and their parents fail to prevail upon them to yield.

A sad case has just happened: a band of young maidens ended their existence in this world by drowning themselves in the Dragon River because one of them was forced by her parents to be married. She was engaged in her childhood before she joined this sisterhood. When her parents had made all the necessary arrangements for her marriage she reported the affair to the other members of her sisterhood who at once agreed to die for her cause, if she remained constant to her sworn vows to be single and virtuous. Should she violate the laws of the sisterhood and yield to her parents, her life was to be made most unpleasant by the other members and she was to be taunted as a worthless being. She consulted with them as to the best mode of escaping this marriage, and they all agreed to die with her, if she could plan to run away from her parents on the night of the marriage.

As there were many friends to watch her movements, it was almost impossible for her to escape, so she attempted her life by swallowing a gold ring, but any serious consequence that might have resulted was prevented by the administration of a powerful emetic. She was finally taken by force and made over to the male side, to her great grief. According to the usual custom she was allowed to return to her parents. During all this time she was planning a way to escape to her sisters. By bribing the female servants she was taken one night to her sisters under the cover of darkness. The sisters at once joined with her in terminating their lives by jumping into the Dragon River with its swift currents, which rapidly carried them off.

This kind of tragedy is not uncommon in this part of the land. The officials have from time to time tried to check the formation of such sisterhoods, but all their efforts were in vain. Girls must have reasons of their own for establishing such societies. Married life must have been proved by many in that region to have been not altogether too sweet. However, such wholesale suicide must be prevented by law if the parents have no control over their daughters.

It is well known that Chinese law recognizes seven grounds for the divorce of a wife, as follows: childlessness, wanton conduct, neglect of husband's parents, loquacity (to yen), thievishness, jealousy, malignant disease. The requisites for a Chinese wife are by no means sure to be exacting. A man in the writer's employ, who was thinking of giving up his single life, on being questioned as to what sort of a wife he preferred, compendiously replied, "It is enough if she is neither bald nor idiotic." In a country where the avowed end of marriage is to raise up a posterity to burn incense at the ancestral graves, it is not strange that "childlessness" should rank first among the grounds for divorce. It would be an error, however, to infer that simply because they are designated in the Imperial code of laws, either this or any other of the above mentioned, are the ordinary occasions of divorce.

It is always difficult to arrive at just conclusions in regard to facts of a high degree of complexity, especially in regard to the Chinese. But so far as we can perceive, the truth appears to be that divorce in China is by no means so common as might be expected by reasoning from the law just quoted. Probably the most common cause is adultery, for the reason that this is the crime most fatal to the existence of the family.

But it must be distinctly understood that in every case of divorce, there is a factor to be taken into account which the law does not even consider. This is the family of the woman, and, as we have seen, it is a factor of great importance, and by no means to be disregarded. It is very certain that the family of the woman will resist any divorce which they consider to be unjust or disgraceful, not merely on account of the loss of "face," but for another reason even more powerful.

In China a woman cannot return to her parent's home after an unhappy marriage, as is often done in Western lands, because there is no provision for her support. Enough land is set apart for the maintenance of the parents, and after that has been provided for, the remainder is divided among the brothers. No lot or portion falls to any sister. It is this which makes it imperative that every woman should be married, that she may have some visible means of support. After her parents are dead, her brothers, or more certainly her brothers' wives, would drive her from the premises, as an alien who had no business to depend upon their family when she "belongs" to another. Under this state of things, it is not very likely that a husband would be allowed to divorce his wife except for a valid cause, unless there should be some opportunity for her to "take a step," that is, to remarry elsewhere.

Next to adultery, the most common cause of Chinese divorce is thought to be what Western laws euphemistically term incompatibility, by which is meant, in this case, such constant domestic brawls as to make life, even to a Chinese, not worth living. It is needless to remark that when things have reached this pitch, they must be very bad indeed. Every one of the above cited causes for divorce evidently affords room for the loosest construction of the facts, and if the law were left to its own execution, with no restraint from the wife's family, the grossest injustice might be constantly committed. As it is, whatever settlement is arrived at in any particular case, must be the result of a compromise, in which the friends of the weaker party take care to see that their rights are considered.

We have repeatedly referred to the imperative necessity that every Chinese youth should be married. To a foreigner there is a mixture of the ludicrous and the pathetic in the attitude of the average parent, in regard to a marriage of a son who has nearly reached the age of twenty and is still single. It is a Chinese aphorism of ancient times that when sons and daughters are once married, "the great business of life has been despatched." Chinese parents look upon the marriage of their sons just as Western parents look upon the matter of taking young boys out of their early dresses and putting them into trousers. The serious part of life cannot be begun until this is done, and to delay it is ridiculous and irrational.

There is a sentiment of false modesty which forbids the persons most interested in a marriage, even to refer to it. It is often impossible for any one but the mother to hint to a girl that it is time she were betrothed, an announcement which is naturally the frequent occasion for stormy scenes.

A Chinese teacher well known to the writer, having graduated from a missionary college at the age of twenty-three, remembered that he was not betrothed. When matters had been arranged without his appearing to be aware of the fact (although he was consulted at each step) it became necessary to visit his home to arrange with his parents the time of the marriage. But the sensitive young man refused to go on this errand himself, and posted off a "yard uncle," urging as a more than sufficient reason: "How could I speak to my father and mother about such a thing as that?"

Since this paragraph was written a Chinese friend called on the writer with an air of pleased embarrassment about "a little matter" which seemed to interest him. He is more than forty years of age, and had never been married. He has two brothers, all three sharing in common a property amounting to less than two English acres. This brother had been at home for some months, during which there was no mention of matrimony, nor any thought of it. Having left home for a few weeks, before the time was nearly expired the elder brother posted off a special messenger to a distance of more than 300 li to mention to him the fact that he had suddenly arranged a betrothal for this forty years old bachelor, to a girl of seventeen, whose friends were now pressing for an immediate execution of the contract. The interview closed with the expression of an earnest wish on the part of the Chinese that his foreign friend would see his way clear to "a loan" of twenty strings of cash for the bride's outfit, the bridegroom having no independent property whatever, and no income. The comment of ninety-nine out of an hundred Chinese on this match, or on any other in similar circumstances would be compendiously condensed in the single word "hao," meaning when fully explicated, "It is well; this is what certainly ought to be done now." Questions of expense appear to them as irrelevant as they would to us if the matter was the burial of a parent.

Chinese parents are never willing to run the risk of having the marriage of any of their children, especially the sons, postponed until after the death of their parents. They often feel uncertain whether the children already married will be willing to make the proper provision for the event, or indeed that they will let it take place at all. Affairs of this sort involve the partition of the land, with a portion to each married son, and it is not in human nature to wish to multiply the sharers in a property which is too often at the best wholly inadequate. For this cause, every prudent parent wishes to see this "main business of life," put through while he is able to superintend the details.

The inexorable necessity for the marriage of sons is not suspended by the fact that the child is wholly unsuited for a real marriage, or indeed incapable of it. Cases constantly occur, in which a boy who is a hopeless and helpless cripple is married to a girl, whose family only assent to the arrangement, because of the advantageous terms which are offered. Children who are subject to epileptic or other forms of fits, those who are more or less insane, and even those who are wholly idiotic, all may have, and do have, wives, provided only that the families of the boys were in good circumstances. The inevitable result of this violation of the laws of nature, is an infinity of suffering for the girls whose lives are thus wrecked, and the evolution of a wealth of scandal.

There is another feature of Chinese married life, to which little attention seems to have been paid by foreigners, but which is well worth investigation. It is the kidnapping of legally married wives. The method by which this may be accomplished, and the difficulty of tracking those who do it, may be illustrated by the following case, with the principal parties in which, the father and father-in-law of the bride, the writer is acquainted, having been present at the wedding in December, 1881.

The bride herself, was, as so often, a mere child. On her frequent visits to her native village, which local custom allows, the bride did not spend much of her time at her own home, where she was probably not made very welcome by her step-mother, but went instead to her grandmother's, who was old, half blind, and ill supplied with bedding. In a neighbouring yard lived a cousin of the girl, who was a "salt inspector," that is, one whose duty is to seize dealers in smuggled salt. His wife was the daughter of a widow, who was reported to be herself a dealer in smuggled salt, of course with the connivance of her son-in-law. This couple were said to have been married without the intervention of go-betweens, and hence the most flagitious conduct was to be expected from them. The girl got into the habit, whenever she visited her village, of going to the house of this cousin, and not to that of her father. The cousin was absent much of the time, on his business in connection with the suppression (or the sale) of smuggled salt. Upon one occasion, after a ten days' visit to her native village she returned to the home of her husband (also a mere child), where she stayed five days, and then went again to her own village. A younger sister-in-law, sixteen years of age, went with her two-thirds of the way, at which point the bride sent her escort back and proceeded alone. Some days after this the own sister of the bride met the father-in-law at a fair, and inquired why the bride did not return to her own village as agreed. Her absence from both homes was thus for the first time discovered. The steps taken to follow her are an excellent illustration of certain phases of Chinese life. It is almost impossible in China for any one to do anything so secretly that some other persons do not know of it, and in an affair so serious as the disappearance outright of a young bride, the chances of successful concealment would seem to be very slight.

The father-in-law of the girl went to the village where she had lived, and learned that upon the occasion of her home visits the child had been allowed to go where she pleased, and that once after coming in from her cousin's, she had been heard to remark that she herself was worth as much as five ounces of silver. It was also reported that the wife of the cousin had been observed waiting for the missing girl, on the night she was last seen at the time when she dismissed the sister-in-law who had accompanied her. This was all the clue that could be got.

The father-in-law now presented a petition to the District Magistrate, reciting the facts and accusing the girl's father, and others. This was followed by counter accusations from the father, the cousin, and his mother-in-law. The official reply to the complaint was an order to the local constable to find the girl. The constable was a wholly incompetent person, and could not have found her if he had tried. A second petition to the Magistrate was followed by the same reply. This signified that there was no hope from that official, who took no interest in the matter.

After these repeated failures of justice, the poor father-in-law resolved to make one more trial, a desperate expedient, but the only one which was left. He seized the occasion of the passing of the District official through that village, to kneel in Front of the sedan-chair and proclaim his grievance. The Magistrate merely repeated what had been said in court, that he knew nothing about the matter; that it was not his business to find the cattle of those who might lose them, neither was it his function to recover daughters-in-law. He also expressed the opinion that the father-in-law was lacking in proof of his case, and was falsely accusing parties who were innocent, and then ordered his chair to proceed.

The only remaining hope of tracing the missing person was to follow up chance dues. In such a case, no one will give any information whatever, no matter what he may know, for the reason that the possible effect may be to drag him as witness into a fearful lawsuit, which is only one step removed from being the principal victim oneself. This is so universal a deterrent in a quest of this sort as almost to bar all progress. Those who were interested in this particular case were led to recall another, which occurred many years before in a village immediately contiguous, where the wife of a man who was working for some one else was taken off (of course with her consent) while he was absent. In this instance, although the husband was able to ascertain to what village she had been taken, yet as it was a large one he could never get any further trace of her, and she died there. The writer is personally acquainted with two families in which such occurrences have taken place, and with a third, the wife in which, when living with her first husband who divorced her, was to have been kidnapped, if the plan could have been carried out.

It is of course impossible to form any correct idea as to the extent to which the kidnapping of married women is carried in China, but there are a few little windows through which glimpses may be had of regions beyond our ordinary vision. Such glimpses may be frequently gained from accounts published in Chinese native newspapers, in which such accounts often form a staple topic. In the absence of any acquaintance with the wider interests of the empire, these piquant personalities seem to many Chinese very entertaining, as items of a similar sort do to certain readers in Western lands. Such gossip is collected at the yamêns, where many of the cases reported have already reached the stage of a prosecution, and others are quietly adjusted by "peace-talkers." Similar information may also be obtained from occasional memorials printed in the Peking Gazette. It not seldom happens that these kidnapping cases lead to murder, and perhaps to wholesale fighting, ending in many deaths, which render it necessary for a Governor to report the facts and proceedings to Peking. From data of this sort one would infer that, as the proverb says, "The crow is everywhere equally black."

We have spoken of the sale of girls by their parents, and have now to refer to the more or less common cases of the sale of wives by their husbands. This is generally due to the press of poverty, and the writer is acquainted with a Chinese who, being deeply in debt, was thrown into prison from which he found deliverance hopeless. He accordingly sent word to his relatives to have his wife sold, which was done, and with the proceeds the man was able to buy his escape. The frequency of such sales may be said to bear a direct ratio to the price of grain.

There is another method of selling wives, with which the Chinese are acquainted, which can be adopted whenever the pressure of life at home becomes too hard to be borne. The husband and wife then start off on a begging expedition toward a region in which the crops have been good. In a bad year, there are thousands of such persons roaming about the country, picking up a scanty subsistence wherever they can. The man who wishes to sell his wife represents her as his sister, and declares that they are forced by hunger to part company. He reluctantly makes up his mind to sell her to some one who is in need of a wife, and who can get one more cheaply by this process than by any other. To this arrangement the woman tearfully assents, the money is paid to her "brother," and he departs, to be seen no more. After a few days or a few weeks in her new home, the newly married "sister" contrives to steal out in the evening with all of her own clothes and as many more as she can collect, and rejoins her "brother," setting out with him for "fresh woods and pastures new." With that keen instinct for analogy which characterizes the Chinese, they have invented for this proceeding the name of "falconing with a woman," likening it to the sport of a man who places his hawk on his wrist, and releases it when he sees game in sight, only that the bird may speedily return. It is a popular proverb, that "playing the falcon with a woman" implies a plot in which two persons are concerned.

An inquirer is told that in some districts this practice of "falconing" is exceedingly common, for the supply of gullible persons who hope to buy a wife at a cheaper rate than usual never fails.

The Chinese ridicule any one who seems to be infatuated with a bargain in which a woman is concerned, but it is not improbable that under similar circumstances they themselves would do the same. An old fellow living in the same village as the writer bought a woman under what he considered exceptionally profitable conditions, and lest she should escape, he anchored her in the yard fastened to a peg like a donkey. His neighbours laughed at him, and he at them, until the woman suddenly disappeared, an event which reduced him to a more sober view of the "five relations."

Chinese public sentiment is altogether on the right side of this question, but Chinese practice is not under the guidance of sentiment of any kind. It is proverbial that a judicious man will never marry a woman who has a living husband, for the sufficient reason that he never can foresee the consequences, which are often serious. But the instinct of trying to cheat Fate is in all Chinese most vigorous. "Cheaper than an animal," was the self-complacent comment of a Chinese friend of the writer's in regard to his own second marriage where he had paid no money for his wife, but only an allowance for outfit. But when the elder sister-in-law had been heard from, this same individual was dissolved in tears for many moons, since his future peace seemed to have been wrecked.

It is a natural sequence to the Chinese doctrine of the necessity of having male children that, in case this becomes unlikely, a secondary wife, or concubine, should be taken, with that end in view. As a matter of fact this practice is confined to a comparatively small number of families, mainly those in fairly good circumstances, for no others could afford the expense. The evils of this expedient are well recognized, and it is fortunate for Chinese society that resort is not had to it on a much greater scale than appears to be the case. The practical turn of the Chinese mind has suggested to them a much simpler method of arriving at the intended results, by a much less objectionable method. This is the well-known adoption of children from collateral branches of the family, already mentioned, so as to keep the line of succession intact, and prevent the extinction of any particular branch.

It not infrequently happens that the son in a family dies before he is married, and that it is desirable to adopt, not a son, but a grandson. There is however, to the Chinese, a kind of paradox in adopting a grandson, when the son has not been married. To remedy this defect after the boy had died unmarried would, to the practical Occidental, appear impossible, but it is not so to the sentimental Chinese. To meet this exigency they have invented the practice of marrying the dead, which is certainly among the most singular of the many singular performances to be met with in China.

In order to keep the line of succession unbroken, it is thought desirable that each generation should have its proper representatives, whether they really were or were not links in the chain. It is only in families where there is some considerable property that this question is likely to arise. Where it does arise, and where a lad has died for whom it is thought desirable to take a post-mortem wife, the family cast about to hear of some young girl who has also died recently. A proposition is then made, by the usual intermediaries, for the union of these two corpses in the bonds of matrimony! It is probably only poor families to which such a proposition in regard to their daughter would be made; to no others would it be any object. If it is accepted, there is a combination of a wedding and a funeral, in the process of which the deceased "bride" will be taken by a large number of bearers to the cemetery of the other family, and laid beside her "husband"! The newly adopted grandson worships the corpse of his "mother," and the other ceremonies proceed in the usual way.

The writer was personally acquainted with a Chinese girl who after her death was thus "married" to a dead boy in another village. Upon being questioned in regard to the matter, her father admitted that it was not an entirely rational procedure, but remarked that the girl's mother was in favour of accepting the offer. The real motive in this case was undoubtedly a desire to have a showy funeral at the expense of another family, for a child who was totally blind, and whose own parents were too poor at her death to do more than wrap her body in a mat.

The practice of marrying one dead person to another is very far from uncommon to China. Its ultimate root is found in the famous dictum of Mencius, that of the three lines of unfilial conduct the chief is to leave no posterity. This utterance is one upon which the whole domestic life of the Chinese seems to have rested for ages. It is for this reason that those Chinese who have not yet married are accounted as of no importance. When they die, they are, if children, "thrown out" either literally or figuratively, and are not allowed a place in the family graveyards. These belong exclusively to those who are mated, and occasional bachelors must expect no welcome there. The same principle seems to be applicable to those who have died, and whose wives have remarried. It is for such cases that the strange plan of marrying a living woman to a dead husband has been invented. The motive on the part of the woman could be only that of saving herself from starvation, a fate which often hangs imminent over poor Chinese widows who do not remarry. The motive on the part of the family of the deceased husband is to make the ancestral graves complete. If the family of the deceased is not moderately well off, they would not go to the expense and trouble of bringing in a wife for a dead husband. But if she were well off, the widow would probably not have remarried. It thus appears the marriage of a living woman to a dead man is likely to be confined to cases where the family being poor, the widow remarried, but where the family circumstances having subsequently materially improved, it became an object to arrange as already explained to fill the threatened graveyard gap.

It is perhaps for this reason that cases of such marriage appear to be relatively rare, so rare indeed, that many even intelligent and educated Chinese have never heard of them at all, and perhaps stoutly deny their existence. Sufficient inquiry, however, may not improbably develop here and there specific cases of conformity to this custom, so repellent to our thought, but to the Chinese natural and rational.

As already mentioned, in cases where it has been decided to adopt a son, and where there are no suitable candidates within the family circle, a lad may be taken from a different family, sometimes related, sometimes connected, sometimes neither related nor connected, and sometimes he may even be a total stranger merely "picked up." The result of this latter practice especially is often very disappointing and painful for the couple who have gone to so much trouble to find an heir, and who too often discover that they have spent their strength in vain, and that filial piety is not a commodity to be had for the asking.

But whatever its attendant evils, which are undoubtedly many and great, the Chinese plan of adoption is always incomparably preferable to that of bringing into the yard a "little wife." It is by no means singular that the Chinese have given to the relations between the real wife and the supplementary one, the significant name of "sipping vinegar."

We happen to have been personally acquainted with several families in which a concubine had been introduced. In two of them, the secondary wives had been bought because they were to be had at a cheap rate in a year of famine. One of these poor creatures came one day running into the yard of a Chinese family with whom the writer was living, screaming and dishevelled, as the result of "vinegar sipping." The man who had taken her openly reviled his mother in the most shameless way, upon her remonstrance at the act.

In a second instance, a man past middle-life thought by this means to make sure of a son, but was greatly disappointed in the result. He was in the habit of inviting elderly Chinese women of his acquaintance to go to his house, and "exhort" his wives to stop "sipping vinegar," a labour which was attended with very negative results. When he died, the last wife was driven out to return to her relatives, although for a country villager her husband was reputed to be a fairly rich man. In cases where the concubine has a son, in the event of her husband's death, if affairs are properly managed, she has a portion of land set apart for her like any other wife.

In a third case a neighbour of the writer, a man in middle-life, had a wife about forty years of age, two others having died, one of them leaving a daughter now twenty years of age. The father was absent from home much of the time, engaged in business in Peking. With Chinese thus situated, it often appears to be a particularly happy solution of a difficulty to have two wives, the legal wife at home, and the "small one" at the place where the husband spends most of his time. When the man returned to his home, he brought this secondary wife with him, an act very well adapted to promote "vinegar sipping." This additional wife was a mere child much younger than the daughter of her husband.

At the next New Year it was reported that the man would not allow his proper wife to go to the ancestral graves, but insisted upon taking his young concubine to do the sacrificing. Other injurious reports, true or false, were circulated in regard to his behaviour toward his proper wife, and his intentions in the future to abandon or divorce her, and these soon reached the village of which she was a native. The result was a deputation of a considerable number of elderly men from that village to the one in which the husband lived. This deputation instituted proceedings by summoning the head of the husband's clan to meet them. But a large number of young men from that same village, having heard of the affair, could not wait for the elders to adjust the matter by slow Chinese diplomacy, but came in a body to the house of the husband, and without any ceremony made an attack upon it, breaking down the barred door and throwing themselves with violence upon the defenceless husband.

The attacking party had armed themselves with awls, but not, according to their own account, with knives. It was late at night when the onslaught was made, and it was impossible to distinguish friend from foe. The husband was at once over-powered, and was subsequently found to have seventeen awl-stabs on his chest, and two savage knife-cuts on his back, penetrating to the lungs. It was alleged by the attacking party that the latter wounds must have been made by some of the man's immediate neighbours who were personal enemies, and who, hearing the outcry, rushed in only to find that their enemy was defenceless and open to their attack (which could not be proved against them), a circumstance of which they took care to avail themselves. The attacking party having thus placed themselves in the wrong, were obliged, upon being prosecuted at law, to get an influential company of intermediaries to help them out of the difficulty. This was at last accomplished according to the usual Chinese method—a great deal of head knocking and a great many feasts for the injured party.

Notwithstanding such instructive object-lessons as these, with which all parts of China must to a greater or less extent abound, many of those who think that they can afford to do so continue to repeat the experiment, although the adage says: "If your wife is against it, do not take a concubine." If this advice were to be adopted, it is not improbable that the practice of concubinage in China would become practically extinct.

A traveller through China often notices in the villages along his route that in the early morning most of the men seem to be assembled by the roadside, each one squatting in front of his own door, all busily engaged in shovelling in their food with chopsticks (appropriately called "nimble-sons"), chatting meantime during the brief intervals with the neighbour nearest. That the entire family should sit down to a table, eating together and waiting for one another, after the manner of the inhabitants of Western lands, is an idea so foreign to the ordinary Chinese mind as to be almost incomprehensible.

This Chinese (and Oriental) habit is at once typical and suggestive. It marks a wholly different conception of the family, and of the position of woman therein, from that to which we are accustomed. It indicates the view that while man is yang, the male, ruling, and chief element in the universe, woman is yin, "dull, female, inferior." The conception of woman as man's companion is in China almost totally lacking, for woman is not the companion of man, and with society on its present terms she never can be. A new bride introduced into a family has visible relations with no one less than with her "husband." He would be ashamed to be seen talking with her, and in general they seem in that line to have very little to be ashamed of. In those unique instances in which the young couple have the good sense to get acquainted with each other, and present the appearance of actually exchanging ideas, this circumstance is the joke of the whole family circle, and an insoluble enigma to all its members. We have heard of cases in which members of a family where there was a newly married couple, kept a string in which was tied a knot, every time that they were heard to speak to one another. This cord would be subsequently exhibited to them in ridicule of their intimacy!

A Chinese bride has no rational prospect of happiness in her new home, though she may be well dressed, well fed, and perhaps not abused. She must expect chronic repression through the long years during which she is for a time in fact, and in theory always, a "child." Such rigorous discipline may be necessary to fit her for the duties of her position, when she shall have become herself a mother-in-law, and at the head of a company of daughters-in-law, but it is a hard necessity. That there are sometimes genuine attachments between mothers-in-law and daughters-in-law it would be a mistake to deny, for in such rare cases human nature shows its power of rising superior to the conventional trammels in which it finds itself by iron customs bound.

To defend herself against the fearful odds which are often pitted against her, a Chinese wife has but two resources. One of them is her mother's family, which, as we have seen, has no real power, and is too often to be compared to the stern light of a ship, of no service for protection in advance, and only throwing a lurid glare on the course which has been passed over, but which cannot be retraced.

The other means of defence which a Chinese wife has at her command is—herself. If she is gifted with a fluent tongue, especially if it is backed by some of that hard common sense which so many Chinese exhibit, it must be a very peculiar household in which she does not hold her own. Real ability will assert itself, and such light as a Chinese woman possesses will assuredly permeate every corner of the domestic bushel under which it is of necessity hidden. If a Chinese wife has a violent temper, if she is able at a moment's notice to raise a tornado about next to nothing, and to keep it for an indefinite period blowing at the rate of a hundred miles an hour, the position of such a woman is almost certainly secure. The most termagant of mothers-in-law hesitates to attack a daughter-in-law who has no fear of men or of demons, and who is fully equal to any emergency. A Chinese woman in a fury is a spectacle by no means uncommon. But during the time of the most violent paroxysms of fury, Vesuvius itself is not more unmanageable by man.

If a Chinese husband happens to be a person of a quiet habit, with no taste for tumults, he may possibly find himself yoked to a Xantippe who never for an instant relaxes the reins of her dominion. In such cases the prudent man will be glad to purchase "peace at any price," and whatever the theory may be, the woman rules. Such instances are by no means infrequent. This is witnessed as well by what one sees and hears in Chinese society as well as by the many sayings which refer to the "man-who-fears-what-is-inside," that is, the "hen-pecked man." Although it is an accepted adage that

"A genuine cat will slay a mouse,

A genuine man will rule his house,"

yet there are numerous references to the punishment of "kneeling-by-the-bedside-holding-a-lamp-on-the-head," which is the penalty exacted by the regnant wife from her disobedient husband.

If a Chinese woman has the heaven-bestowed gift of being obstreperous to such a degree that, as the sayings go, "people do not know east from west"; that "men are worn out and horses exhausted"; that "the mountains tremble and the earth shakes,"

315

this is unquestionably her surest life-preserver. It is analagous to the South American toucan, which is said to frighten away enemies by the mere exhibition of itself, they not caring to wait for further and detailed proofs of its capacities of execution. But if such an endowment has been denied her, her next best resource is to pursue a course exactly the opposite, in all circumstances and under all provocations holding her tongue. To most Chinese women, this seems to be a feat as difficult as aërial navigation, but now and then an isolated case shows that the difficult is not always the impossible.

The present position of woman in China is a heritage of the remote past, as is illustrated by the most ancient Chinese literature, an example of which heads the present chapter. The instructions and the prohibitions in the Book of Rites, one of the oldest and most venerated classical works, embody fundamental principles which have always governed the Chinese in their treatment of women. The essence of the Chinese classical teaching on this subject is, that woman is as inferior to man as the earth is inferior to heaven; and that she can never attain to full equality with man.

According to Chinese philosophy death and evil have their origin in the Yin, or female principle of Chinese dualism, while life and prosperity come from the subjection of it to the Yang, or male principle; hence it is regarded as a law of nature to keep woman completely under the power of man, and to allow her no will of her own. The result of this theory and the corresponding practice is that the ideal for women is not development and cultivation, but submission. Women can have no happiness of their own, but must live and work for men, the only practical escape from this degradation being found in becoming the mother of a son. Woman is bound by the same laws of existence in the other world. She belongs to the same husband, and is dependent for her happiness on the sacrifices offered by her descendants.[5]

It is occasionally objected that to attribute the evils attending the lot of woman in China to the moral system which has molded and preserved that empire, is as inaccurate as it would be to hold Christianity responsible for all the moral evils found in Christian lands. Between the two cases there is, however, this fundamental difference. Every moral evil has from the beginning been antagonized by Christianity. Those evils that still flourish do so in spite of it, and against its unceasing efforts and incessant protest. Christianity acting upon the relatively lofty conception of woman, held by the Teutonic races, has gradually brought about that elevation of the sex which we now witness in full development. The theory of Confucianism, on the other hand, is both erroneous and defective. It is therefore no exaggeration to charge a large part of the evils from which Chinese women suffer to this efficient cause. It is moreover highly important to remember that neither for evils arising from wrong moral teaching nor for others, has Chinese ethics ever furnished either preventive or remedy.

We must, therefore, regard the position of women in China, as the ultimate outcome and a most characteristic fruitage of Confucianism. In our view it has been a bitter fruit, and in recapitulation we would lay emphasis upon seven deadly sins in the relation of that system to woman.

I. Viewed from a purely Chinese point of view there is no inherent objection to the education of Chinese women. In one of the huge Chinese encyclopedias, out of 1,628 books, 376 are devoted to famous women, and of these four chapters treat of female knowledge, and seven others of the literary productions of women, works which have been numerous and influential. But as compared with the inconceivable numbers of Chinese women in the past, these exceptional cases are but isolated twinkles in vast interstellar spaces of dense darkness. Yet in view of the coming regeneration of China, their value as historical precedents to antiquity loving Chinese is beyond estimation.[6]

Rare and unimportant exceptions aside, Chinese women are provided with no education. Their minds are left in a state of nature, until millions of them are led to suppose that they have no minds at all, an opinion which their fathers, husbands and brothers often do much to confirm, and upon which they then habitually act.

II. The sale of wives and daughters. This comes about so naturally, and it might almost be said so inevitably, when certain conditions prevail, that it is taken by the Chinese as a matter of course. Except in years of famine it appears in some parts of the empire to be rare, but in other parts it is the constant and the normal state of things for daughters to be as really sold as are horses and cattle.

There are sections of northern China in which it is not uncommon for a man who has contracted debts which he cannot otherwise pay, to part with a daughter as a last resort. But there are other districts where the practice cannot be exceptional, as is evident from the great number of girls who, one is told, have been procured from this region. If the Chinese themselves are questioned about the matter, the fact is always admitted, the custom is reprobated, but the universally conclusive inquiry is propounded: "What help is there for it?" In the present condition of the empire this interrogatory is unanswerable.

III. Too early and too universal marriages. A considerable part of the unhappiness caused by Chinese marriages may fairly be charged to the immaturity of the victims. To treat children as if they were adults, while at the same time treating them as children who require the same watch and ward as other children, does not appear to be a rational procedure, nor can it be claimed that it is justified by its results. That a new pair constitute a distinct entity to be dealt with independently, is a proposition which Confucianism treats with scorn, if indeed it ever entertains such a conception at all. The compulsory marriage of all girls forces all Chinese society into cast-iron grooves, and leaves no room for exceptional individual development. It throws suspicion around every isolated struggle against this galling bondage, and makes the unmarried woman seem a personified violation of the decrees of heaven and of the laws of man.

IV. Infanticide of female infants. This is a direct, if not a legitimate result of the tenet that male children are absolutely indispensable, applied in a social system where dire poverty is the rule, and where an additional mouth frequently means impending starvation. In a chapter in her "Pagoda Shadows," on "The Extent of a Great Crime," Miss Fielde combines a great variety of testimony taken from several different provinces, in the following paragraph. "I find that 160 Chinese women, all over fifty years of age, had borne 631 sons, and 538 daughters. Of the sons, 366, or nearly sixty per cent., had lived more than ten years; while of the daughters only 205, or thirty-eight per cent., had lived ten years. The 160 women, according to their own statements, had destroyed 158 of their daughters; but none had ever destroyed a boy. As only four women had reared more than three girls, the probability is that the number of infanticides confessed to is considerably below the truth. I have occasionally been told by a woman that she had forgotten just how many girls she had had, more than she wanted. The greatest number of infanticides owned to by any one woman is eleven."

Infanticide will never cease in China, until the notion that the dead are dependent for their happiness upon sacrifices offered to them by the living shall have been totally overthrown.

V. Secondary wives. Concubinage is the natural result of the Confucian theory of ancestral worship. The misery which it has caused and still causes in China is beyond comprehension. Nothing can uproot it but a decay of faith in the assumption underlying all forms of worship of the dead.

VI. Suicides of wives and daughters. The preceding causes, operating singly and in combination, are wholly sufficient to account for the number of suicides among Chinese women. The wonder rather is that there are not more. But whoever undertakes to collect facts on this subject for any given district will not improbably be greatly surprised at the extraordinary prevalence of this practice. It is even adopted by children, and for causes relatively trifling. At times it appears to spread, like the smallpox, and the thirst for suicide becomes virtually an epidemic. As already mentioned, according to the native newspapers, there are parts of China in which young girls band themselves into a secret league to commit suicide within a certain time after they have been betrothed or married. The wretchedness of the lives to which they are condemned is thoroughly appreciated in advance, and fate is thus effectually checkmated. It would be wrong to overstate the evils suffered by woman in China, evils which have indeed many alleviations, and which are not to be compared to those of her sisters in India or in Turkey. But after all abatements have been made, it remains true that the death-roll of suicides is the most convincing proof of the woes endured by Chinese women.

VII. Overpopulation. The whole Chinese race is and always has been given up with a single devotion to the task of raising up a posterity, to do for the fathers what the fathers have done for the grandfathers. In this particular line, they have realized Wesley's conception of the ideal church in its line, where, as he remarked, the members are "All at it, and always at it." War, famine, pestilence sweep off millions of the population, but a few decades of peace seem to repair the ravages of the past, which are lost to sight, like battlefields covered with wide areas of waving grain.

However much we may admire the recuperative power of the Chinese people as a whole and individually, it is difficult not to feel righteous indignation toward a system which violates those beneficent laws of nature which would mercifully put an end to many branches of families when such branches are unfitted to survive. It is impossible to contemplate with equanimity the deliberate, persistent, and uniform propagation of poverty, vice, disease and crime, which ought rather to be surrounded with every restriction to prevent its multiplication, and to see this propagation of evil and misery done, too, with an air of virtue, as if this were of itself a kind of religion, often indeed the only form of religion in which the Chinese take any vital interest.

It is this system which loads down the rising generation with the responsibility for feeding and clothing tens of thousands of human beings who ought never to have been born, and whose existence can never be other than a burden to themselves, a period of incessant struggle without respite and without hope.

To the intelligent foreigner, the most prominent fact in China is the poverty of its people. There are too many villages to the square mile, too many families to the village, too many "mouths" to the family. Wherever one goes, it is the same weary tale with interminable reiteration. Poverty, poverty, poverty, always and evermore poverty. The empire is broad, its unoccupied regions are extensive, and its undeveloped resources undoubtedly vast. But in what way can these resources be so developed as to benefit the great mass of the Chinese people? By none, with which we are acquainted, or of which we can conceive, without a radical disturbance of the existing conditions. The seething mass of over-population must be drawn off to the regions where it is needed, and then only will there be room for the relief of those who remain.

One of China's Parasites—a Beggar.

One of her Sources of Strength—a Carpenter.

It is impossible to do anything for people who are wedged together after the manner of matches in a box. Imagine a surgeon making the attempt to set the broken leg of a man in an omnibus in motion, which at the time contained twenty other people, most of whom also had broken legs which likewise require setting! The first thing to do would be to get them all unloaded, and to put them where they could be properly treated, with room for the treatment, and space for breathing. It is, we repeat, not easy to perceive how even the most advanced political economy can do anything of permanent benefit for the great mass of the Chinese without a redistribution of the surplus population. But at this point practical Confucianism intervenes, and having induced the begetting of this swarm of human beings, it declares that they must not abandon the graves of their ancestors, who require their sacrifices, but must in the same spot continue to propagate their posterity to continue the interminable process.

The world is still large, and it has, and for ages will doubtless continue to have, ample room for all the additional millions which its existing millions can produce. The world was never so much in need of the Chinese as to-day, and never, on the other hand, were the Chinese more in need of the world. But if China is to hold its own, much more if it is to advance as other nations have advanced and do advance, it must be done under the lead of new forces. Confucianism has been a mighty power to build up, and to conserve. But Confucianism with its great merits has committed many "Deadly Sins," and of those sins it must ultimately suffer the penalty. Confucianism as a developing force is a force, which is spent. Sooner or later it must give way to something stronger, wiser, and better.

XXIV

THE MONOTONY AND VACUITY OF VILLAGE LIFE

It is difficult to project ourselves backward to the times of our great-grandfathers when mails were carried on horseback, the postman leisurely knitting stockings as he rode. Yet however slow, measured by modern standards, the rural life of a century and more ago, it was a varied life, ultimately anastomosing with the great currents of the age. The rate of progress of thought has no necessary correlation to the versatility or the virility of mental processes. Our ancestors may perhaps have been peasants, but they were an integral part of the land in which they dwelt, and they rose and fell with the national tides of life like boats in a harbor.

A Chinese village is physically and intellectually a fixture. Could one gaze backward through a vista of five hundred years at the panorama which that vast stretch of modern history would present, he would probably see little more and little less than he sees to-day. The buildings now standing are not indeed five hundred years old, but they are just such houses as half a millennium ago occupied the same sites, "similar and similarly situated." Some families that then lived in adobe dwellings now flourish under roofs of tile in houses of brick. Other families have become extinct. Now and then a new one may have appeared, but this is irregular and exceptional. Those who now subsist in this collection of earth-built abodes are the lineal descendants of those who lived there when Columbus discovered America. The descendants are doing just what their ancestors did, no more, no less, no other. They cultivate the same fields in the same way (albeit a few of the crops are modern); they go to the same markets

325

in the same invariable order; buy, sell, and wear the same articles; marry and are given in marriage according to the same pattern.

It was a shrewd suggestion of a philosopher that if we wish to understand a people, we should note what things they take for granted. The pre-suppositions of a Chinese villager are the same as those of his ancestry near and remote. There is in a Chinese village as such no intellectual life. If there happen to be literary men living in it, they form a little clique by themselves, largely out of relation to their neighbours, and likewise to most of their own families. It is an ancient aphorism that "Scholars talk of books—butchers of pigs." We have already abundantly seen that the processes of Chinese education are narrowing processes, fitting the accomplished student to run only in grooves. It is almost incredible how narrow these ruts become. Each literary examination is a crisis at which one either becomes a graduate or does not; in either case the result, whether appertaining to the student himself, the pupils whom he has coached, or his own sons, is contemplated purely as a personal and an individual matter. It is a literary lottery upon which much has been risked, and out of which it is desirable to recover if possible a prize. If that is out of the question all interest in the literary business is at an end.

Unlike his representative in Western lands, the Chinese village scholar is not a centre or source of illumination to others. His life is the ideal of "subjectivity"—the quintessential essence of selfishness. It is a venerable superstition of the Chinese that though the graduate does not emerge from his own door, he knows the affairs of all under heaven. As we have already had occasion to point out, among the many rhetorical exaggerations of Chinese proverbial philosophy this aphorism may be held to take the lead. The typical scholar knows nothing whatever about all-under-heaven. He has no decided opinions one way or the other as to whether the earth is round or flat, for it is no concern of his. Neither is the current history of his own country. National affairs belong to the mandarins who get their living by them; what have such matters to do with a literary man who has taken his degree?

The writer is acquainted with an ex-schoolmaster who went into a business which often led him to a distance from home. About a year after peace had been concluded with Japan, this much-travelled merchant inquired during the progress of a call if we could inform him how the war turned out, explaining that he had heard such contradictory accounts at the capital of his province and at Tientsin that he knew not what to believe, and had judiciously held his mind entirely in suspense until he had an opportunity to see his foreign friend, who might, he thought, know for certain!

Linked with this dense ignorance and more impenetrable indifference is a most unbounded credulity. Faith in the fêng-shui, or geomancy of a district is still as firmly rooted as ever in the minds of the leading literary men of the empire, as is shown by memorials in the Peking Gazette calling for changes in buildings, the erection of lucky towers, etc., because the number of successful competitors is not greater.

A scholar who thinks it necessary to beat drums in order to save the sun in an eclipse from the "Dog" which is devouring it, receives with implicit faith the announcement that in Western lands the years are a thousand days in length, with four moons all the time. If some one who has dabbled a little in chemistry reports to him a rudimentary experiment in which carbonic dioxide poured down a trough extinguishes a row of burning candles, he is at once reminded that The Master refused to speak of feats of magic, and he dismisses the whole topic with the verdict: "Of course it was done by malign spirits."

In this fertile soil every kind of mischievous tale takes root downward, and in due time bears its bitter fruit, as many foreigners in China know to their cost. Were it not for the credulity of the literary men in China, riots against foreigners would seldom or never occur. It is a melancholy fact that vast numbers of this class, especially in the rural districts, are profoundly convinced of the truth of the worst allegations made against the men of the

West, while still greater numbers are absolutely indifferent to the matter unless it happens in some way to affect themselves.

The learned and semi-intelligent vacuity of the village scholar is more than matched by the ignorant vacuity of his illiterate neighbours. If he happens to have travelled, the latter has indubitably the better education of the two, for the reason that it is based (as far as it goes) upon facts. But if he is a typical villager he has never been anywhere to speak of, and knows nothing in particular. His conversation is filled with unutterable inanities till he is gathered to his fathers. In every Chinese village one sees, except at the busiest times, groups of men sitting in the sunshine in winter, in the shade in summer, on some friendly stick of timber, and clustered in the little temples which constitute the village exchange. Even in the depth of winter they continue to huddle together in a vain effort to be comfortable as well as sociable, and chatter, chatter all the day, or until it is time to go to their meals. The past, present, and future state of the weather, the market prices, local gossip, and especially the details of the latest lawsuit form the warp and woof of this unending talk. What the Magistrate asked of Chang when he was examined, what Chang replied, what Wang retaliated, as well as what the Official had to say to that, with interminable iterations and profuse commentary furnish the most interesting and the most inexhaustible themes for discourse.

For any official changes unless it be that of his own District Magistrate the villager cares very little. At a time when it was supposed that His Majesty Kuang Hsü had been made way with, the writer remarked to a Chinese friend that there was reason to fear that here was an empire without an Emperor. A villager of the sluggish type just mentioned, who had heard nothing of the news from Peking, inquired of what country the observation had been made, and when the answer had been given that it was the Central Empire, he reflected for a moment, and merely replied, "Oh", with the air of one who had feared it might be worse! Yet the rustic of this class is shrewd in his own affairs, and by no means deficient in practical intelligence. He is passionately fond of hearing story-tellers and of witnessing plays having for their heroes the great men of the Three Kingdoms seventeen hundred years ago, and on occasion he might be able to tell us much about these characters and their deeds. But modern and contemporaneous history is out of his line, and lacks flavour. It is most literally none of his business, and he knows nor cares nothing about it. The whole map of Asia might be reconstructed, and it would have for him no interest whatever, provided it did not increase his taxes nor raise the price of grain.

We have already mentioned that the villager who has been far from home is a conspicuous exception to the general vacuity of mind so often to be met. He has a rich and a varied experience which he is willing although not forward to relate. But it is a striking fact that the man of this sort when he returns to go abroad no more, tends speedily to relapse into the prevailing type. He may have been in every one of the Eighteen Provinces, or possibly in foreign lands, yet on his settling down to his old ways he has no more curiosity to know what is going on elsewhere, than a man who had at some time in his life been shipwrecked would have to know what had become of the schools of fish with which for a time he was in fortuitous proximity. When it is considered how vast a proportion of the whole population live in villages, and when we contemplate in detail the meagreness and poverty of the mental output, an impressive conception is gained of the intellectual barrenness of the Flowery Empire. The phenomena which we everywhere see are the outward expression of inner forces which have been at work for more than two thousand years. The longer they are considered and the more thoroughly they are understood the more profoundly will it be seen and felt that the "answer to Confucianism is China."

XXV

UNSTABLE EQUILIBRIUM OF THE CHINESE FAMILY

The family is the unit of Chinese social life and, as we have often had occasion to observe, the Chinese Family is a highly complex organization, with many aspects which sometimes appear mutually contradictory. To the consideration of one of these polyhedral faces we now turn, asking the reader to bear well in mind that while what we have to say contains important truth, this is but one out of many points of view.

The instability of the equilibrium of the Chinese family arises from its constitution, from its environment, and from the relation between the two. Let us first glance at some of the exterior causes. In a large portion of the empire the rain-fall is more or less uncertain, rendering famine a perpetual possibility. Within the past quarter of a century foreigners in China have had superabundant opportunities to study the phenomena of famine upon a great scale. The misery thus occasioned is inconceivable, but we wish to refer only to the resultant disruption of families. Nothing is more common than to find that the father has gone to some distant region hoping to secure a bare sustenance leaving the wife and children to shift for themselves. This is not because he does not care for them, nor because he desires the separation, but because there is literally "no help for it."

Large portions of the empire are liable to inundation, often with little or no warning. Those who contrive to save themselves wander off whither they can, generally in family groups, but not infrequently one by one.[7] Children are born and children die on these haphazard journeys nowhither. The elders die too, and sometimes a marriageable girl is disposed of for life to some husband who could not afford the expense of an ordinary wedding. It is proverbial that there are no ceremonies for a second marriage, and whenever a family is broken up, it is highly probable that all the widows will soon find partners, the union liable to be discontinued whenever there is again a scarcity of food.

Political disturbances which often rise to the dignity of small rebellions operate in the same way as famines and floods. In any of these cases families once widely dispersed are not likely again to recombine.

It is not in times of special stress only that families are parted. In several of the provinces of China a considerable proportion of the adult males earn their living at great distances from home.

Myriads of Chinese from the northern portion of China get such a livelihood as they can in Manchuria or elsewhere beyond the Great Wall, hundreds or thousands of miles from home, to which multitudes never return. Innumerable Chinese mothers never learn what has become of their sons, who went away in early youth to be heard of no more. Communication is irregular and uncertain, and uniformly untrustworthy. No wonder the current adage declares that when the son has gone a thousand miles the mother grieves.[8] The Chinese Enoch Arden perhaps returns from an absence of possibly ten or it may be twenty years, enters his house, throws down his bundle and without a question or a greeting to any one, proceeds to take a solacing smoke. He may have been away so long that no one recognizes him, and perhaps he is taken for a tramp and warned off. But he merely replies "Why should I not make myself at home in my own house?" and resumes his smoking, leaving details to be filled in later.

The equilibrium of every Chinese family is liable to be disturbed by an evil which may not unlikely work more mischief than an ordinary earthquake—to wit, a lawsuit. There is not a day in the life of any Chinese when his peace, his prosperity, and possibly his life may not be endangered by some complication for which he is not in any way responsible, but from which escape is practically impossible. Let not the reader suppose that most

Chinese are entangled in the meshes of the law, for this is not the case. But there is always the unavoidable liability. A moment of uncontrollable passion on the part of any one of a score of persons, may precipitate a crisis involving the expenditure of the greater part of one's resources, subjection to protracted detention in jail, to torture, to punishment of immeasurable barbarity, and to virtual starvation in prison unless the means of the family are drained to prevent it. Not every lawsuit has within it such phenomena as these, but they are everywhere potential, for no one can predict where or how any suit will end. It is not alone the principals who suffer in cases of this sort, for, as the current saying runs, "When one family has trouble none of the four neighbours are in peace."

Attention has been repeatedly called to the familiar fact that practically no Chinese can maintain financial independence. To a foreigner nothing is more amazing than the reckless manner in which a debt is contracted which subsequently proves to have within it the fruitful seeds of ruin for the whole family. It is vain to ask why the money was borrowed. One might as well inquire why one is so wet who has been out all night in a Scotch mist. Ages of experience have made the Chinese relentless creditors, and woe to him who owes but cannot pay. China is full of small dealers with a limited capital, who do well enough in ordinary years. A very small percentage contrives to get so far ahead as to buy land, and thus the family is rooted to the soil. But a far larger number lose the capital invested, are obliged to sell their little holdings to pay their dues, and thenceforth they join the great, hopeless, landless class. A single failure of one important crop may carry with it consequences of this kind to many small dealers. In China the man or the family which is loaded with a debt beyond the recuperative power of the debtor, finds itself upon an oiled toboggan-slide at the bottom of which is remediless ruin.

In the families of the poor there is no margin of any kind for sickness, but sickness comes impartially to every grade of life. When the bread-winner is laid aside, when the mother of a little flock is no longer able to keep the simple domestic machinery in motion, then indeed trouble has arrived. If a young married woman is sick, the first step is to send for her mother; for ordinarily no one in the family into which she has married has the time or disposition to take care of her, least of all the husband, who regards himself as aggrieved by her disability, and who is often far more inclined to expect the family of his wife to bear all the resultant expenses, than to meet them himself. One of the legal occasions for divorce is chronic illness, although we have never heard of a single instance where formal steps were taken for that reason. It is a current saying that in the presence of a long continued sickness there is no filial son. How great the family strain often is, there are many things to prove. In the midst of it all one is sometimes agreeably surprised to find an amount of tenderness and forbearance worthy of all praise. But in the constitution of Chinese society these exhibitions are and must be in a great minority. A man well known to the writer in speaking of the serious symptoms of a disease of his wife, remarked that he had asked her how long she expected to keep up the groans called forth by the intolerable agonies of terrible and incurable ulcers, and that for his part he had offered to provide her with a rope that she might relieve him of his inconvenience, and herself of her miseries, though upon being remonstrated with for such an inhuman view of the case, he frankly admitted that his troubles had made him "stupid." It is a significant saying in such instances that the sufferer although poor has contracted a rich man's malady.

The disintegrating forces which operate in the Chinese family are more efficient in the homes of the poor than of the rich, because there is less power of resistance. But there are two of these agencies which imply a certain degree of prosperity ere they can be fully developed, the gambling and the opium habit, twin vices of the Chinese race. Each leads by swift and relentless steps to destruction, and in each case there ensues at last what is virtually a paralysis of the will, making amendment impossible.

Against these gigantic evils there is in Chinese society no safeguard whatever, no preventive influences, and no remedies. It would be easy to illustrate in terrible detail how these forces act insidiously, universally and irresistibly. The wonder is that the track of devastation is not even wider. They take rank among the most destructive instrumentalities in Chinese social life. It is very rare indeed to hear of reform from either of these vices, when there has been no impulse imparted from without, and it is rarer that there is any one who can and who will impart it.

To this dark catalogue of maleficent forces must be added one more, violation of social morality. To what extent this prevails in any given place it is impossible for any Chinese—much less for any foreigner—to say with authority. There is among the people, despite their loquacity—an instinct of reticence in every way commendable. Little value is placed upon infant life. The air is always full of rumors and suspicious whispers, so that the judicious will believe nothing of which there is not positive evidence. The Chinese code of morals is a lofty one, both in theory and in practice. The social arrangements are all made with a carefulness which to the Occidental seems mere prudery, but which the accumulated experience of millenniums has convinced the Chinese to be not only wise, but indispensable.

Yet in the conditions of everyday life it is simply impossible that theoretical regulations should be reduced to practice. The elderly women die, and courtyards are left from sheer necessity in a condition to invite catastrophe. Against a bad father-in-law especially if he be a widower—there is in the Chinese social economy no provision and no defence. It is proverbial that insinuations lurk about the dwelling-place of widows. In a word it may almost be said that no one has absolute confidence in any one else.

In spite of all apparent evidence to the contrary, there is adequate reason to believe that Chinese social morality at its best is fully equal to that of any Western land. Yet it is necessary to take careful note of the circumstance that the consequences of a lapse from virtue are destitute of the ameliorations with which we have become familiar. The principal concern of every one interested is the "face" of the family involved, and to save this imaginary self-respect it may be necessary for some one to commit suicide, which is done with the smallest provocation at all times. No Chinese is ever quite free from the dread that some one of his household may take this step. Provision is expressly made in Chinese law for the punishment of those who can be proved to have "urged to death" others; a crime which is treated as manslaughter. This fact alone would serve as a gauge of the wide interval between the civilizations of the west and of China.

All Chinese may be said to have strongly developed an attachment to the family in which they were born, and most of them have also strong family affections running in specific and limited channels, and by no means evenly distributed. They share with the rest of the race a desire to make their families perpetual, and when they fail, as they so frequently do, their failure is the more conspicuous by reason of their inalienable attachment to their natal soil. In order more deeply to explore some of the causes of their want of success, it will be necessary to go farther below the surface of the Chinese family.

XXVI

INSTABILITY FROM FAMILY DISUNITY

To give a correct diagnosis of the inner causes of the disunity of Chinese social and family life without at the same time grossly misrepresenting both the Chinese character and society, is a hopeless undertaking. Merely to note even the most authentic and typical facts is to convey an impression which is incorrect because it is not proportional. Every family contains within itself the seeds of disunity, and if they do not in all cases produce their appropriate harvest, it is because they are mercifully blighted or counteracted in their development.

Of each Chinese family a full half has had or will have interests largely at variance with those of the other half. Every Chinese wife came by no choice of her own from some other family, being suddenly and irrevocably grafted as a wild stock upon the family tree of her husband. As we have already seen, she is not received with enthusiasm, much less with affection (the very idea of which in such a connection never enters any Chinese mind) but at best with mild toleration, and not infrequently with aggressive criticism. She forms a link with another set of interests from which by disruption she has indeed been dissevered, but where her attachments are centred. The affection of most Chinese children for their mothers is very real and lasting. The death of the mother is for a daughter especially the greatest of earthly calamities. Filial piety in its cruder and more practical aspects constantly leads the married daughter to wish to transfer some of the property of the husband's family to that of her mother. The temptation to do so is often irresistible, and sometimes continues through life, albeit with many dramatic checks. The

Chinese speak of this habit in metaphorical phrase as "a leak at the bottom" which is proverbially hard to stop. It is a current saying that of ten married daughters, nine pilfer more or less. It is not uncommon to hear this practice assigned as one of the means by which a family is reduced to the verge of poverty. The writer once had occasion to acquaint a Chinese friend with the fact that a connection by marriage had recently died. He replied thoughtfully: "It is well she is dead; she was gluttonous, she was lazy; and beside she stole things for her mother!"

Visits to the mother's family constitute by far the most substantial joys in the life of a young Chinese married woman. It is her constant effort to make them as numerous as possible, and it is the desire of her husband's family to restrict them, since her services are thus partially lost to them. To prevent them from being wholly so, she is frequently loaded down with twice as much sewing as she could do in the time allowed, and sent off with a troop of accompanying children, if she has reached so advanced a stage as to be a mother of a flock. An invasion of this kind is often regarded with open dissatisfaction by her father and brothers, and what could be more natural than her desire to appease them by the spoils which she may have wrested from the Philistines?

After the death of her mother the situation has materially altered. The sisters-in-law have now no restraint on their criticisms upon her appearance with her hungry brood, and her whole stay may not improbably be a struggle to maintain what she regards as her rights. It is one of the many pathetic sights with which Chinese society abounds to witness the effort to seem to keep alive a spark of fire in coals which have visibly gone out. Not to have any "mother's family" to which to go is regarded as the depth of misery for a married woman, since it is a proclamation that she no longer has any one to stand up for her in case she should be abused. To discontinue altogether the visits thither is to some extent a loss of face, which every Chinese feels keenly. We have known an old woman left absolutely alone in the world, obliged at the age of ninety-four to gather her own fuel and do whatever she wanted done for herself, except draw water, which was furnished her by a distant relative as an act of special grace. Her poverty was so abject that she was driven to mix fine earth with the little meal that sufficed for her scanty food, that it might last the longer. Yet this poor creature would sometimes be missed from her place, when it was reported that she had gone on a visit to her "mother's family" consisting of the great-grandchildren of those whom she had known in youth!

By the time a married woman had reached middle life her interest in her original home may have greatly weakened. There are now young marriageable girls of her own growing up, each of whom in turn repeats the experience of her mother. To their fathers and also to their brothers these girls are at once a problem and a menace. Could the birth-rate of girls be determined by ballot of all the males of full age, it is probable that in a few generations the Chinese race would become extinct. The expression "commodity-on-which-money-has-been-lost," is a common periphrasis for a girl. They no sooner learn a little sewing, cooking, etc., than they are exported, and it is proverbial that water spilled on the ground is a synonym for a daughter. "Darnel will not do for the grain-tax, and daughters will never support their mothers." These modes of speech represent modes of thought, and the prevailing thought, although happily not the only thought of the Chinese people.

Girls as a rule have next to no opportunities for cultivating friendships with one another. The readiness with which under favourable condition such attachments are formed and perpetuated, shows how great a loss is their persistent absence. When it is considered that each Chinese family consists not of a man and his wife and their children, but of married sons, and of their several wives, each one introduced into the circle in the same compulsory way, each with a strong and an uncurbed will, yet powerless to assert herself except by harsh speeches and bad temper, it is evident that the result is not likely to be unity.

In the eye of Chinese law brothers are equal, and though the elder has some advantages, a portion larger than that of the others is not one of them. Sometimes the young married pair are given an outfit, say of cotton, for spinning and weaving, and are thenceforth expected to support themselves by this capital and their own added labour. Not infrequently an unequal distribution of the land is made among several brothers by the father while living, a wrong for which there is no remedy other than remonstrance. Neither if the father should conceive the idea of depriving a son of any portion at all in the land, is there effective redress.

Should the property be held in common according to Chinese traditions, it is a physical, a psychological, and a moral impossibility that there should not be ceaseless friction among so many claimants for what is often at best a most inadequate support.

The Chinese ideal is to hold the family property in common indefinitely. But the Chinese themselves are conscious that theirs is not an ideal world, so that division of the land cannot always be postponed. It not infrequently happens that one of the sons becomes discontented, and commissions one of the neighbours to tell the father that it is time to effect a division. At such times the family affairs are put into the hands of third parties who are supposed to be entirely disinterested, but sometimes the family has itself so well under control as to be able to dispense with this important assistance. The middlemen who have to conduct operations, begin by taking an inventory of the numerous pieces of land, the buildings, etc., which they then appraise roughly, endeavouring to separate these assets into as many portions as there are to be shares. A certain part of the land is set aside for "nourishing the old age" of the parents; and perhaps another section is reserved for the wedding expenses of unmarried daughters or younger sons. What remains is to be divided, which is accomplished by grouping the portions, and writing the descriptions of the several pieces of land, houses, etc., on pieces of paper which are rolled up and placed in a rice-bowl. This is shaken up and it is a courtesy to allow the youngest son to draw first. Whatever is noted on his bit of paper represents his share, and so on until all are drawn. The household furniture, water-jars, utensils of every kind, and all the grain and fuel on hand must be all taken out in public in the presence of the middlemen to be sure that nothing is secreted. We have known a particularly obstreperous son to come to his father's house the day after a division, and under pretence of looking for something which he had lost, to feel in every jar and pot to be sure that no beans or millet had escaped him. In a family where harmony reigns, all this trouble is avoided, but such are altogether exceptional. Shrewd Chinese estimate that out of every ten families which "divide" seven, if not nine, will have a domestic tempest as a concomitant, and these storms vary all the way from a short, sharp squall, to a hurricane which leaves everything in a wreck.

It is the Chinese theory that parents are to be taken care of in old age by their children either in combination or in rotation. But cases in which aged mothers have a portion to themselves, doing all their own cooking and most of the other necessary work are everywhere numerous. A Westerner is constantly struck with the undoubted fact that the mere act of dividing a property seems to extinguish all sense of responsibility whatever for the nearest of kin. It is often replied when we ask why a Chinese does not help his son or his brother who has a large family and nothing in the house to eat, "We have divided some time ago." The real explanation is perhaps to be found in the accumulated exasperations of the larger part of a lifetime, once delivered from which, a Chinese feels that he can judiciously expend his energies in looking out for Number One, leaving the rest of the series to do the same as best they may.

If a member of a family is absent when a division is made, it is common to hear that advantage has been taken of that fact to assign to him a portion which he would not have quietly accepted had he been present. This is particularly the case with the family debts, often aggregating a large sum. Sometimes a young man is forced to begin life weighted down with several hundred thousand cash worth of these liabilities due to some unprofitable partnership of his father with his uncles—which may have extended over a period of perhaps many years.

Another most undesirable but unavoidable asset is "empty grain-tax land!" This means a liability to pay the tax on land which is non-existent, but which has been made to appear to exist by mismeasurements in former years, either by accident or design. Suppose, for example, that a family has a hundred acres of land, which has to be sold in small pieces from time to time as occasion arises. Each surveying party works from such indefinite boundaries as the stump of an aged mulberry bush to another stump which may prove to be missing. The one who buys the land will use his best efforts to see that he gets good measure, which it is no concern of the measurers to refuse. No one knows exactly what is left until some final measurement becomes necessary, when it often appears that there is a shortage of a considerable amount. From deficits like this there arises the necessity of paying "empty taxes," and though the tax itself is sufficiently solid and substantial, there is no way known to Chinese practice by which such injustice can be rectified. The son who finds himself saddled with this sort of a burden is not likely to contribute to the harmony of the household in future, and were he ever so much inclined to bury the matter in oblivion and "eat a dumb man's loss," his wife would never stop talking about it, unless she chanced to be dumb herself. A complete catalogue of the possible and indeed inevitable occasions which produce family alienations and bitterness would of itself fill a volume, but those which have been suggested may serve as samples of them all.

It deserves mention that when the strain has reached the breaking point, especially when it is difficult for the aggrieved individual to go off to a great distance and escape his woes, he is often seized by the idea of administering poison to the person hated. Were the list of toxic substances available to the Chinese larger, poisoning would be far more frequent than at present.

As it is cases are everywhere to be heard of, and occasionally foreigners are the victims.

While this chapter was in preparation a Chinese friend called to ask advice. He had a nephew thirty-six years of age, who until recently had never been married. He is a dull witted man, with very little property, and had never been regarded as a desirable match. About five months previous to the recent occurrence which led to the request for advice, a girl aged sixteen was found who had a deformity in one limb preventing her from making a match. A go-between proposed her for this bachelor and it was arranged that he should pay her family eight strings of cash for "bridal outfit," and in due time the marriage took place. As might have been expected it was a conspicuously infelicitous one. On the twenty-sixth day of the first moon of the current year, the husband ate a bowl of millet which seemed to him to have a singular taste, but he did not suspect poison until he had taken it all, when he saw arsenic at the bottom. After violent retching he was somewhat relieved. The next day but one the same thing occurred, the symptoms being graver. He vigorously remonstrated, and his bride left for her home some miles away. The husband was now very ill, and was waited on for some days by his uncle, at the times of whose visit for advice the nephew's life was supposed to be out of danger. The uncle wanted to know what should be done about it. In an empire where "talkativeness" is a legal ground for divorce, it naturally appeared to an Occidental that repeated, albeit clumsy attempts at poisoning might be equally so. But the uncle explained that there was a sister-in-law who objected. Why? Apparently because having invested eight strings of cash in a wife it was a pity to lose her for a mere trifle like this! The matter was put into the hands of peace-talkers, who arranged that the relative who had brought the bride the arsenic should kotow to the man poisoned by the arsenic, and that the family of the bride should pay the injured husband fifteen strings of cash wherewith to recruit his depleted vitality. Meantime the bride remained at her mother's home, where one of the women was said to have beaten her a little. She is not divorced, her husband being reluctant to proceed to such extremities, in part on account of the large investment originally made, and in part for fear of ridicule. In due time she will probably be sent back to his home to resume her experiments in the art of making home happy.

Thus far we have spoken of disunity of Chinese families as promoted by that intense subjectivity to which we give the name selfishness. There are, however, many other factors to be taken into account, which have to do with racial habits and race traits.

To affirm that every Chinese is a natural liar is a grievous error. On the contrary we believe the Chinese to be by far the most truthful of Asiatics. Yet there can be no doubt that disingenuousness is to them a second nature. It runs through the warp and woof of their life.

A witness in a Chinese lawsuit (where veracity is more than ordinarily important) usually begins his mixture of three-tenths fact with seven-tenths fiction with the remark: "I will not deceive Your Honour." In this he speaks the truth, for His Honour knows perfectly well that the witness is lying, and the witness knows that His Honour knows it. The only question is in regard to the percentage of falsehood, and as to which particular statements come under that head. The same principles are in operation in the family life as in court. Most husbands know better than to confide the real state of their affairs to their wives. Children in turn constantly conceal from their parents what ought to be known, and are themselves deceived whenever it becomes convenient to do so. A Chinese woman known to the writer when a mere child was one day told by her mother that she must not go upon the street to play as usual, but must remain in the house and have her clothes changed. This was done, and before she knew it, she was thrust into a sedan-chair, and was on the way to the house of her "husband," for this was her marriage! The conditions which would make such an occurrence possible, would produce quite naturally many phenomena of a disagreeable description. It is a popular adage that "She who knows how to behave as a daughter-in-law will prevaricate at both her homes, while the inexpert daughter-in-law reveals what she knows at each of them"—and is in constant trouble in consequence.

Despite their disadvantages wives may contrive to conceal from their husbands the fact that they have a little property in the hands of some member of the wife's family. The writer is acquainted with a Chinese almost sixty years of age, who has a flock of grandchildren, but who will have nothing to do with his wife nor she with him. During all their married life, between thirty and forty years, he has cherished the suspicion that she has somewhere at interest a considerable sum of money which she will not share with him. It is certainly not true that all Chinese deceive one another, but it is surely true that there is always danger of it, which everywhere begets unrest and suspicion. It is also an allied phenomenon that the principals in a matter may be totally unable to ascertain the real facts with which every one else is perfectly acquainted, but which no one will tell.

Mencius remarked that the feeling of pity is common to all men, and what was true in his day is no less so now. At the same time there are wide differences in its exhibition. Every Chinese is a seasoned soldier in the warfare of life and is accustomed to every form and grade of misery. His first thought at such a spectacle is not, Cannot something be done about it? but if he has a thought at all it is far more likely to be, Why should I do anything about it? Ages of hereditary experience have taught him not too rashly to indulge in sentimental benevolence which may have disagreeable sequelæ. A Chinese remarked in the writer's hearing while glancing at the corpse of a man who had died far from home under painful circumstances: "This plaything will be hard to transport." Of what we call sympathy he had not the smallest conception. A few years later this same individual was seized by the District Magistrate of the county in which he lived, thrust into the standing-cage (a punishment far more horrible than the slicing process, since the victim is conscious but is in a position of acute agony without food or water until he miserably perishes) with no definite charge of any kind against him, and with no trial whatever. The only comment of many of these who had once known him well, was either that it was just what might have been expected, or that it was probably just what he deserved.

The typical Chinese is a good-natured, even-tempered, peaceable individual, ready to do his part in life without shirking, and asking only for fair treatment. But as the placid surface of many lakes is often lashed into fury by sudden and violent winds pouring down through mountain gorges, so the equilibrium of the Chinese is liable to be destroyed by gusts of terrible passion, instantly transforming him from a quiet member of a well ordered society, into an impressive object-lesson on the reality of demon possession. Whether life is worth living has been thought "to depend upon the liver." In China one might rather affirm that it hinges upon the spleen. Some of our readers may not be unfamiliar with a legend of a distinguished American who was provided by his kind father with a little hatchet which he tried upon a favourite cherry tree with marked success. When the father discovers this, he asks who did the deed, upon which the child handsomely confesses, and is clasped to his father's arms with the remark that he would rather lose many cherry trees than to have his son tell a lie. The whole occurrence probably did not consume more than ten minutes. To illustrate some of the traits of disunity already mentioned, let us translate this incident into Chinese.

Mr. Hua Hsing-tun was a well-to-do farmer, who had in his courtyard a handsome pomegranate tree of which he was very proud. His youngest son one day got hold of a sickle, which had been sharpened ready to cut wheat the next morning. With this implement he chopped at everything he saw, and among the rest, at the pomegranate tree which fell at the third blow. Seeing what mischief he had done, he ran to the other end of the village where he played with some boys whom he told that a cousin (the third son of his fourth uncle) had done the deed. This was overheard by a neighbour who passed on to the other end of the village just in time to hear Mr. Hua angrily roaring out the inquiry who had spoiled his pet tree. During a lull in the storm the neighbour, who had stepped into the courtyard to see what was the matter, confided to another neighbour that it was the nephew who had done the mischief. The neighbours soon depart. As no one in the yard knows anything about the tree, Mr. Hua, white with rage, continues his bawling upon the village street, denouncing the individual who had killed his tree. An older son who has just come up, having heard the story of the two neighbours, repeats it to his father, who gaining at last a clue, rushes to his fourth brother's yard, only to find no one at home but his sister-in-law, whom he begins to revile in the most outrageous manner. For an instant only she is surprised, then takes in the situation and screams at her brother-in-law, returning his revilings with compound interest added. He retreats into the alley and thence to the street, whither she follows him, shrieking at the top of her voice.

At this juncture the unfortunate nephew alleged to be the author of the mischief attracted by the clamour comes home, when the infuriated uncle administers a great deal of abusive language relative to his illegitimate descent from a base ancestry, as well as a stunning blow with a stick. This drives the mother of the child to frenzy, and she attacks her brother-in-law by seizing his queue, being immediately pulled off by the second brother, and some neighbours, there being now fifty or more spectators. The fourth sister-in-law is forcibly dragged back to her own yard by several other women, screaming defiance as she goes, and ends by scratching her own face in long furrows with her sharp nails, being presently covered with blood. Her husband has now come in furious at the insult to his family, reviles the elder brother (and his ancestry) declaring that he will immediately go to the yamên and lodge a complaint. He takes a string of cash and departs on this errand, but is subsequently followed several miles by six men, who spend two hours in trying to get him to return, with the promise that they will "talk peace." About midnight they all reach home. Most of the next five days is spent in interviews between third parties, who in turn have other conferences with the principals. At the expiration of this period all is settled. Mr. Hua the elder is to make a feast at an expense of not less than ten strings of cash, at which he shall admit that he was in error in reviling this sister-in-law at that time; the younger brother is to accept the apology in the presence of fourteen other men who have become involved in the matter at some of its stages. When the feast has been eaten, "harmony" is restored. But what about the author of all this mischief? Oh, "he is only a child." With which observation the whole affair is dismissed, and forgotten.

Chinese quarrels are objectionable by reason of their suddenness, their violence, and their publicity. The last named feature is the one most repugnant to Western civilization which has not yet learned how to avoid domestic disputes itself. As every occurrence immediately becomes public property, the element of "face" at once enters in, demanding an adjustment which shall put the injured party right in the presence of the rest of creation always conceived as looking critically on.

One of the most melancholy phenomena of Chinese life is the suddenness, the spontaneity, the inexorableness with which natural affection and all kindly relations under certain conditions seem absolutely to wither up. If a member of a clan comes into collision with the prejudices of the generation above his own, or even with that to which he himself belongs, his grandfather, father, great uncles, uncles, cousins, and brothers often promise to break his legs, rub out his eyes with quick-lime, and the like, and not infrequently carry these threats into execution. It is constantly mentioned as a mitigation of an attack with violence, that there was no intention to kill the individual, only to maul him till he had so many broken bones that he could not stir!

If the matter comes to a lawsuit, it is a common cry that no compromise shall ever be made, until the opponent has parted with his last piece of land. The suspense of mind under which many Chinese habitually live, uncertain whether these menaces will be carried into execution, would drive an Occidental to insanity or to suicide, or both. A frequent ending to a stormy conference is the dark hint: "We shall see about this later."

The Chinese are firm believers in the doctrine of rewards and punishments. A man who has been conspicuous for his evil deeds will meet no shadow of sympathy when trouble of any sort overtakes him. He is a tiger in a pit. Such an one who was attacked with worm-breeding corrosive ulcers, dragged himself to the terrace of one of the temples of his native village, where he lay sometimes in a coma, and at others screaming with pain. His neighbours would revile him as they passed with the comment: "It is heaven's vengeance!"

The Chinese character often abounds in amiable alleviations of conditions which would seem at first sight to make existence intolerable. In the breasts of the Chinese, as in ours, Hope springs eternal. His generalizations from the experience of others as well as his own, render him measurably certain that in the long-run almost nothing will go right. He expects to meet insincerity, suspicion, and neglect, and he is rarely disappointed. He will often be dependent upon those who would be glad to get rid of him, and who keep him constantly aware of this fact. He knows as certainly before as after the event that the loans which he is obliged to make will not be repaid at the proper time, nor in full; that the promised assistance if given at all will be rendered grudgingly, and perhaps turned into open hostility. It is proverbial that he has in his mind "two hundred next years" but he is not infrequently perfectly aware that no number of "next years" will ever suffice to get him straight with the world. Yet amid all this he generally maintains a serene cheerfulness which to us would be as impossible as comfortable respiration in the foul atmosphere of a Chinese sleeping-room. He is used to it—we are not. A man of this type weighted with a termagant wife, who had become exasperated by the unexpected remarriage of a brother of her husband for twenty years a widower, and who filled the house with a tempest in consequence, said to the writer that for the past three months he had not drawn "one peaceful breath!" This was not mentioned by way of complaint, but as one might refer in reply to an inquiry about a troublesome corn on the toe. Under stress of this sort many Chinese exhibit a degree of forbearance to which it is to be feared we have no counterpart in the West, where individual rights have not for ages been merged in those of the family. Such persons are said to "eat a dumb man's injury," and the number of them is proverbially unlimited, for the class is immortal.

No one who is intimately acquainted with their real life is likely to exaggerate the evils from which the Chinese suffer, since the strongest representation often seems to come short of the truth. But every one finds himself asking by what means it would be possible to forefend some of these evils. Since many of them appear to be inseparably associated with that poverty which is apparently the keynote of Chinese discords, one is tempted to imagine that if poverty were abolished, family disunity also would largely disappear. Something may be said in favour of this theory, but it fails in presence of the undoubted fact that the evils to be remedied are perhaps quite as prevalent among those Chinese who are fairly well off, as among the poor, besides being much more conspicuous and irrepressible.

Moral discord can be cured only by radical and not by superficial remedies. Yet there is one prescription of an economic as distinguished from a moral type which were it tried on a large scale for a generation or two might work such a revolution that China would hardly know itself. If marriages could be invariably postponed until the partners had arrived at mature age, and if on occasion of the marriage of each son the family property were divided so that a conflict of interests were no longer unavoidable, a whole continent of evils would be nipped in the bud.

At the inquiry held in marine courts as to the reasons for the wreck of great steamers with all their passengers and cargo, in the Formosan Channel, it is often shown that the vessel was acted upon by a powerful but hidden current which made ruin inevitable. The hereditary habits of the Chinese in the agglomeration of large numbers of individuals under one head constitute a drift toward disunity and disintegration. We firmly believe that the strain upon the temper and the disposition incident to the mechanical collocation of so many human beings in one compound-family on the Chinese plan is one which no society in the world could endure, because it is more than human nature can bear. It is certain that the resultant evils are inevitable, insufferable, and by any means at the command of the Chinese incurable.

PART III

Regeneration of the Chinese Village

XXVII

WHAT CAN CHRISTIANITY DO FOR CHINA?

However inadequate or imperfect our survey of the life of the Chinese Village may have been, it must at least have shown that it has defects of a serious character. It is therefore a legitimate question how they are to be remedied, on the supposition that they can be remedied at all.

It is certainly conceivable that there might be many remedial agencies set at work with varying degrees of success; but as a matter of fact, so far as we are aware, there is but one the friends of which have been stimulated to try on any extended scale. That sole agency is Christianity. It thus becomes an inquiry of great moment, what effect the introduction into China of Christianity in its best form may be rationally expected to exert upon the springs of the national life and character of the Chinese. What can Christianity do for the Chinese family? What can it do for the Chinese boy and girl?

In the first place it can take better care of them. The dense and impenetrable ignorance which sacrifices so large a proportion of Chinese infants during the first two years of their life, might perhaps be counteracted in other ways, but it is probably safe to predict that it never would be. To the Chinese girl the practical introduction of Christianity will mean even more than to her brother. It will prevent her from being killed as soon as she is born, and will eventually restore her to her rightful place in the affections of her parents. It is never enough merely to point out the folly, danger, or sin of a given course of action. There must be moral as well as intellectual enlightenment, coöperation in a new social order, the stimulus both of precept and example, and adequate moral sanctions. This can be furnished by Christianity alone. History testifies that if Christianity begins to lose its power, the dormant forces of human selfishness, depravity and crime reassert themselves in infant murder.

Christianity will call into existence a sympathy between parents and children hitherto unknown, and one of the greatest needs of the Chinese home. It will teach parents to govern their children, an accomplishment which in four millenniums they have never made an approach to acquiring. This it will do, not as at present by the mere iterative insistence upon the duty of subjection to parents, but by showing parents how first to govern themselves, teaching them the completion of the five relations by the addition of that chiefest one hitherto unknown, expressed in the words Our Father. It will redeem many years during the first decade of childhood, of what is now a mere animal existence, filling it with fruitfulness for a future intellectual and spiritual harvest.

It will show Chinese parents how to train as well as how to govern their children—a divine art of which they have at present no more conception than of the chemistry of soils. It will put an end to the cruelty and miseries of foot-binding. Toward this great reform there was never in China the smallest impulse, until it had long been urged by Christian forces. If it shall prove at length to have successfully taken root in China apart from Christianity, that fact would be a luminous star in the East showing that there are no Chinese walls which may not ultimately fall before the blast of Christian trumpets.

Christianity will revolutionize the Chinese system of education. Such a revolution might indeed take place without reference to Christianity. The moral forces which have made China what it is, are now to a large extent inert. To introduce new intellectual life with no corresponding moral restraints, might prove far more a curse than a blessing, as it has been in the other Oriental lands. Christian education will never make the mistake so often repeated of seeking for fruits where there have been no roots. It starts from a fixed point and moves onward to a definite end.

Little Old People.

Going to a Christian School.

Christian education will teach the Chinese child his own tongue in a rational manner. It will abbreviate to the greatest possible extent "the toils of wandering through the wilderness of the Chinese language to arrive at the deserts of Chinese literature." It will awaken the child's hibernating imagination, enormously widen his horizon, develop and cultivate his judgment, teach him the history of mankind, and not of one branch only. Above all it will arouse his conscience, and in its light will exhibit the mutual interrelations of the past, the present, and the future. It will create an intellectual atmosphere in the home, causing the children to feel that their progress at school is intimately related to instruction at home, and has a personal interest to the parents and to the family as a whole. The value of such a stimulus, now totally lacking in most Chinese homes, is beyond calculation, and would of itself easily double the mental output of every family into which it entered.

Christianity will provide for the intellectual and spiritual education of girls as well as boys, when once the Christian point of view has been attained. The typical Chinese mother is "an ignorant woman with babies," but she is not the Chinese ideal woman as the long list of educated ladies in many dynasties (a number too considerable to be ignored but too insignificant to be influential) abundantly shows. A Chinese girl told her foreign friend that before Christianity came into her life, she used to go about her work humming a ballad, consisting of the words: "The beautiful teacup; the painted teacup; the teacup, the teacup, the beautiful, beautiful teacup." Contrast the outlook from such an intellectual mouse-hole with the vista of a maiden whose thoughts are elevated to the stars and the angels. By developing the neglected spiritual nature, Christianity will broaden and deepen the existing rills of natural affection into glorious rivers wide and deep, supplementing the physical and the material by the intellectual and the divine. By cultivating a fellowship between mothers and daughters in all these and in other lines, it will make it easier for children to love their fathers and respect their mothers, and will fill the lives of both parents and children with new impulses, new motives and new ambitions. It will impel mothers to give their daughters much needed instruction in their future duties as daughters-in-law and as wives, instead of throwing them overboard as now, often in mere childhood, expecting them to swim untaught, against the current, and in the dark.

It will for the first time provide and develop for the daughters girl friendships, adapted to their long-felt but uncomprehended needs. The education of Chinese women is a condition of the renovation of the empire. No nation, no race can rise above the status of its mothers and its wives. How deftly yet how surely Christianity is beginning to plant its tiny acorns in the rifts of the granitic rock may be seen in the surprising results already attained. When the present isolated and initiatory experiments shall have had time to bring forth fruit after their kind, it will be clearly perceived that a new and an Imperial force has entered into the Chinese world.

Christianity wherever introduced tends to a more rational selection of partners for its sons and daughters than has ever been known before. In place of the mercenary considerations which alone find place in the ordinary practice of the Chinese, it naturally and inevitably leads to the choice of Christian maidens for daughters-in-law, and Christian youths for sons-in-law. It attaches weight to character, disposition and acquirements instead of to wealth and to social position alone. A Christian community is the only one in China where it is possible to learn with certainty all important facts with regard to those who may be proposed for matrimonial engagements, because it is only in such a community that dependence can be placed upon the representations of third parties. As Christian communities come more and more to distinct self-consciousness, more and more care will be exercised in making matches. Christians are indeed the only Chinese who can be made to feel that caution in this direction is a religious duty. The result of this process continued for an extended period will produce by "natural selection" a distinctly new type of Chinese, physically, intellectually, and morally the superiors of all types about them and therefore more fitted to survive.

Chinese customs will not be rashly invaded, but the ultimate tendency will be to postpone marriage to a suitable age, to consider the preferences of the principal parties—so far as they may have any—and to make wedlock a sacred solemnity instead of merely a social necessity.

Christianity will make no compromise with polygamy and concubinage, but will cut the tap-root of a upas-tree which now poisons Chinese society wherever its branches spread. Christianity will gradually revolutionize the relations between the young husband and his bride. Their common intellectual and spiritual equipment will have fitted them to become companions to one another, instead of merely commercial partners in a kettle of rice. The little ones will be born into a Christian atmosphere as different from that of a non-Christian household as the temperature of Florida from that of Labrador. These forces will be self-perpetuating and cumulative.

Christianity will purify and sweeten the Chinese home, now always and everywhere liable to devastating hurricanes of passion, and too often filled with evil-speaking, bitterness and wrath. The imperative inhibition of all manner of reviling would alone do more for domestic harmony than all the wise maxims of the sages mechanically learned and repeated could accomplish in a lifetime. Indeed, Christianity will take these semi-animate precepts of the dead past, breathe into them for the first time the breath of life, and then reinforce them with the Word of the Lord and the sanctions of His Law.

Christianity will introduce a new and a potent factor into the social life of the Chinese by its energy as a prophylactic. Chinese society has a virtuous talent for "talking peace" when there is no peace, and when matters have come to such a pitch that a catastrophe appears inevitable. But the remedy almost invariably comes too late. Chinese "peace-talking" is usually a mere dust-storm, unpleasantly affecting the eyes, the ears, the nostrils of every one exposed to it, thinly covering up the surrounding filth with even impartiality, while after all leaving the whole of it just where it was before. Christianity is an efficient sanitary commission which aims at removing everything that can breed pestilence. In this it will not, indeed, entirely succeed, but its introduction upon a large scale will as certainly modify Chinese society, as a strong and steady north-east wind will eventually dissipate a dense fog.

As has been already remarked, perhaps there is no single Chinese custom which is the source of a larger variety of mischief than that of keeping large family organizations in a condition of dependence upon one another and upon a common property, instead of dividing it up among the several sons, leaving each free to work out his own destiny. The inevitable result is chronic discontent, jealousy, suspicion, and on the part of many indolence. This is as clearly perceived by the Chinese as by us, indeed far more so, but hereditary cowardice, dread of criticism, and especially of ridicule prevent myriads of families from effecting the desired and necessary division, lest they be laughed at. Christianity is itself a defiance of all antecedent public opinion, and an appeal to a new and an illuminated understanding. Christian communities will probably more and more tend to follow the Scriptural plan of making one man and one woman a new family, and by this process alone will save themselves an infinity of misery. This will be done, not by the superimposition of any force from without, but by the exercise of a common sense which has been at once enlightened to see and emboldened to act, attacking with courage whatever needs amendment.

Christianity will introduce an entirely new element into the friendships of the Chinese, now too often based upon the selfish considerations suggested by the maxim of Confucius, "Have no friends not equal to yourself." Friendship is reckoned among the Five Relations and occupies a prominent place in Chinese thought as in Chinese life. But after all is conceded in regard to it which can be reasonably claimed, it remains true that its benefits are constantly alloyed by mutual insincerity and suspicion, and not infrequently by jealousy. This the Chinese themselves are ready to admit in the frankest manner; but as they have no experience of friendships which arise from conditions above and beyond those of the material issues of everyday life, no remedy for existing evils is ever thought of as possible. Those Chinese who have become intimate with congenial Christian friends, recognize at once that there is a flavour and a zest in such friendships not only unknown before, but absolutely beyond the range of imagination. Amid the poverty, barrenness, and discouragements of most Chinese lives, the gift of a wholly new relationship of the sort which Christianity imparts is to be reckoned among the choicest treasures of existence.

The theory of the Chinese social organization is admirable and beautiful, but the principles which underlie it are utterly inert. When Christianity shows the Chinese for the first time what these traditional principles really mean, the theories will begin to take shape as possibilities, even as the bones of Ezekiel's vision took on flesh. Then it will more clearly appear how great an advantage the Chinese race has enjoyed in its lofty moral code. The Classical but not altogether intelligible aphorism that "within the Four Seas all are Brethren," requires the Christian teaching regarding a common Father to make it vital to Chinese consciousness. When once the Chinese have grasped the practical truth of the Fatherhood of God and the Brotherhood of Man, the starlight of the past will have been merged into the sunlight of the future.

In China the family is a microcosm of the empire. To amplify illustrations of the modus operandi of Christianity on a wider scale beyond the family is superfluous. What Christianity can do in one place it can do in another. Though soils and climate vary, the seed is the same. For the changes which Christianity alone can affect, China is waiting to-day as never before. Her most intelligent thinkers—too few alas, in number—recognize that something must be done for her. They hope that by the adoption of certain formulæ, educational, industrial, economical, China may be saved, not perceiving that her vital lack is neither Capital nor Machinery, but Men. The New China is to be penetrated by numerous railways, and by steam navigation of its inland waters. Vast industrial enterprises such as mines and factories will call for great supplies of labour from the most numerous people on earth. In the management of these immense and varied interests, in the conduct of the new education which China cannot dispense with, in the administration of all branches of its government China must have men of conscience, and of sterling character. It has hitherto been impossible to secure any such men except by importation; how is it to be otherwise in the future? Only by the cultivation of conscience and character as they have been cultivated in lands to which China is at last driven to turn for help. Like all processes of development this will be a slow one, but it will be sure; and aside from it there is literally no hope for China.

With its other great benefits Christianity will confer upon China real patriotism, at present existing almost entirely in the blind impulses of the bias of national feeling. During the political crises of the past few years, the great mass of the Chinese people have been profoundly indifferent to the fate of their country, and in this respect there has been little distinction between scholars, farmers, merchants, and coolies. Each individual has been chiefly occupied in considering how in any cataclysm impending he could make with fate the best bargain for himself. If there are any exceptions to this generalization, so far

as we know they consist exclusively of those who have been acted upon by forces from outside of China.

The Christian converts are now sufficiently numerous to show in what direction their influence will be felt in the not distant future. They are keenly alive to what is taking place in the empire, and they may almost be said to be the only Chinese in it who are so. China will never have patriotic subjects until she has Christian subjects, and in China as elsewhere Christianity and patriotism will be found to advance hand in hand.

It must be distinctly understood that all which we have said of the potency of Christianity as of "unwasting and secular force" is based upon the conception of it as a moral power "producing certain definite though small results during a certain period of time, and of a nature adapted to produce indefinite similar results in unlimited time." It is therefore eminently reasonable to point out that under no circumstances can it produce its full effects in less than three complete generations. By that time Christian heredity will have begun to operate. A clear perception of this fundamental truth would do much to abate the impatience alike of its promotors and its critics.

There are some Occidentals with large knowledge of China who seriously raise the question, What good can Christianity do in China? Of what use is it for a Chinese to be "converted"?

To infer from any phenomena of Chinese life that the Chinese do not need a radical readjustment of their relations is to judge most superficially. Patient and long continued examination of these phenomena in their endless variety and complexity, shows clearly the imperative necessity of a force from without to accomplish what all the forces from within operating unimpeded for ages have been powerless to effect. To those who know the Chinese people as they are the question what good Christianity can do them, answers itself. Of the necessity of a new power the Chinese themselves are acutely conscious. If what has been already set forth in proof of the proposition that there is imperative need of renovation is regarded as irrelevant or inadequate, then further debate is indeed vain.

But it may be objected that the views here taken of the efficacy of the remedy are exaggerated. Those Chinese who have had the best opportunity to become acquainted with the nature of the benefits which Christianity affords, perceive its adaptation to China's need. All that is required to render the proof to every reasonable inquirer as complete as evidence can be made, is a searching and scientific analysis of known facts. The case for Christianity in China may rest solely upon the transformations which it actually effects. These are not upon the surface, but they are as real and as capable of being accurately noted as the amount of the rain-fall, or the precession of the equinoxes. They consist of revolutionized lives due to the implanting of new motives and the influence of a new life. They occur in many different strata of society, and with the ever widening base-line of Christian work they are found in ever increasing numbers. At first few and isolated, they are now counted by scores of thousands. Among them are many immature and blighted developments, as is true of all transitional phenomena everywhere; but the indisputable residuum of genuine transformations furnish a great cloud of witnesses in the presence of which it is unnecessary to inquire further what good Christianity will do the Chinese, and of what use it will be to a Chinese to be converted. It will make him a new man, with a new insight and a new outlook. It will give back his lost soul and spirit, and pour into all the avenues of his nature new life. There is not a human relation in which it will not be felt immediately, profoundly, and beneficently.

It will sanctify childhood, ennoble motherhood, dignify manhood, and purify every social condition. That Christianity has by no means yet done for Western lands all that we expect it to do for China, we are perfectly aware. Christianity has succeeded wherever it has been practiced. It is no valid objection to it that it has been misunderstood, misrepresented and ignored. Whatever defects are to be found in any Christian land, not the most unintelligent or the most sceptical would be willing to be transplanted into the non-Christian conditions out of which every Christian land has been evolved. It must be remembered also that although the lessons of Christianity are old, the pupils are ever new. Each generation has to learn its lesson afresh. It has well been said that heredity, so mighty a force for evil, has not yet been captured for Christianity on any large scale, and its reserves turned to the furtherance of Christian forces. When it has been so taken captive, progress upward will be greatly accelerated.

How long it will take Christianity to renovate an empire like China, is a question which may be answered in different ways, but only hypothetically. First by historical analogies. It took eight centuries to develop the Roman Empire. It has taken about as long to mold Saxon, Danish, and Norman elements into the England of to-day. Each of these race-stocks were at the start barbarous. The Chinese are an ancient and a highly civilized race, a fact which may be in some respects a help in their Christianization, and in others a hindrance. Taking into account the intensity of Chinese prejudices, the strength of Chinese conservatism, the vast numbers involved and their compact, patriarchal life, we should expect the first steps to be very slow. Reckoning from the general opening of China in 1860, fifty years would suffice for a good beginning, three hundred for a general diffusion of Christianity, and five hundred for its obvious superseding of all rival faiths. Reasoning from history and psychology this is perhaps a probable rate of progress, and its realization would be a great result.

There is however a different sort of forecast which appeals to many minds more powerfully. It must be remembered that spiritual development, like that of races, is slow in its inception, but once begun it takes little account of the rules of ratio and proportion. The intellectual, moral, and spiritual forces of Christianity are now far greater than they have ever been before. The world is visibly contracted. The life of the man of to-day is that of "a condensed Methusaleh." The nineteenth century outranks the previous millennium. Great material forces are but types and handmaids of the great spiritual forces which may be reinforced and multiplied—as they have been at certain periods of the past—to a degree at the present little anticipated.

Putting aside all consideration of the time element, we consider it certain that what Christianity has done for us it will do for the Chinese, and under conditions far more favourable, by reason of the high vitalization of the age in which we live, its unfettered communication, and the rapid transfusion of intellectual and spiritual forces. The forecast of results like these is no longer the iridescent dream which it once appeared. It is sober history rationally interpreted. When Christianity shall have had opportunity to work out its full effects, it will be perceived to have been pervasive leaven in the individual heart, in society, and in the world. Whether it is to take five centuries or fifty to produce these results appears to be a matter of altogether minor importance in view of certain success in the end.

There are in China many questions and many problems, but the one great question, the sole all-comprehending problem is how to set Christianity at work upon them, which alone in time can and will solve them all.

END

Selections from
Fleming H. Revell Company's
Missionary Lists

MISSIONS, CHINA.

Chinese Characteristics.

By Rev. Arthur H. Smith, D.D., for 25 years a Missionary in China. With 16 full-page original Illustrations, and index. Sixth thousand. Popular edition. 8vo, cloth, $1.25.

"The best book on the Chinese people."—The Examiner.

A Cycle of Cathay;

Or, China, South and North. With personal reminiscences. By W. A. P. Martin D.D., LLD., President Emeritus of the Imperial Tungwen College, Peking. With 70 Illustrations from photographs and native drawings, a Map and an index. Second edition. 8vo, cloth decorated, $2.00.

"No student of Eastern affairs can afford to neglect this work, which will take its place with Dr. William's 'Middle Kingdom,' as an authoritative work on China."—The Outlook.

Glances at China.

By Rev. Gilbert Reid, M.A., Founder of the Mission to the Higher Classes. Illustrated. 12mo, cloth, 80c.

Pictures of Southern China.

By Rev. James MacGowan. With 80 Illustrations. 8vo, cloth, $4.20.

A Winter in North China.

By Rev. T. M. Morris. With an Introduction by Rev. Richard Glover, D.D., and a Map. 12mo, cloth, $1.50.

John Livingston Nevius,

For Forty Years a Missionary in Shantung. By his wife, Helen S. C. Nevius. With an Introduction by the Rev. W. A. P. Martin, D.D. Illustrated. 8vo, cloth, $2.00.

The Sister Martyrs of Ku Cheng.

Letters and a Memoir of Eleanor and Elizabeth Saunders, Massacred August 1st, 1895. Illustrated, 12mo, cloth, $1.50.

China.

By Rev. J. T. Gracey, D.D. Seventh edition, revised. 16mo, paper, 15c.

Protestant Missions in China.
By D. Willard Lyon, a Secretary of the Student Volunteer Movement. 16mo, paper, 15c.

MISSIONS, CHINA AND FORMOSA.

James Gilmour, of Mongolia.
His Diaries, Letters and Reports. Edited and arranged by Richard Lovett, M.A. With three photogravure Portraits and Illustrations. 8vo, cloth, gilt top, $1.75.
"It is a vivid picture of twenty years of devoted and heroic service in a field as hard as often falls to the lot of a worker in foreign lands."—The Congregationalist.
Among the Mongols.
By Rev. James Gilmour. Illustrated. 12mo, cloth, $1.25.
James Gilmour and His Boys.
Being Letters to his Sons in England. With facsimiles of Letters, a Map and other Illustrations. 12mo, cloth, $1.25.
Griffith John,
Founder of the Hankow Mission, Central China. By William Robson. Missionary Biography Series. Illustrated. 12mo, cloth, 75c.
John Kenneth Mackenzie,
Medical Missionary to China. With the Story of the first Chinese Hospital. By Mrs. Mary I. Bryson. With portrait. 12mo, cloth, $1.50.
The Story of the China Inland Mission.
By M. Geraldine Guinness. Introduction by J. Hudson Taylor, F.R.G.S. Illustrated, 2 volumes, 8vo, cloth, each, $1.50.
From Far Formosa:
The Island, its People and Missions. By Rev. G. L. Mackay, D.D., 23 years a missionary on the island. Well indexed. With

many Illustrations from photographs by the author and several Maps. Fifth thousand. Popular edition. 8vo, cloth, $1.25.

China and Formosa.

The Story of the Mission of the Presbyterian Church of England. By Rev. James Johnson, editor of "Missionary Conference Report, 1888." With 4 Maps and many Illustrations, prepared for this work. 8vo, cloth, $1.75.

MISSIONS, JAPAN.

Rambles in Japan,

The Land of the Rising Sun. By Rev. Canon H. B. Tristram, D.D., F.R.S. With forty-six illustrations by Edward Whymper, a Map, and an index. 8vo, cloth, $2.00.

"A delightful book by a competent author, who, as a naturalist, writes well of the country, while as a Christian and a humanitarian he writes with sympathy of the new institutions of new Japan."—The Independent.

The Gist of Japan:

The Islands, their People, and Missions. By Rev. R. B. Peery, A.M., Ph.D., of the Lutheran Mission, Saga. Illustrated. 12mo, cloth decorated, $1.25.

This book does not pretend to be an exhaustive treatise of an exhaustless topic; it does pretend to cover the subject; and whosoever is eager to know the "gist" of those matters Japanese in which Westerners are most interested—the land, the people, the coming of Christianity, the difficulties and prospects of her missions, the condition of the native Church—will find it set down in Dr. Peery's book in a very interesting, reliable, instructive, and condensed form.

The Ainu of Japan.

The Religion, Superstitions, and General History of the Hairy

Aborigines of Japan. By Rev. John Batchelor. With 80 Illustrations. 12 mo, cloth, $1.50.

"Mr. Batchelor's book, besides its eighty trustworthy illustrations, its careful editing, and its excellent index, is replete with information of all sorts about the Ainu men, women, and children. Almost every phase of their physical and metaphysical life has been studied, and carefully noted."—The Nation.

The Diary of a Japanese Convert.

By Kanzo Uchimura. 12mo, cloth, $1.00.

"This book is far more than the name indicates. It is the only book of its kind published in the English language, if not in any language. It is something new under the sun, and is as original as it is new. It has the earmarks of a strong and striking individuality, is clear in diction, forceful in style, and fearless in criticism."—The Interior.

A Maker of the New Japan.

Joseph Hardy Neesima, the Founder of Doshisha University. By Rev. J. D. Davis, D.D., Professor in Doshisha. Illustrated. Second edition. 12mo, cloth, $1.00.

"The life is admirably and spiritedly written, and its hero stands forth as one of the most romantic and inspiring figures of modern times, a benefactor to his own country and an object of tender regard on our part; for it was to the United States that Mr. Neesima turned for light and help in his educational plans."—The Examiner.

MISSIONS, PACIFIC ISLANDS.

John G. Paton,

Missionary to the New Hebrides. An Autobiography, edited by his brother. With an Introductory Note by Rev. A. T. Pierson, D.D. Illustrated. Tenth thousand. 2 vols., 12mo, cloth, gilt top, boxed, net, $2.00; cheaper edition, 1 vol., 12mo, cloth, $1.50.

"We commend to all who would advance the cause of Foreign Missions this remarkable autobiography. It stands with such books as those Dr. Livingstone gave the world, and shows to men that the heroes of the cross are not merely to be sought in past ages."—The Christian Intelligencer.

Bishop Patterson,

The Martyr of Melanesia. By Jessie Page. Missionary Biography Series. Illustrated. Thirteenth thousand. 12mo, cloth, 75c.

James Calvert;

Or, From Dark to Dawn in Fiji. By R. Vernon. Missionary Biography Series. Illustrated. Tenth thousand. 12mo, cloth, 75c.

From Darkness to Light in Polynesia.

With Illustrative Clan Songs. By Rev. William Wyatt Gill, LL.D. Illustrated. 12mo, cloth, $2.40.

John Williams,

The Martyr Missionary of Polynesia. By Rev. James J. Ellis. Missionary Biography Series. Illustrated. Thirteenth thousand. 12mo, cloth, 75c.

Among the Maoris;

Or, Daybreak in New Zealand. A Record of the Labors of Marsden, Selwyn, and others. By Jessie Page. Missionary Biography Series. Illustrated. 12mo, cloth, 75c.

Pioneering in New Guinea,

1877-1894. By James Chalmers. With a Map and 43 Illustrations from Original Sketches and Photographs. 8vo, cloth, $1.50.

"It reveals a splendid character, and records a noble apostolic work. It is a notable addition to our missionary literature of the high class."—The Standard.

James Chalmers,

Missionary and Explorer of Rarotonga and New Guinea. By William Robson. Missionary Biography Series. Illustrated. Fourteenth thousand. 12mo, cloth, 75c.

MISSIONS, AFRICA.

The Personal Life of David Livingstone.

Chiefly from his unpublished journals and correspondence in the possession of his family. By W. Garden Blaikie, D.D., LL.D. With Portrait and Map. New, cheap edition. 508 pages, 8vo, cloth, $1.50.

"There is throughout the narrative that glow of interest which is realized while events are comparatively recent, with that also which is still fresh and tender."—The Standard.

David Livingstone.

His Labors and His Legacy. By A. Montefiore, F.R.G.S. Missionary Biography Series. Illustrated. 160 pages, 12mo, cloth, 75c.

David Livingstone.

By Mrs. J. H. Worcester, Jr., Missionary Annals Series. 12mo, paper, net, 15c.; flexible cloth, net, 30c.

Reality vs. Romance in South Central Africa.

Being an Account of a Journey across the African Continent, from Benguella on the West Coast to the mouth of the Zambesi. By James Johnston, M.D. With 51 full-page photogravure reproductions of photographs by the author, and a map. Royal 8vo, cloth, boxed, $4.00.

The Story of Uganda.

And of the Victoria Nyanza Mission. By S. G. Stock. Illustrated. 12mo, cloth, $1.25.

"To be commended as a good, brief, general survey of the Protestant missionary work in Uganda."—The Literary World.

Robert Moffat,

The Missionary Hero of Kuruman. By David J. Deane. Missionary Biography Series. Illustrated. 25th thousand. 12mo, cloth, 75c.

Robert Moffat.

By M. L. Wilder. Missionary Annals Series. 12mo, paper, net, 15c.; flexible cloth, net, 30c.

The Congo for Christ.

The Story of the Congo Mission. By Rev. John B. Myers. Missionary Biography Series. Illustrated. Tenth thousand. 12mo, cloth, 75c.

On the Congo.

Edited from Notes and Conversations of Missionaries, by Mrs. H. Grattan Guinness. 12mo, paper, 50c.

Samuel Crowther, the Slave Boy

Who became Bishop of the Niger. By Jesse Page. Missionary Biography Series. Illustrated. Eighteenth thousand. 12mo, cloth, 75c.

"We cannot conceive of anything better calculated to inspire in the hearts of young people an enthusiasm for the cause,"—The Christian.

Thomas Birch Freeman.

Missionary Pioneer to Ashanti, Dahomey and Egba. By John Milum, F.R.G.S. Missionary Biography Series. Illustrated. 12mo, cloth, 75c.

"Well written and well worth reading."—The Faithful Witness.

Seven Years in Sierra Leone.

The Story of the Missionary Work of Wm. A. B. Johnson. By Rev. Arthur T. Pierson, D.D. 16mo, cloth, $1.00.

Johnson was a missionary of the Church Missionary Society in Regent's Town, Sierra Leone, Africa, from 1816 to 1823.

Among the Matabele.

By Rev. D. Carnegie, for ten years resident at Hope Fountain, twelve miles from Bulawayo. With portraits, maps and other illustrations. Second edition. 12mo, cloth, 60c.

Peril and Adventure in Central Africa.

Illustrated Letter to the Youngsters at Home. By Bishop Hammington. Illustrated, 12mo, cloth, 50c.

Madagascar of To-Day.

A Sketch of the Island. With Chapters on its History and Prospects. By Rev. W. E. Cousins, Missionary of the London Missionary Society since 1862. Map and Illustrations. 12mo, cloth, $1.00.

Madagascar.

Its Missionaries and Martyrs. By Rev. W. J. Townsend, D.D. Missionary Biography Series. Illustrated. Tenth thousand. 12mo, cloth, 75c.

Madagascar.

By Belle McPherson Campbell. Missionary Annals Series. 12mo, paper, net, 15c.; flexible cloth, net, 30c.

Madagascar.

Country, People, Missions. By Rev. James Spree, F.R.G.S. Outline Missionary Series. 16mo, paper, 20c.

MISSIONS, AMERICA.

On the Indian Trail,

And Other Stories of Missionary Work among the Cree and Saulteaux Indians. By Egerton R. Young. Illustrated by J. E. Laughlin. 12mo, cloth, $1.00.

Mr. Young is well known to readers of all ages as the author of "By Canoe and Dog Train," "Three Boys in the Wild North Land," and other very popular books describing life and adventure in the great Northwest. The stories in this new book tell of some very exciting incidents in his career, and describe phases of life among the American Indians which are fast becoming things of the past.

Forty-two Years Among the Indians and Eskimos.

Pictures from the Life of the Rt. Rev. John Harden, first Bishop of Moosonee. By Beatrice Batty. Illustrated. 12mo, cloth, $1.00.

Vikings of To-Day;

Or, Life and Medical Work among the Fishermen of Labrador. By Wilfred T. Grenfel, M.D., of the Deep Sea Mission. Illustrated from Original Photographs. Second edition. 12mo. cloth $1.25.

"The author has been in charge of the work since its inception, and writes, accordingly, with special authority and wealth of detail, both as to the methods of work and as to the people—the

fearless, patient Vikings—to whom he has dedicated his life."—
The Examiner.

Amid Greenland Snows;

Or, The Early History of Arctic Missions. By Jesse Page.
Missionary Biography Series. Illustrated. Tenth thousand. 12mo,
cloth, 75c.

Kin-da-Shon's Wife.

An Alaskan Story. By Mrs. Eugene S. Willard. Illustrated.
Third edition. 8vo, cloth, $1.50.

"From beginning to end the book holds the attention. Mrs.
Willard has shown herself peculiarly well qualified to write such
a book."—Public Opinion.

David Brainerd,

The Apostle to the North American Indians. By Jesse Page.
Missionary Biography Series. Illustrated. Twelfth thousand.
12mo, cloth, 75c.

South America, the Neglected Continent.

By Lucy E. Guinness and E. C. Millard. With a Map in colors
and many other illustrations. Small 4to, paper, 50c.; cloth, 75c.

Footnotes:

[1] A consideration of the important crisis through which the
Chinese Empire is passing at the close of the century, does not fall
within the scope of a work like the present. All who are interested
in that subject should not omit to read attentively Mr. Colquhoun's
"China in Transformation," London and New York, 1898,
embodying the matured convictions of an accomplished traveller,
and an experienced Oriental administrator, with an exceptional
first-hand acquaintance with China.

[2] A Chinese woman for many years employed in the writer's
family, remarked that for a long time after she was married she was

never allowed to leave the narrow courtyard in her hamlet. The wife of a Tao-t'ai told a foreign lady that in her next existence she hoped to be born a dog, that she might go where she chose!

[3] We have known occasional instances in which a betrothed girl was not required to attend the funeral of her future father-in-law or mother-in-law, a trying ordeal which she must be glad to escape. Sometimes when she does attend, she merely kneels to the coffin, but does not "lament," for usage is in this, as in other particulars, very capricious.

[4] A Chinese woman whose parents are living, is constantly referred to not only as a "girl," but as an unmarried girl (ku-niang), although she may be herself the mother of half-a-dozen children.

[5] See a small pamphlet on "The Status of Woman in China," by Dr. Ernst Faber, Shanghai, 1889, containing many illustrative classical citations.

[6] For ample illustration of this subject see Dr. Ernst Faber's "The Famous Women of China," Shanghai, 1890, and "Typical Women of China," by the late Miss A. C. Safford, an abridged translation of a famous and authoritative Chinese work.

[7] An extreme case of chronic misery from this cause is found in the Hsiên District of Chih-li, where there is a section wedged in between the high artificial banks of two rivers. Every year many villages are deluged as matter of course, and the houses have been repeatedly destroyed. No autumn crop can ever be raised here, but wheat is put in after the waters have subsided. In the winter one sees many of the houses with doors and windows plastered up, almost all the inhabitants having gone off in droves to beg a living where they can, returning the next spring to look after their wheat. This has become a regular practice even with families who own fifty or sixty acres of land, and who elsewhere would be called well off.

[8] A case of this sort came to the writer's notice in which a man from Ho-nan had gathered a stock of goods amounting to more than the value of fifty Mexican dollars, and departed for Manchuria, nearly 1,500 miles distant, in order to learn what had

become of his sister's son who had left home in anger. The goods were disposed of to pay travelling expenses, but the journey of a few months as planned, was lengthened to more than a year. The poor man fell sick, his goods were spent, and he was many months slowly begging his way back, and after all had learned nothing of his nephew.

Transcriber's Notes:

Images have been moved from the middle of a paragraph to a nearby paragraph break.

The text in the list of illustrations is presented as in the original text, but the links navigate to the page number closest to the illustration's loaction in this document.

Other than the corrections noted by hover information, inconsistencies in spelling and hyphenation have been retained from the original.